The Antarctica Protocol

Reflections on Humanity's Purpose in a Cosmic Research Station

Viren Shah

COPYRIGHT PAGE

The Antarctica Protocol: Reflections on Humanity's Purpose in a Cosmic Research Station

By **Viren B. Shah**

Copyright © 2025 Viren B. Shah

All rights reserved.

No part of this book may be copied, reproduced, distributed, or transmitted in any form or by any means electronic, mechanical, photocopying, recording, or otherwise without prior written permission from the author, except in the case of brief quotations for reviews, educational use, or scholarly research as permitted under applicable copyright law.

First Edition: 2025

U.S. Copyright Registration Number: TXu 2-472-679

Registration Decision Date: March 5, 2025

Published by:

fundae University

Printed in the United States of America

10 9 8 7 6 5 4 3 2 1

Contents

Preface 8

Acknowledgements..11

Disclaimers and Notes on Errors and Omissions 13

Chapter 1: The Human Paradox..14

    Introduction..14

    The Programming of Consciousness................................17

    From Infinite Potential to Chosen Patterns 22

    The Evolution of Meaning: How Humanity's Search for Purpose Shapes Understanding..................................26

    Mind and Matter: Between Observable Reality and Infinite Possibility..30

    Conclusion: Where Value Systems Meet Universal Questions.......34

Chapter 2: Evolution of Human Consciousness and Society............37

    Introduction..37

    Development of Societal Structures and Control Mechanisms......41

    Divided Wisdom: How Humanity's Quest for Truth Amplified Its Inherent Divisions 50

    Confined Consciousness: The Paradox of Seeking Intelligence Through Constraint..61

    Conclusion: Born Free, Yet Bound, The Circle of Human Consciousness 67

Chapter 3: The Architecture of Certainty: From Infinite Potential to Prescribed Reality..70

Introduction..70

Bonds Beyond Time: The Triumvirate of Transcendent Purpose.75

Beyond the Bonds: The Triumvirate of Controlled Thought 110

Bonds Beyond Time: The Triumvirate of Dominion and Might.138

Conclusion: Beyond the Paradigm, Reconciling Free Will and Universal Order in the Quest for Intelligence..................................159

Chapter 4: Beyond Purpose: Decoding Humanity's Role in the Infinite Design..168

Introduction..168

Hypothesis Statement: Earth As A Cosmic Research Station for Intelligent Civilizations 171

The Antarctica Protocol: Exploring Earth's Cosmic Paradigm ...175

    The Divine Tapestry: The Abrahamic Threads of Faith...........184

    The Divine Tapestry: The Dharmic Threads of Enlightenment 188

    The Divine Tapestry: The Eastern Threads of Wisdom...........194

    The Divine Tapestry: The Ancestral Threads of Zoroastrian, African, and South American Faiths...200

Between the Threads: Global Faiths and the Cosmic Research Station Hypothesis..205

Question: Understanding the Scope of Divine Power and Control..207

What Are We Trying to Determine?...207

How Divine Systems Define the Soul: Unseen Energy Mirroring Antarctic Experiments 217

Comparative Perspectives on the Soul's Creation Across Diverse Divine Systems 222

Synthesizing Definitions: Earth as Lab, Refinement Station, or Cosmic Chance? 230

One Humanity, Many Cultures: Does Divinity Clarify Shared Biology and Diverse Lives? 233

Divine Communications: Genuine Revelations or Mental Illusions? 242

Heavenly Oversight: How Divine Systems Link Celestial Bodies to Earthly Life 249

Beyond the Temporal: Divine Views on the Afterlife Continuum 256

Divine Narratives of Earth's End: Why Sacred Teachings Foresee Civilizations' Dissolution 264

Earth's Divine Tapestry: Affirming the Cosmic Research Station Hypothesis? 270

Beyond Equations: Does Science Support the Cosmic Research Station Hypothesis? 276

The Big Bang: From Singularity to Cosmic Birth 280

Darwinian Evolution: Nature's Experiment in Adaptation and Intelligence 284

Multiverse Theory: Infinite Realities and the Quest for Purpose 289

Steady State Theory: Eternal Universe, Continuous Creation, and Infinite Observation 296

    The Fermi Paradox: Silent Cosmos, Hidden Civilizations, and the Quest for Intelligence 303

    Dark Forest Hypothesis: Silent Universe and the Hidden Struggle Among Civilizations..312

    Simulation Hypothesis: Programmed Universes and the Illusion of Existence 322

Pragmatic Thought: Bridging Observation, Utility, and Measurable Truth 328

Conclusion: Divinity, Science, and Pragmatism Converge in Earth's Cosmic Hypothesis 340

Chapter 5: Beyond the Script: Free Will and Cosmic Uncertainty Drive Revolutionary Change..369

    Introduction...369

    All Opinions Are Valid But Ours Is Valid-er: A Cheery Nod to the Rules of 'No Rules..377

    Love, Legacy, or Legislation? Exploring the Cultural Alchemy of Marriage...382

    From Twilight Whispers to Midnight Screams: Why We Believe in the Unseen 386

    Blaming Mercury's Retrograde Again? Perhaps We Just Hit Snooze Twice..391

    Martians Have Better Wifi: What Humanity Really Wants to Ask Our Cosmic Cousins 396

Filters, Followers, and FOMO: Tales from the Digital Parade 401

From Santas to Subpoenas: When Holidays Demand You Hand Over Your Last Brownie 405

When Test Tubes Meet Testaments: How Atheists, Believers, and Scientists End Up in the Same Chatroom Brawl 410

Free Will vs. Fill-in-the-Blank: Are They Marking Down Your Creativity With a #2 Pencil? 415

Carrying Receipts Beyond the Exit: The Curious Notion of Deeds Echoing Elsewhere 418

CSI: Common Sense Investigation In Case Anyone Wonders Why Our Brain's on a Vacation Without Us 424

Chapter 6: Convergence at Infinity: Humanity's Journey from Paradox to Cosmic Understanding 430

Concepts Used in the Books 460

Preface

I have often marveled at how astonishingly suited Earth is for human life. A slight shift in its axis could plunge us into chaos, disrupting seasons and agricultural cycles, while even minor fluctuations in its magnetic field might leave life vulnerable to devastating cosmic radiation. Then consider Jupiter, our celestial guardian, tirelessly absorbing cosmic debris that could otherwise threaten our existence. With each observation, I became increasingly convinced that our planet's equilibrium was not merely convenient it seemed, in a quiet, profound way, intentional.

Though my professional journey has been rooted firmly in the world of finance and entrepreneurial ventures, questions about Earth's unique qualities and humanity's place within this vast universe continuously captivated my imagination. Motivated by an enduring curiosity and a growing sense that we overlook countless subtle wonders in our everyday lives, I embarked upon the endeavor of writing this book. It became my earnest exploration into a bold yet inviting hypothesis: might Earth, in some profound sense, serve as a kind of cosmic research station?

As I delved deeper, I quickly recognized how expansive this question truly is, stretching across disciplines such as astrophysics, religious traditions, philosophy, and historical patterns of human thought. My ambition was not to make sweeping claims or assert definitive truths but rather to thoughtfully unpack an intriguing concept and present it as a starting point for meaningful contemplation and dialogue.

Preface

Writing became an immersive experience, one that challenged my assumptions and encouraged rigorous investigation into realms far beyond my initial familiarity. As I navigated topics ranging from quantum physics to ancient mythologies and philosophical treatises, I experienced a form of intellectual humility: the realization that, while no single field held the ultimate answer, each offered invaluable insights that enriched the broader narrative.

Central to this inquiry emerged a compelling theme: the extraordinary nature of human free will. Whether examining Earth's precise position in our solar system or contemplating ancient texts hinting at unseen cosmic observers, it became clear how profoundly our understanding of existence hinges on the decisions we make. We frequently speak of destiny, fate, or inevitability, yet within each moment lies our capacity to shape outcomes, large and small. Reflecting upon this notion illuminated what I call the "*singularity of perspective*" the narrowing of our vision by daily routines and pressures, obscuring the immense potential embedded in human freedom.

The guiding metaphor for this exploration is what I term "*The Antarctica Protocol*" inspired by Antarctica's distinctive global status. Despite political and territorial divisions worldwide, nations have collaboratively preserved Antarctica as a space dedicated to scientific exploration and minimal exploitation. To me, this arrangement offers a compelling parallel: perhaps Earth itself exists as a sphere designed to cultivate varied forms of life and consciousness within a vast cosmic framework. The idea became my metaphorical compass, guiding my reflections and inquiries throughout this narrative.

This book is my humble attempt to weave together diverse threads modern scientific discoveries, ancient spiritual insights, philosophical considerations, and historical patterns to examine whether the concept of Earth as a cosmic research station holds intellectual and existential value. While no definitive answers emerged, the exploration itself proved illuminating, continuously nudging me toward deeper understandings.

If you choose to journey through these pages, my hope is that you find within them a stimulating blend of old wisdom and contemporary thought, as well as a sincere invitation to reconsider the mysteries surrounding our existence. This book makes no grand claims to revelation; rather, it represents an honest sharing of curiosity, reflection, and openness to possibility. In nurturing an open mind and a spirit willing to question the world around us, perhaps we can rediscover perspectives that quietly transform how we see ourselves and our remarkable place in the cosmos.

Acknowledgements

First and foremost, I extend heartfelt gratitude to my family, whose unwavering support, boundless patience, and unconditional love have provided a steadfast anchor throughout this journey. Their enduring belief in my aspirations and constant encouragement have illuminated my path, transforming challenges into achievable milestones.

In the creation of this book, I delved profoundly into the expansive reservoir of my accumulated knowledge. This reservoir is enriched by countless extraordinary teachers encountered throughout life's diverse and extensive classrooms. From the structured environments of school and university, where foundational principles and disciplined inquiry were imparted, to the spontaneous and unpredictable corridors of everyday existence, every lesson, each interaction, and even subtle observations have intricately contributed to shaping my intellectual and philosophical perspectives.

My sincere appreciation extends further to the innovative content creators on platforms such as YouTube and TikTok, whose brief yet remarkably insightful contributions continually challenged my assumptions and reshaped my understanding in impactful ways. Likewise, profound conversations with brilliant minds, though sometimes fleeting, have left lasting and indelible marks upon my consciousness, providing perspectives that persistently influence my thoughts and reflections.

Acknowledgements

To all educators, both known and unknown, whose teachings have intentionally or inadvertently impacted my journey, I express my deepest gratitude. Your wisdom, whether imparted consciously or unknowingly, has allowed me to harness and distill profound universal truths, enabling the conception and realization of this literary endeavor. Your collective influence has been instrumental in translating ideas into tangible expression, guiding me toward deeper comprehension and appreciation of our shared human experience.

A special thanks is extended to the pioneering scientists behind Artificial Intelligence (AI). Without AI, this book may not have come into existence. AI has been invaluable in clarifying complex concepts such as the laws of physics, aiding in meticulous text review, and supporting extensive research efforts. It is through the groundbreaking work of such visionary individuals across all fields that humanity is continually propelled forward, evolving toward an increasingly intelligent civilization.

Disclaimers and Notes on Errors and Omissions

The endeavor of bringing this book together has required extensive research, meticulous attention to detail, and diligent effort to ensure both factual accuracy and comprehensive coverage of the varied subjects explored within its pages. Despite the rigorous and careful approach employed throughout the creation process, it is possible that some inadvertent errors or omissions may remain. These mistakes, should they exist, are entirely unintentional, and it is not the intention of the author to cause offense, discomfort, or harm to any individual or group.

Given the vast scope of topics addressed in this work, which encompasses intricate and profoundly sensitive concepts from religion, science, and pragmatism, every precaution has been undertaken to ensure the material is presented with the utmost respect, fairness, and impartiality. If any inaccuracies or oversights inadvertently result in offense, misunderstanding, or distress, I wish to express my deepest and most sincere apologies. The core objective of this book is to cultivate thoughtful, meaningful dialogue and foster deeper comprehension among diverse perspectives, honoring and celebrating the rich variety of insights and ideas that collectively drive our intellectual, ethical, and spiritual advancement.

Chapter 1: The Human Paradox

Introduction

In the vast tapestry of life on Earth, humans emerge as extraordinary beings of boundless potential. While most living organisms, roughly 95% of all species, complete their entire life cycles within 16 years, humans at this same age stand merely at the threshold of self-discovery. This extended period of development grants humanity a rare and invaluable gift: the opportunity to learn, evolve, and actively shape our perception and understanding of the world.

Consider how a newborn individual enters the world brimming with limitless possibilities. Humans are inherently born free yet soon find themselves constrained not by physical shackles but by the invisible constraints imposed by inherited systems of values and beliefs. The human mind resembles a sophisticated quantum computer, inherently equipped to process, assimilate, and adapt to any given environment, culture, or intellectual tradition.

This extraordinary adaptability is vividly illustrated through cross-cultural adoption studies. Imagine a child born into Mongolia's nomadic society, rich in traditional wisdom, strong community bonds, and intricate environmental stewardship. If adopted and raised by a family in Copenhagen, renowned for its social cooperation, technological innovation, and urban sustainability, the individual naturally embodies the cultural outlook of their adopted surroundings. Meanwhile, biological siblings raised within the Mongolian tradition retain their distinct and equally valuable nomadic heritage. Such remarkable flexibility underscores that our value systems, frameworks defining right and wrong, importance and triviality, meaning and irrelevance, are not hardwired but learned.

At its core, a value system functions as the operating framework of human consciousness, forming an intricate tapestry of beliefs, priorities, and guiding principles that shape our interpretation of and responses to the surrounding world. Similar to how a computer's operating system dictates how all software functions, our value systems govern how we perceive information, make decisions, build relationships, and define our life's purpose. This foundational framework becomes the lens through which reality is perceived, the filter through which experiences are processed, and the structure within which choices are ultimately made.

The last five centuries have provided compelling examples of the dynamic evolution of value systems. Consider the profound transformation in Japan, where a rigid feudal society rapidly transitioned into a modern democracy within just a century. Observe the sweeping shift in gender equality, moving within a few generations from denying women basic voting rights to celebrating female leadership across governments, science, and industry. Perhaps most dramatically, South Africa's transition from apartheid to becoming a "*rainbow nation*" exemplifies a remarkable change in how people perceive and value one another.

Yet herein lies humanity's central paradox. Picture a quantum computer, inherently capable of simultaneously running an infinite number of complex processes yet deliberately constrained to performing only basic calculations. This analogy mirrors the human mind, born with infinite potential for exploration and innovation, yet frequently confined within a narrow scope of predetermined beliefs and thoughts. How does a being endowed with boundless possibilities for discovery become limited by rigid frameworks? Why does a creature capable of envisioning countless opportunities often choose to operate within restrictive boundaries of conventional thinking?

This observation is not intended as criticism but as an invitation to investigate one of humanity's most captivating traits. Our capacity to establish robust value systems has facilitated significant achievements: the creation of civilizations, advancements in science, and flourishing artistic expression. Nevertheless, these very systems can occasionally restrict our openness to novel ideas and perspectives that challenge entrenched worldviews.

As we embark on this journey of exploration, we may discover that this apparent contradiction is not a deficiency but rather a defining trait that uniquely characterizes humanity. Approaching this paradox with curiosity and awe, we can delve deeper into understanding how it has shaped, and continues to shape our collective past, present, and future.

The Programming of Consciousness

Human consciousness has been systematically shaped since long before recorded history. Unlike other social species, humans uniquely create and perpetuate complex societal norms across generations, a remarkable ability reflected clearly in our earliest archaeological records.

In caves within South Africa, archaeologists have unearthed deliberately engraved ochre fragments dating back approximately 70,000 years. These early markings represent humanity's foundational efforts toward external information storage and intergenerational transmission. Despite the absence of formal institutions, these nascent societies already employed structured methods like artistic expression, sophisticated tool-making, and ritual practices to communicate essential knowledge and social expectations.

The intricate nature of ancient value systems becomes especially clear when observing contemporary hunter-gatherer communities. Far from arbitrary, their social codes are maintained meticulously through oral traditions and experiential teachings, deliberately structured to ensure social cohesion and practical survival.

The progression from these primitive methods to more complex societal forms highlights a compelling evolution in how consciousness has been systematically cultivated. Around 10,000 BCE, the advent of settled communities introduced heightened complexity into value transmission, manifesting through elaborate symbolic behaviors and increasingly refined learning methodologies.

This evolution is vividly demonstrated through specialized craftsmanship. Early metallurgical cultures established apprenticeship systems that went beyond mere skill acquisition, embedding within them frameworks for imparting social values, defining community roles, and reinforcing hierarchies. These foundational practices laid essential groundwork for more sophisticated consciousness programming in subsequent civilizations.

With the rise of urban centers, consciousness cultivation further deepened. Societies developed tailored methods, adapting to their distinct environmental and cultural contexts, from Chinese oracle bones and Mesopotamian clay tablets to Mesoamerican codices and African talking drums. These systems transcended mere administrative tools, becoming sophisticated instruments for codifying and disseminating societal expectations.

As social complexity escalated, the techniques for programming consciousness evolved in parallel across continents. East Asia developed intricate civil service structures designed to shape mindsets and behaviors. South Asia demonstrated remarkable urban planning in Mohenjo-daro and Harappa, purposefully creating environments that fostered learning and cultural interchange. Concurrently, in the Americas, Maya and Inca civilizations integrated astronomical and mathematical principles into their physical and social architectures, profoundly influencing societal perceptions.

The invention of writing systems marked another pivotal advancement. Research by archaeologist Denise Schmandt-Besserat reveals that writing was more than a method for documentation, it became a powerful mechanism for standardizing cognition and embedding value systems across extensive populations, extending their impact through time and geography.

Formal education systems represent an additional significant leap in consciousness programming. Beginning in the 15th century, humanity experienced unparalleled acceleration in developing and disseminating values, paralleling the exponential technological growth encapsulated by Moore's Law.

The Age of Exploration catalyzed humanity's first comprehensive global exchange of values. Portuguese navigators adopted Arab navigation techniques, Spanish conquistadors integrated Aztec astronomical insights, and Italian merchants employed Chinese financial practices, collectively forming hybrid systems that propelled humanity toward globalized consciousness programming.

The Scientific Revolution further transformed societal approaches to consciousness cultivation. Advocated by figures such as Francis Bacon in his "*Novum Organum*" the scientific method emerged as a universal cognitive framework, transcending cultural boundaries and dramatically reshaping the human intellectual landscape.

Industrialization accelerated this transformation even further, reshaping perceptions of labor, time, and social hierarchy. German manufacturing approaches adapted uniquely within Japanese cultural contexts, and American mass production techniques influenced Soviet industrial methodologies, generating novel organizational hybrids grounded in distinct value systems.

The 20th century witnessed perhaps the most profound acceleration in consciousness programming, facilitated by mass media such as radio, television, and later the internet. Social movements promoting environmental consciousness, digital rights, and social justice spread globally at unprecedented speeds, signaling rapid evolutionary shifts in collective awareness.

Today, digital media sustains this momentum, enabling instantaneous global dissemination and reinterpretation of values. Events occurring in one region immediately influence global perceptions, reflecting a quantum leap in the dynamics of consciousness programming. Contemporary thought leaders suggest we stand on the precipice of even deeper transformative shifts driven by biotechnology, artificial intelligence, and global interconnectedness. Changes that will challenge our ability to thoughtfully and intentionally guide the evolution of consciousness.

We now actively shape ourselves, not merely our environments. Thus, future frameworks must be exceptionally adaptable, capable of evolving in real-time, while preserving essential human values crucial for social coherence.

Ultimately, these scholarly insights point toward a future where consciousness programming is increasingly dynamic and interactive. The essential challenge ahead lies not simply in transmitting values but in designing flexible, responsive systems capable of navigating rapid technological and societal transformations while safeguarding the core attributes of humanity itself.

From Infinite Potential to Chosen Patterns

From the moment we awaken into consciousness, intricate value systems quietly yet decisively embed themselves within our minds. Comparable to an expertly designed program operating invisibly beneath our awareness, these structures become thoroughly integrated through repeated interactions: first familial, then social, educational, and cultural. Their seamless installation rarely attracts scrutiny, subtly transforming our ostensibly boundless potential into a carefully delineated array of permissible choices and acceptable behaviors. What initially appears as unrestricted freedom thus becomes quietly channeled through frameworks that shape our moral boundaries, perceptions, and engagements with reality itself. Acting as powerful filters, these internalized norms continually direct our experiences and decisions, crafting a facade of autonomous choice atop deeply ingrained behavioral patterns.

Remarkably, this phenomenon is not characterized by uniformity; instead, human cultures have generated a rich tapestry of diverse and often opposing frameworks to interpret existence. Rather than converging toward a universal set of values, humanity has cultivated a mosaic of philosophies and ethics, each uniquely influencing social interactions and historical trajectories. This diversity will be further examined, underscoring how different cultures' interpretative frameworks profoundly impact societal structures.

Yet, amid this multiplicity lies humanity's extraordinary cognitive trait: an unparalleled adaptability and ceaseless learning capability.

While other species such as ants persisting in identical routines across millennia or primates consistently adhering to established social patterns, remain fixed, humans possess the distinct capacity for continual intellectual evolution. Our ability not only fuels technological advancement and scientific breakthroughs but also perpetually reshapes our collective consciousness and value systems.

Certain transformative individuals stand apart by employing free will not merely for personal fulfillment but for collective progression. Analogous to quantum computing's capacity for simultaneous processing, these visionaries comprehend both the intricacies of established norms and the possibilities inherent in innovation. They grasp society's complex structures, visualizing not only current realities but also viable pathways toward future evolution. Truly reshaping value systems demands courage to challenge entrenched norms combined with the wisdom to create inclusive, sustainable alternatives that elevate society as a whole.

Societal coherence, much like a harmonious symphony performed by skilled musicians, relies upon aligned value systems facilitating cooperative progress. If individuals were guided solely by their isolated values, societal interactions would dissolve into incompatible fragments, rendering communication, collaboration, and advancement impossible. Historically, meaningful transformation has often arisen when visionaries skillfully merged existing paradigms with novel insights. Gandhi intertwined ancient spiritual teachings with contemporary civil rights advocacy; Martin Luther King Jr. fused democratic principles with innovative social justice strategies.

Modern adaptations, such as the shift to remote work environments, similarly demonstrate how traditional organizational norms evolve seamlessly alongside technological innovation.

In contemporary societies, individuals routinely navigate complex intersections of multiple value frameworks, smoothly transitioning among corporate ethics, family traditions, civic duties, and societal expectations. Executives fluidly shift between competitive corporate cultures, nurturing family dynamics, and collaborative community activities. Educators similarly balance institutional requirements with personal pedagogical beliefs and broader social responsibilities, demonstrating adaptability across varying contexts.

Historically, visionary individuals capable of imagining alternative possibilities have significantly reshaped societal value systems. Workplace standards swiftly adapted following the widespread introduction of remote work, rapidly altering organizational expectations. Environmental awareness transitioned from fringe activism to mainstream consciousness, dramatically reshaping corporate and governmental policies worldwide. Public health strategies have similarly demonstrated remarkable flexibility, swiftly responding to urgent crises, highlighting humanity's resilience in evolving values to address critical needs.

Ultimately, the narrative of human consciousness is defined by perpetual evolution, driven by the dynamic interplay between established structures and the deliberate exercise of individual autonomy. The human mind continuously seeks equilibrium, balancing preservation of existing frameworks with creative adaptation toward emerging possibilities. This vibrant tension between conformity and innovation, stability and change, constitutes the profound complexity observed within human consciousness today. Rather than fragmenting society, the deliberate practice of free will harmoniously guides collective evolution toward ever more inclusive and enlightened value systems.

The Evolution of Meaning: How Humanity's Search for Purpose Shapes Understanding

Deep in our earliest narratives, we discover traces of humanity's perpetual quest to grasp its role within the cosmos. As consciousness arose and humans began moving beyond mere survival, they encountered profound mysteries demanding explanation. Through this exploration emerged two distinct yet equally profound pathways for finding meaning and purpose.

In cave depths, beneath expansive starry skies, and during moments of transcendent insight, individuals from diverse cultures experienced what they perceived as divine inspiration. These moments of profound revelation led to belief frameworks providing comprehensive explanations for existence itself. Initially arising from direct experiences, these insights gradually crystallized across generations into structured systems, preserved first through oral traditions and later in meticulously safeguarded texts. These frameworks didn't merely guide individual behavior, they delivered complete blueprints for comprehending existence, defining humanity's place in the cosmic order, and establishing rules for personal and societal conduct.

As belief frameworks matured, their initial inspired wisdom evolved into sophisticated traditions, ultimately underpinning social structures. Abstract spiritual insights solidified into tangible guidelines for daily life, forming boundaries within which individuals navigated existence while maintaining connections to something transcendent.

Simultaneously, another understanding emerged through careful observation of the natural world. Early humans, noting patterns in seasons, animal behaviors, and natural events, began constructing an empirical framework. From humble beginnings, this observational approach progressively evolved into complex systems of knowledge. The human mind naturally developed to recognize patterns, retain outcomes, and anticipate future occurrences, fundamentally shaping our empirical approach to reality.

Curious minds discovered something profound: the universe follows discernible patterns, suggesting an underlying order accessible through meticulous study. Practical survival knowledge transformed into deeper inquiries about existence itself. Early astronomers tracking celestial movements, healers cataloging plant properties, and philosophers pondering cause-and-effect relationships all contributed to an expanding systematic understanding.

Both the inspired and observational pathways share a common evolutionary trajectory. Each began with individual insights that eventually grew into comprehensive frameworks for understanding life's purpose. As societies increased in complexity, these frameworks transitioned from flexible guidelines into structured systems formalized in laws and institutions. This progression wasn't simply about exerting control, it reflected humanity's inherent need for coherent, dependable frameworks that clarify existence.

Today, these dual pathways continue their parallel evolution, each illuminating unique aspects of human experience. Like complementary lenses focusing on the same landscape, they offer distinct yet interrelated perspectives on life's fundamental questions. The human mind is inherently inclined to seek both patterns and meaning, continually balancing the desire to understand how things function with the need to grasp their significance.

Intriguingly, these frameworks parallel contemporary simulation concepts. Much as simulations establish parameters within which infinite variations occur, these frameworks define boundaries for human behavior, preserving individual agency. Whether guided by divine ordinance or natural law, both approaches recognize meaningful existence requires structure alongside freedom, constraint balanced with choice.

This realization yields a profound insight: humanity's pursuit of meaning involves not merely discovering answers but constructing frameworks wherein answers can emerge. Through divine inspiration or empirical observation, humans have built sophisticated meaning architectures continuously evolving alongside our expanding understanding of existence.

Remarkably, these frameworks exhibit inherent dynamism. Answers provided by each system inevitably generate deeper questions. Similar to a fractal pattern revealing endless complexity under magnification, human understanding continually expands. Solving one mystery invariably uncovers new ones, perpetuating an infinite cycle of discovery. This cycle signifies not a failure but rather robustness, demonstrating adaptive evolution alongside human consciousness.

The evolutionary interplay between questions and answers illuminates a remarkable dynamic between free will and value systems. Rather than value systems simply constraining free will, we observe a sophisticated reciprocal interaction. Value systems create a structured environment where free will can meaningfully function, while free will constantly evaluates these boundaries, driving the evolution of the systems themselves. It's analogous to a river and its banks, each shaping and defined by the other, neither meaningful in isolation.

This dynamic interplay clarifies humanity's distinct evolutionary path. Unlike other species maintaining static behaviors across millennia, humans exhibit exceptional adaptability and growth. This distinction lies less in physical evolution than in conceptual evolution, our ability to question, comprehend, and reconstruct frameworks of meaning. Consciousness provides us the unique ability to reflect upon ourselves and our relationship with the world around us, driving continuous evolution in our understanding and perspective.

Similar to simulations prompting increasingly sophisticated models, human understanding continually evolves toward greater complexity. Each iteration of inquiry and understanding builds upon previous frameworks rather than discarding them, constructing increasingly refined architectures of meaning. This iterative process underscores the uniquely human capacity for cultural and intellectual evolution, distinguishing our species not merely by degree but fundamentally by kind.

Mind and Matter: Between Observable Reality and Infinite Possibility

Gaze upward at the night sky from anywhere on Earth, and you'll share an experience that has shaped human consciousness since our earliest times: the profound realization that we are part of something vastly larger than ourselves. Long before telescopes and modern mathematics, humans documented extraordinary insights about reality and their place within it, often received through divine inspiration.

These early understandings revealed concepts remarkably modern in essence: multiple universes coexisting simultaneously, consciousness extending beyond physical bodies, energy transcending space and time, and realities existing in dimensions beyond immediate perception. Through visions, meditation, and what was perceived as direct divine communication, individuals across cultures gained insights into various realms of existence, consciousness flowing across multiple realities, cyclical time, and a shared cosmic awareness. These weren't mere speculations, but structured cosmological frameworks forming the foundations of value systems guiding humanity for millennia.

Remarkably, these ancient understandings of transcendent realities and infinite existence emerged long before humans developed the technological means to peer deeply into space. Everywhere on Earth, divine inspiration consistently indicated a universe more complex and expansive than human senses could grasp, suggesting that consciousness and existence stretch far beyond earthly comprehension.

Only recently has structured scientific inquiry begun reaching similar understandings. As humanity developed tools to explore the cosmos, the universe revealed itself as far grander than initially measured. Earth, once perceived as the universe's center, became recognized as a small life-filled planet orbiting an ordinary star among billions within a galaxy itself among billions.

The scientific journey into these realms reveals a fascinating narrative of rediscovering what divine insights long suggested. Initially viewing consciousness strictly as biological, a fleeting phenomenon between birth and death, scientific exploration uncovered deeper mysteries. Quantum physics blurred clear distinctions between mind and matter, observer and observed, echoing ancient conceptions of consciousness.

Yet humanity remains paradoxically fixated on its immediate physical existence despite expansive insights from both divine and scientific sources. Our daily lives focus narrowly on our brief physical embodiment, while our value systems reference infinite realms and eternal consciousness.

This intriguing disconnect extends into our approach to consciousness itself. Divine traditions have always depicted consciousness transcending physical form and interacting across multiple dimensions. Modern physics, with quantum theories and multiverse hypotheses, similarly suggests realities beyond immediate perception. The universe, it seems, consistently defies not only our current understanding but also the very limits of our imagination, suggesting that reality might be far more extraordinary than we can ever fully conceive.

Value systems derived from divine inspiration emphasize consciousness extending beyond the physical, operating in diverse existential realms. Likewise, scientific inquiry increasingly hints that consciousness might be fundamental rather than incidental, possibly operating at quantum levels across dimensions currently barely understood

Resistance to broader understandings of consciousness might stem from our inclination to favor familiar experiences, dismissing the unexplored simply because it lies beyond immediate perception. Even as our frameworks consistently point toward boundless potential, many individuals gravitate toward established limits, treating the unknown as something to avoid rather than an opportunity for exploration.

This limitation is striking given humanity's remarkable evolution. Within a mere blink of cosmic time, we transformed from basic tool users into creators of quantum computers and interplanetary explorers. This exponential growth distinguishes humanity through unmatched development and adaptability.

Yet this success might highlight a deeper limitation. While mastering our immediate environment, we remain curiously confined by current tools and comprehension. Both divine insights and scientific exploration suggest realities beyond current understanding, yet civilization often prioritizes material mastery over embracing the infinite.

This raises profound questions about humanity's maturity as a civilization. Have we evolved sufficiently to engage meaningfully with potential cosmic consciousnesses? Despite advancements beyond other Earth species, vast realms of existence and consciousness remain beyond current interaction. As technology reaches toward the stars, are we prepared for discoveries anticipated by ancient wisdom and modern science?

Perhaps the true measure of a civilization's advancement lies less in physical mastery and more in its readiness to embrace infinite possibilities. As our understanding advances, we might discover that reality continually surpasses our capacity to fully comprehend it, suggesting that deeper truths lie perpetually just beyond our grasp.

Conclusion: Where Value Systems Meet Universal Questions

In our exploration of human consciousness and value systems, we repeatedly return to a fundamental observation: humanity perpetually stands at the intersection of the known and the unknown, the finite and the infinite. Value systems, whether inspired by divine revelation or pragmatic observation, consistently point to existence beyond immediate perception, yet humanity often remains tethered to the familiar even while yearning to comprehend what lies beyond.

This dynamic emerges clearly when we face phenomena that challenge established understanding. Consider Antarctica, where physicists' equations and thermodynamic predictions occasionally falter in the face of observable realities. Here, researchers from nations with widely varying value systems collaborate, illustrating a universal truth: when confronted by phenomena that challenge comprehension, humanity achieves its greatest potential by cooperating across diverse value systems in pursuit of deeper truths.

Throughout history, from ancient cave paintings to contemporary quantum laboratories, we discern a persistent pattern: humans consistently push against the boundaries of their knowledge while simultaneously holding onto familiar frameworks. This observation is not merely philosophical but practical, shaping societal development and consciousness evolution. Throughout every era, those who explore beyond accepted intellectual limits navigate between the security of established understanding and the uncertainties of expanded awareness.

The paradox of human existence might not lie in inherent limitations, but in our hesitation to embrace the infinite even as we seek limitless meaning within finite dimensions. This tension, arising from our vast capacity for understanding juxtaposed with self-imposed constraints, has consistently influenced human consciousness from its earliest stages. As societies transitioned from purely survival-driven concerns to reflections on their cosmic significance, this pattern has endured with remarkable consistency.

Yet this paradox also illuminates a deeper facet of human potential. Although value systems can restrict understanding when viewed as absolute boundaries, they also function as frameworks through which infinity becomes comprehensible, analogous to mathematical notation, humanly devised yet capable of representing infinite concepts. The solution lies not in discarding value systems but in recognizing their role as instruments of comprehension rather than limitations. Approached with this perspective, these systems become gateways to broader insights rather than restrictive barriers. As our understanding expands, so too does our appreciation for the unknown. Each discovery, whether related to consciousness or the physical universe, inevitably unveils additional mysteries. This cyclical journey toward deeper comprehension indicates that our exploration is spiral in nature, repeatedly revisiting foundational questions with increasingly profound insight.

Crucially, this iterative process has driven the co-evolution of human consciousness and frameworks of understanding. As our cognitive abilities have grown in complexity, from early intuitive insights to contemporary sophisticated interpretations, these systems have adapted accordingly. This mutual evolution points toward an unfolding trajectory of future developments that, at present, we can scarcely imagine.

Chapter 2: Evolution of Human Consciousness and Society

Introduction

In our earlier examination of value systems, we uncovered the fascinating process by which humanity's limitless potential gradually became organized into structured modes of understanding. Advancing further, we now explore how these frameworks have deeply influenced human consciousness itself, transforming unbounded free will into carefully delineated binary choices comparable to the fundamental categorizations of day and night or moral distinctions between right and wrong.

At its core, human perception fundamentally relies on binary oppositions. The significance of these dualities lies not in their specific terms, but in their inherent relational structures. Evidence of this foundational cognitive pattern permeates every layer of human society, from basic survival instincts such as distinguishing edible from inedible, safe from dangerous to contemporary societal divisions like work and leisure that define our daily routines.

This evolutionary transformation underscores a profound paradox inherent in humanity: despite our innate capacity for boundless imagination and complexity, our collective interpretation of reality frequently resorts to simplistic dualistic categories such as good versus bad, acceptable versus forbidden. Rather than embracing the universe's diverse potential, our consciousness increasingly imposes restrictive binary frameworks, shaping experiences into clearly defined boundaries.

Tracing this extraordinary evolution through distinct societal stages reveals humanity's intricate dance between consciousness and control. Initially, nomadic hunter-gatherers operated within fluid, unrestricted communities, mirroring their expansive movement across open landscapes. With the rise of agricultural settlements, the demands of cultivation imposed regularity on human behaviors and thought processes. Gradually, the human body and mind became objects of systematic scrutiny and regulation, resulting in extensive organizational frameworks. Modern manifestations of this control permeate our institutions: schools dictate structured schedules, workplaces meticulously manage productivity, and urban planners guide societal movement through deliberate design.

In contemporary nation-states, control mechanisms have reached unprecedented sophistication, implementing complex frameworks of permissions and restrictions. Just as ancient temples once regulated entry into sacred spaces through detailed rituals, modern societies now oversee individuals' mobility via passports, visas, and rigorous security procedures. While these mechanisms ensure stability and order, they represent a substantial departure from our ancestors' experience of unrestricted consciousness and free movement. What originated as free expression has evolved into a tightly managed system of predefined choices.

Chapter 2: Evolution of Human Consciousness and Society - Introduction

The ongoing dialogue between divine inspiration and practical necessity imbues this evolutionary journey with particular fascination. Ancient agricultural communities, for instance, transformed practical irrigation techniques into rituals symbolizing divine order, intertwining tangible survival methods with sacred ceremonial practices. Religion, deeply embedded within social structures, embodies collective beliefs, reinforcing communal values and shared realities through its inherently social nature.

Humanity's progression from boundless potential to standardized consciousness signifies more than mere social advancement, it reflects a fundamental shift in our perception and interaction with reality. As societies grew more complex, the expansive potential of human consciousness gradually narrowed, becoming increasingly aligned with socially sanctioned thought and behavior. This standardization marks the emergence of collective frameworks that deeply influence our individual interpretations of the world.

Upon close observation, this evolutionary trajectory appears less arbitrary and more intentional than previously recognized. Each societal stage, from primitive value systems to sophisticated nation-states, exhibit discernible patterns, suggesting an overarching design. This notion parallels the precision of mathematical constants that govern the universe, hinting at a profound, underlying order beyond current human comprehension.

As we journey through each phase of this evolution, we will carefully examine the intricate interplay between divine guidance and practical necessity, exploring how these elements combined to create increasingly advanced systems of consciousness and societal regulation. We will recognize how each stage offered both empowerment and constraint, simultaneously expanding collective capacities and restricting individual autonomy. By undertaking this exploration, we aim to illuminate not only humanity's past trajectory but also the possible future directions of our collective consciousness.

Development of Societal Structures and Control Mechanisms

The transformation of human free will into regulated consciousness stands as one of history's most fascinating paradoxes. Early human societies, observing the raw power of nature like lightning splitting ancient trees, floods reshaping landscapes, fire consuming forests, first encountered divinity not as an abstract concept, but as a direct experience of awe-inspiring natural forces. This early sense of the divine revealed itself through the rhythm of seasons, the mystery of birth, and the finality of death, phenomena that defied early human understanding yet demanded acknowledgment and respect, compelling humanity toward worship and reverence.

Archaeological evidence from every continent narrates a remarkable story: our ancestors didn't initially conceive of gods in human form. Instead, they recognized divinity within natural phenomena, the sun's life-giving warmth, the moon's rhythmic cycles, the earth's fertile abundance. This divine force remained fundamentally unknowable yet undeniably present, manifesting through observable patterns in nature rather than through anthropomorphic representations. Early rock art and artifacts suggest a worldview wherein humans perceived themselves as participants within this divine natural order, rather than separate from or superior to it.

> *In our quest to understand the divine, we transformed our gaze from the infinite patterns of nature to the finite structures of*

human organization, perhaps the first and most profound constraint we placed upon our own consciousness

Human free will's transformation into regulated consciousness stands as one of history's most fascinating paradoxes. Early human societies, observing the raw power of nature like lightning splitting ancient trees, floods reshaping landscapes, fire consuming forests, first encountered divinity not as an abstract concept, but as a direct experience of awe-inspiring natural forces. This early sense of the divine revealed itself through the rhythm of seasons, the mystery of birth, and the finality of death, phenomena that defied early human understanding yet demanded acknowledgment and respect, compelling humanity toward worship and reverence.

This divine authority provided something unprecedented, a coherent framework for comprehending existence itself. Through various global traditions, it introduced the concept of the soul or life force, an eternal energy transcending physical existence, providing humanity with its first unified theory of consciousness and being. This allowed individuals to perceive their lives as part of a larger cosmic narrative, resonating deeply with their innermost sense of self and reality.

Soul as a concept emerged not merely as a philosophical construct but as a practical framework for understanding human experience. Ancient texts describe this essence as simultaneously intimate and universally connected, suggesting that individual consciousness represents a localized expression of greater cosmic awareness. This understanding elegantly addressed humanity's profound questions about individuality and unity, elucidating how beings could simultaneously exist as unique individuals and integral parts of a greater whole. The Vedic concept of Atman-Brahman, the Taoist principle of individual consciousness emerging from and returning to the Tao, and the Neo-Platonic notion of the soul emanating from and returning to the One all articulate this fundamental insight.

The notion of the soul emerging from and ultimately reuniting with the One profoundly articulates a foundational insight. This sophisticated conceptualization of consciousness as energy is especially striking, as ancient wisdom traditions intuited concepts that modern physics would confirm millennia later. Long before Einstein unveiled the interchangeability of matter and energy, these traditions described consciousness as an eternal, indestructible force, capable of transformation but immune to annihilation. Symbols such as the Egyptian ankh, the Chinese qi, and the Hindu prana vividly represent this enduring understanding of life as an eternal energetic presence temporarily inhabiting physical form.

This insight provided humanity with its earliest systematic explanations for the profound mysteries of existence: our origins, our purpose, and our ultimate fate. Far from depicting life as a random or meaningless phenomenon, these traditions viewed human existence as a deliberate, meaningful journey of consciousness through physical embodiment. Rather than something to be transcended or escaped, the physical world was framed as an educational stage, a means through which the soul could experience, learn, and evolve. Contemporary theories similarly propose that consciousness forms the underlying fabric of reality, continuously connecting our conscious awareness to deeper subconscious or even universal dimensions. Consequently, physical life becomes more than mere existence, it is transformed into a purposeful vessel for conscious experience and growth.

Consistently, these traditions described human consciousness as a fragment of universal energy, temporarily embodied but ultimately destined to reunite with a broader cosmic consciousness. Yet, despite initially emphasizing harmony between humanity and the divine, a dramatic shift in this relationship soon emerged.

At some pivotal juncture, the divine perception evolved dramatically. Initially seen as awe-inspiring and benevolent, the divine gradually acquired associations of fear and retribution. Religious practice, once guided by reverence for divine wisdom, increasingly became dominated by fear of divine punishment. Ancient texts originally celebrating universal love and cosmic unity began incorporating stark warnings of divine wrath. The creative force behind existence transformed into a deity capable of withdrawing favor, suggesting that human free will required regulation not through enlightened wisdom but through the anticipation of severe consequences.

> *The greatest triumph of institutional control lies not in its ability to enforce restrictions, but in its success at making the unnatural appear inevitable, transforming the infinite possibilities of human consciousness into a carefully curated set of acceptable choices*

This transformation first materialized through the concept of divine judgment, whereby actions performed during physical life carried profound implications extending into eternity. Ancient texts meticulously detailed systems of post-life accountability, scrutinizing every thought and deed. The boundless potential inherent in freedom thus became entwined with anxiety about responsibility and consequence. Works like the Egyptian Book of the Dead outlined precise rituals necessary for safe passage through the afterlife. Similar frameworks appeared across cultures, from the Chinese Diyu courts to the Greek realm of Hades, each emphasizing the soul's vulnerability to divine judgment.

Fear embedded itself within the paradox of eternal consequences emerging from fleeting actions. Although defined as immortal energy, the soul's brief physical experience was laden with everlasting repercussions. This introduced a profound psychological dimension: actions performed visibly carried invisible, enduring significance. Concepts such as karmic debt in Eastern philosophies and moral sin in Western traditions significantly reshaped perceptions of free will.

Crucially, this fear transcended physical death itself. Religious doctrines introduced a deeper terror, spiritual death or eternal separation from divine essence. This profound anxiety became humanity's fundamental and universal dread, significantly more potent than any worldly punishment. Depictions of eternal torment, such as Abrahamic Hell, Buddhist Naraka, and Norse Helheim, illustrated states of perpetual anguish, elevating spiritual fears above worldly threats.

This shift notably redefined the relationship between consciousness and physical form. The body, previously seen merely as a transient vessel, evolved into a proving ground where souls either accrued divine favor or judgment. Religious teachings stressed bodily discipline, cautioning that physical impulses could divert consciousness from its divine path. Spiritual leaders instilled guilt within human awareness, urging introspection regarding desires and behaviors. Thus, the concept of sin became inseparably linked to physical existence, perpetuating anxieties surrounding bodily desires.

This systematic fostering of fear significantly restructured human consciousness, marking a profound transformation in its regulation. Primitive fears of tangible threats evolved into abstract fears independent of physical realities. Divine experience shifted from awe-filled reverence to anxiety-driven judgment, profoundly redefining human consciousness within societal frameworks.

The emergence of empirical thinking represented humanity's first comprehensive challenge to the divine-centric worldview, introducing a radically different method of understanding reality. Originating with ancient Greek thinkers like Thales and Aristotle, who advocated natural explanations for natural phenomena, this empirical approach evolved significantly through subsequent intellectual developments. The Scientific Revolution, led by figures such as Galileo and Newton, established a paradigm wherein truth required empirical verification rather than authoritative endorsement

Though revolutionary, this empirical viewpoint did not simply reject the divine; rather, it proposed an alternative route to understanding reality grounded in systematic observation, experimentation, and logical analysis. Early scientists like Kepler and Newton perceived their work as revelations of divine precision rather than contradictions to faith. Yet their commitment to evidence-based conclusions initiated a pivotal transformation in humanity's pursuit of knowledge. The ongoing interaction between scientific inquiry and spiritual belief thus became critical in determining humanity's future direction.

> *In replacing divine mystery with scientific certainty, we did not free consciousness from its chains, we merely replaced golden shackles with iron ones, exchanging the poetry of infinite possibility for the prose of measurable probability*

The insight that empirical thinking, while challenging religious authority, developed its own distinct forms of social control through mechanisms such as standardized education, bureaucratic organization, and technological surveillance is particularly revealing. Observing natural patterns of movement and freedom makes systematic human restrictions vividly apparent. Every species, from migratory birds traversing continents to salmon returning to ancestral spawning grounds, from wolves roaming expansive territories to butterflies crossing oceans, moves freely within limits set solely by physical capability and natural barriers. Astonishingly, numerous species remain undiscovered even in extensively studied regions, underscoring a fundamental truth: the natural world operates unbounded by artificial barriers, guided instead by ancient, instinctive pathways unaffected by human-imposed territorial concepts.

Throughout Earth's extensive biological history, encompassing millions of species across millions of years, no known instance exists of one species systematically restricting another's freedom and movement, apart from humans. Particularly pronounced within Western tradition is a rationality whose scope and influence have steadily expanded. Humans uniquely established intricate systems of captivity, domestication, and territorial constraints, profoundly altering the natural movements of countless species.

This unprecedented pattern permeates every layer of human society. Pets confined within apartments, livestock contained within industrial agricultural facilities, wildlife displayed in zoos, and marine life housed in aquariums, all exemplify humanity's normalization of constraining other species' innate movements. Even conservation practices, seemingly benevolent, involve extensive tracking, monitoring, and management, interventions absent in pristine ecosystems. Most tellingly, the term "*invasive species*" illustrates our assumed authority to validate or invalidate the natural movements of organisms, disregarding the millennia-old phenomena of migration and range expansion that existed well before human oversight.

The ultimate irony resides in our internalization of these constraints. Initially external controls have become so ingrained within our collective consciousness that we rarely question their artificial origins. Modern humans often mistakenly believe they understand their true desires, despite these desires frequently being shaped by external societal expectations. This internalization manifests in our habitual pursuit of permissions for inherently natural actions, our constant search for explicit indications of what is permissible or forbidden, and our anxiety when personal documentation: licenses, permits, identification, is momentarily inaccessible.

Each new technological advancement introduces fresh possibilities for control, digital surveillance, social credit systems, and behavioral tracking, that we not only accept but enthusiastically adopt. Our tools, originally shaped by human intention, subsequently reshape human behaviors and perceptions. Smartphones, for instance, ostensibly tools of freedom and connectivity, have become sophisticated devices facilitating voluntary self-monitoring.

This evolution encapsulates perhaps humanity's most profound paradox: our transition from unlimited potential to self-imposed limitations. Whether this represents a gain, a loss, or both simultaneously is a complex inquiry. However, a more urgent question arises whether human consciousness, having adapted to accept these constraints, can evolve again to clearly recognize and potentially transcend them. As we approach even more advanced control mechanisms such as artificial intelligence, genetic engineering, and neural interfaces, understanding this dimension of our evolutionary trajectory becomes not merely philosophically intriguing but practically essential for our ongoing development and survival.

Divided Wisdom: How Humanity's Quest for Truth Amplified Its Inherent Divisions

Earth's tapestry of life offers a fascinating exploration into the dynamics of interaction and survival. Across the countless organisms populating our world, ranging from meticulously documented species to those yet undiscovered, there emerges a consistent and elegant pattern of interconnected relationships. Nature orchestrates an intricate web, a layered symphony where each species occupies a distinct role within the delicate boundaries of necessity. Among all life, humans uniquely extend their interactions beyond immediate survival imperatives, performing roles on stages constructed by imagination rather than necessity alone.

> *In nature's grand theater, each species plays its role within the boundaries of necessity, only humans have created a stage where the performance continues long after survival's needs are met*

Interactions in the natural world adhere rigorously to patterns dictated by fundamental needs. On the Serengeti plains, lions engage primarily with their own species to establish territories or pursue prey; interactions with zebras and wildebeests remain strictly centered around predation. Similarly, within India's dense rainforests, tigers live largely solitary lives, interacting mostly during mating or territorial confrontations, their exchanges with prey meticulously choreographed by ancient instincts. In the unforgiving Arctic tundra, polar bears traverse vast expanses driven solely by survival imperatives, whether engaging with seals for sustenance or other bears in territorial disputes.

The compelling simplicity of these natural interactions enhances their intrigue. Elephant herds guarding their young on African savannas, macaws contesting nesting sites within Amazonian forests, and wolves maintaining territorial boundaries in North American wildernesses, all demonstrate engagements clearly linked to survival, reproduction, or territory maintenance.

Humans, by stark contrast, have forged interactions remarkably distinct from this survival-driven paradigm. Perhaps humanity's most striking paradox arises from our relationship with struggle itself. Having mastered the fundamental survival imperatives that compel competition among other species, we have fabricated entirely novel arenas of rivalry existing solely within our cognitive constructs.

> *Perhaps humanity's greatest paradox lies in its relationship with struggle, having conquered the necessities that drive all other species to compete, we have created entirely new realms of competition that exist purely within the architecture of our minds*

Despite lacking the physical prowess of gorillas, the swiftness of cheetahs, or the natural armor of bears, humans have dominated the natural world through intellectual prowess and technological sophistication. Yet, as basic survival became increasingly assured, human interactions paradoxically intensified and expanded, becoming elaborate and multifaceted, disconnected from immediate physical demands.

This divergence becomes palpably evident when individuals step outside human-made environments. Immersed in the tranquility of rainforests, the expansive silence of deserts, or the isolation of mountain peaks, people frequently report profound serenity even amidst wildlife's relentless survival activities. This peace starkly contrasts the perpetual tension inherent to densely populated human communities, where survival necessities are already comfortably met.

Ironically, in a species that has largely neutralized existential threats, achieving unparalleled security and abundance, persistent discord remains pervasive. Unlike other life forms governed strictly by immediate needs, humans developed intricate divisions independent of physical necessity. Consequently, the most profound threats to human well-being stem paradoxically not from environmental pressures or competing species, but from other humans, making our species uniquely self-destructive.

The persistence of human conflict beyond basic survival needs arises from forces deeper than physical exigencies. While behaviors of other species have remained stable over millennia, human consciousness has undergone exponential transformation, developing sophisticated conceptual frameworks. Indeed, human consciousness, striving to decode existence, generated conceptual structures so robust they transitioned from instruments of insight into restrictive boundaries of thought.

Chapter 2: Evolution of Human Consciousness and Society - Divided Wisdom: How Humanity's Quest for Truth Amplified Its Inherent Divisions

Humanity's initial attempts to grasp cosmic reality through divine inspiration marked the inception of this transformation. Across diverse geographic regions, profound existential insights emerged, mediated by individuals who became conduits for cosmic wisdom. Initially personal and experiential, these insights gradually solidified into structured belief systems, codified through sacred texts. These systems dictated extensive human behavior, imposing obligations extending far beyond mortal existence into eternal dimensions.

Geographic isolation significantly shaped the formation of these belief systems. Disparate communities interpreted divine inspirations within unique local contexts, resulting in distinct frameworks guiding life, from daily practices to overarching existential purpose. The profound irony here is that universal truths, filtered through isolated human experiences, fragmented into competing absolutes.

The great irony of human understanding lies in how universal truths, filtered through the prism of isolated experience, fractured into competing absolutes

Simultaneously, human consciousness developed a parallel empirical pathway grounded in systematic observation and verification. Although seemingly opposite to divinely inspired belief systems, empirical methodologies similarly crystallized into rigid structures. Diverse empirical interpretations fostered discrete schools of thought, each forming its own rigid frameworks, demonstrating humanity's repeated inclination toward inflexible dogmatism.

This reveals an intriguing paradox: despite unprecedented mastery over physical challenges and technological advancement, humanity still falls short of embodying a genuinely intelligent civilization. Such a civilization would transcend arbitrary divisions, harmonize diverse existential interpretations, and direct collective energies toward exploration and mutual growth rather than internal conflict.

Yet, human societies remain fragmented by competing claims to absolute truth. Ironically, value systems developed to liberate human potential have become barriers limiting it. Driven by fear of divine reprisal or exclusion from scientific acceptance, these frameworks often enforce conformity rather than encourage exploration.

Uniquely in Earth's biological history, humans subordinated physical reality to conceptual constructs. We alone create invisible barriers, not of physical substance, but of meaning, powerful enough to divide what nature unified and unify what nature separated.

> *Humans alone among Earth's species have mastered the art of creating invisible walls not from matter, but from meaning, walls so powerful they can divide what nature united and unite what nature divided*

Human divisions frequently defy natural patterns. Unlike other species competing for tangible resources, human societies compete for something intangible: the authority to define reality itself. Each conceptual framework, whether divine or empirical, imposes rules extending into realms of eternal consequence, employing sophisticated social controls and existential fears to ensure compliance.

These divisions persist despite our species' unparalleled technological advances. While humanity conquers previously insurmountable challenges: disease, distance, darkness, we remain constrained by ideological divisions established millennia ago. Anthropologist Claude Lévi-Strauss aptly termed this "*the paradox of progress*": our enhanced power to reshape the world contrasts starkly with our persistent inability to transcend conceptual barriers.

The prerequisites of an intelligent civilization highlight this disparity further. Intelligence at a societal level entails harmonizing diverse perspectives, prioritizing exploration over internal conflict, and demonstrating wisdom to transcend artificial boundaries. Yet, humanity, despite possessing near-magical technologies by ancestral standards, remains mired in systems originally designed to deepen existential understanding but now obstruct collective wisdom.

Ultimately, humanity's greatest challenge may lie not in conquering distant stars, but in bridging the intellectual divides we ourselves have created. Becoming genuinely intelligent necessitates unprecedented cognitive flexibility: embracing multiple perspectives, valuing intellectual diversity, maintaining cohesive unity of purpose, and channeling creative energies toward collective exploration rather than division.

> *The measure of civilization's intelligence lies not in its tools but in its unity, not in what it can build, but in what it can transcend*

Yet humanity's current condition stands in stark opposition to these ideals. Despite possessing technology our ancestors would deem magical; we remain entrenched in the very frameworks originally intended to expand our comprehension of existence. Each system whether religious, scientific, or philosophical, tends to enforce conformity within its sphere, often dismissing or actively rejecting alternative viewpoints, thus obstructing authentic collective intelligence. Religious systems frequently utilize the fear of eternal consequences, while empirical frameworks rely on professional isolation and the marginalization of unconventional methods.

This paradox results in humanity occupying a peculiar state of stagnation, advancing at an exponential technological pace yet remaining tethered by deeply entrenched ideological divides. Our remarkable capacity to manipulate matter at an atomic scale, observe distant galaxies, and fundamentally alter biological structures sharply contrasts with our enduring inability to bridge conceptual divides. This growing chasm between technological capability and societal cohesion prompts critical inquiry into the true essence and trajectory of human advancement.

> *Perhaps our greatest challenge lies not in reaching the stars, but in reaching across the chasms we've created between different ways of understanding the same reality*

Advancing toward an intelligent civilization requires more than technological progress alone; it calls for a profound shift in collective consciousness, transcending entrenched absolutes and embracing diverse perspectives. Achieving such evolution involves cultivating an unprecedented ability to value varied viewpoints while maintaining a unified purpose, channeling humanity's immense creativity toward collective exploration instead of internal division.

As technological capabilities rapidly expand: artificial intelligence, genetic engineering, and space exploration, the urgency of aligning social maturity with technological prowess intensifies. Humanity now confronts a critical challenge: not simply inventing more powerful tools but cultivating the wisdom necessary to use those innovations constructively, rather than perpetuating historical divisions.

Historically rooted in geographical isolation and limited mobility, humanity's fragmented understandings originated from diverging interpretations of existence. Viewed from a cosmic perspective, human significance diminishes sharply; our species occupies a modest planet orbiting an ordinary star in an obscure galaxy corner. Despite this shared insignificance, isolated human communities formed increasingly rigid and exclusive views of reality, fostering enduring divisions.

Human consciousness historically evolved along two primary pathways, each illustrating its paradoxical nature. Divine insights, experienced independently across varied cultures, gradually solidified into rigid doctrines demanding strict adherence. Initially flexible and profoundly personal existential insights became transformed into inflexible belief systems.

Human understanding's true tragedy emerges not from inherent limitations but from our stubborn insistence on perpetuating these limits. Concurrently, pragmatic observation developed its distinct form of rigidity. Although the scientific method dramatically enhanced our capacity to interpret reality, it frequently gave rise to its own dogmatic constraints. While inherently advocating skepticism and continual questioning, scientific institutions established hierarchies and orthodoxies resistant to challenges against prevailing theories, echoing patterns of control reminiscent of religious structures.

Both paths, divine revelation and empirical inquiry solidified into intricate mechanisms of social regulation. From ancient Mesopotamian city-states to contemporary nation-states, societies structured themselves around shared frameworks often defined in opposition to one another. Such divisions extended beyond philosophical disagreements, profoundly influencing education, shaping social interactions, and guiding technological innovation. Persistence of these divisions was maintained through sophisticated reward-and-punishment systems: divine traditions promising eternal repercussions for deviations, and empirical frameworks enforcing conformity through social and professional ostracism.

This persistent fragmentation sharply diverges from what the cosmos might deem an intelligent civilization. From a universal viewpoint, intelligence within civilization transcends mere technological accomplishment, reflecting instead the ability to mobilize collective energies toward exploration rather than internal discord. Advancing knowledge requires cultivating a holistic comprehension that synthesizes individual insights into a unified understanding. However, prevailing human frameworks typically resist such integration, preferring distinct boundaries and isolated spheres of influence.

Universally, an intelligent civilization's defining characteristics remain notably consistent. Such a civilization integrates diverse perspectives, values intellectual diversity, prioritizes exploration over domination, and possesses the wisdom to navigate artificial divisions while respecting natural boundaries.

Our quest for understanding has created a paradox, the very frameworks we built to comprehend existence have become barriers to experiencing its fullness

Evidence of such fragmentation becomes apparent when examining humanity's response to emerging challenges and opportunities. Whether addressing environmental crises, technological advancements, or societal changes, human reactions frequently mirror divisive perspectives rather than collective wisdom. Often, established knowledge overshadows the vital capacity for diverse and innovative thinking, stifling genuine progress. Prevailing frameworks commonly favor sustaining their entrenched paradigms instead of embracing new, potentially transformative viewpoints.

To evolve into an intelligent civilization requires overcoming these self-imposed boundaries while still respecting and incorporating the valuable insights that various traditions contribute.

Perhaps the true measure of consciousness lies not in what it knows, but in how it approaches what it doesn't know, not in the certainty of its answers, but in its capacity to remain open to new questions

Achieving such evolution necessitates exceptional cognitive adaptability: simultaneously embracing multiple perspectives, honoring diverse viewpoints while maintaining a shared vision, and channeling humanity's boundless creativity toward exploration rather than conflict.

This transformation gains urgency as technological capabilities grow exponentially. At this unique juncture in history, human capacity to reshape the physical world significantly outpaces our collective wisdom to responsibly guide such influence. Humanity's central challenge lies not simply in developing increasingly potent technologies, but in cultivating the collective wisdom to employ these advancements constructively, overcoming long-standing divisions. Ultimately, the trajectory of human consciousness and perhaps consciousness itself rests on our ability to bridge the deep divides we have created.

Confined Consciousness: The Paradox of Seeking Intelligence Through Constraint

The evolution of human consciousness reveals a profound irony: our quest for order resulted in creating systems that significantly constrained the very freedom distinguishing humanity. As societies grew larger and more intricate, the demand for coordinated effort gave rise to progressively rigid frameworks governing understanding and conduct. Previously, we examined how these frameworks originated from both divine and practical perspectives; however, their profound influence on human consciousness warrants further, deeper examination.

In nature's grand design, chaos and order dance in perpetual balance, yet humans, in their quest for certainty, chose to silence the chaos and formalize the dance, creating rhythms too rigid for innovation to flourish

This departure from nature's inherent flexibility marked a pivotal moment in human evolution. Earth's biosphere thrives on diversity and continual adaptation, yet human societies increasingly leaned toward uniformity and restriction.

Initially experienced as profound, personal revelations about existence, divine inspirations gradually hardened into rigid rules demanding strict compliance. Understanding humanity requires acknowledging the fundamental frameworks that guide and dominate our thoughts. Instead of serving as flexible guides for discovery, these divine insights became rigid doctrines, reinforced through complex systems of social and psychological regulation.

Human consciousness begins shaping remarkably early. From a child's earliest grasp of language, they enter a structured environment emphasizing certainty over curiosity. This structured environment, imparted through family dynamics, community customs, and formal education, does not simply propose ideas; it delivers beliefs as unquestionable truths, frequently invoking divine authority to ensure unwavering adherence.

Perhaps the most subtle constraint on human potential lies in systems where acceptance becomes so complete that questioning itself becomes unthinkable

While structured methods foster societal cohesion and stability, they inadvertently suppress innate curiosity and adaptability essential for human innovation.

Structured mindsets contrast starkly with nature's embrace of diversity and paradox. Across Earth's biosphere, countless life forms thrive precisely through adaptation and variation. Nature inherently encourages cooperation, innovation, and responsiveness to environmental challenges. Conversely, human societies frequently gravitate toward uniformity, unintentionally limiting innovations vital for advancing consciousness.

Divergence between human behavior and natural patterns becomes evident upon examining interactions among other species with their environments. Although all organisms confront survival challenges, only humans impose additional layers of constraints beyond physical necessity. Birds traverse territories freely; wolves howl without seeking permission; trees stretch toward sunlight without approval. Human consciousness, perhaps due to extraordinary potential, operates within carefully delineated boundaries extending beyond physical needs into thought itself.

Standardization of consciousness emerges clearly in societal reactions to innovation and discovery. When new ideas challenge established paradigms, responses typically follow a familiar trajectory: initial dismissal, prolonged resistance, eventually giving way to hesitant acceptance if concepts endure. Such patterns recur from ancient philosophical traditions to modern scientific practices. Effective learning and innovation require openness to relinquishing entrenched knowledge, yet prevailing systems commonly prioritize preserving existing beliefs over exploring novel possibilities.

Such implications become crucial when considering prerequisites for intelligent civilizations. Genuine intelligence involves not merely technological prowess but conceptual flexibility which is an ability to transcend existing paradigms when obstructing collective progress. Mastering paradox may be necessary: holding ideas firmly enough to build upon yet loosely enough to discard when deeper truths emerge.

Balancing stability with adaptability, preservation with evolution, constitutes core challenges in humanity's conscious development. Nature exemplifies systems maintaining coherence without rigid conformity. Ecosystems like forests preserve integrity through continual dynamic adaptation, allowing myriad variations within stable frameworks. Species adhere to ancient behavioral patterns while exploring novel possibilities. Dynamic equilibrium contrasts sharply with human cognitive systems. Although divine frameworks openly enforce adherence, even pragmatic, rational systems originally grounded in objective observation developed mechanisms reinforcing conformity. Despite differing justifications, approaches achieve similar outcomes, constraining intellectual boundaries.

Initially, pragmatic thought appeared as unprecedented intellectual freedom. As societies progressed and education broadened, individuals increasingly questioned traditional doctrines, embracing evidence-based understanding.

> *The greatest irony in human intellectual evolution lies in how systems born from the quest for freedom often become new architectures of constraint*

New ways of thinking, despite rejecting old authorities, soon created their own rigid orthodoxies.

Consider scientific thought in the 19th century. When evolutionary theory emerged, challenging established conceptions of life's origins, proponents encountered substantial opposition from traditional frameworks. Paradoxically, as revolutionary theory gained acceptance, it developed rigid conventions of its own. Rather than sustaining the questioning spirit from which it arose, scientific establishments often created hierarchies discouraging further inquiry. What began as an instrument for deeper understanding occasionally became dogma, as inflexible as beliefs it aimed to replace.

In the 20th century, such patterns appeared even more prominently through social and political ideologies advocating human equality. Movements founded on collective welfare and universal dignity presented rational alternatives to religious doctrines and unchecked capitalism. However, in practice, these ideologies frequently created power structures more absolute than those they intended to dismantle.

Systems that begin by promising universal emancipation often end by demanding universal submission to their interpretation of freedom

Patterns of constraint emerge distinctly when examining treatment of dissent within these frameworks. Traditional doctrines typically acknowledged divine mercy and redemption; however, some modern ideological movements implemented control mechanisms permitting no deviation. Leaders enforced adherence not through divine mandates but by asserting scientific necessity or social justice. Consequently, contemporary systems often imposed constraints surpassing traditional systems, eliminating possibilities for personal or spiritual continuity beyond physical existence.

Liberation movements consistently evolved into restrictive structures across diverse cultures and historical contexts. Initially advocating intellectual and social freedom, economic, social, and scientific movements frequently transitioned into rigid hierarchies punishing dissent severely. Societies aiming to eliminate class distinctions commonly established more inflexible social stratifications. Systems advocating rational governance occasionally deteriorated into personality cults demanding absolute conformity.

Feudal and monarchical systems replaced by modern ideologies operated within recognized frameworks of higher authority and universal principles. Conversely, numerous contemporary systems, despite claims of rationality and humanitarianism, established absolute authorities accountable to no higher standards. Modern structures regulated not only behaviors but thoughts themselves, often surpassing previous eras in scope and authority.

Significantly, throughout human civilization, frameworks originating from varying principles consistently inclined toward restricting consciousness rather than expanding it. Whether derived from divine commandments, scientific orthodoxies, or ideological doctrines, outcomes commonly included limitations on free will and innovative thought. Persistent patterns raise critical inquiries regarding human capacity to nurture adaptive, open consciousness necessary for genuine civilizational intelligence.

Conclusion: Born Free, Yet Bound, The Circle of Human Consciousness

Every human birth signifies a moment brimming with infinite potential, yet systematic examination illustrates how swiftly such potential narrows into predetermined patterns of thought and behavior. From divine frameworks to pragmatic structures, from inherited beliefs to chosen ideologies, human consciousness frequently moves toward constraint rather than expansion.

> *The profound irony of human development lies in how our quest for understanding has led us to create systems that limit our ability to understand anything beyond those very systems*

Patterns of constrained consciousness fundamentally challenge the evolution toward an intelligent civilization. An intelligent civilization inherently requires continuous evolution in thinking, synthesizing diverse perspectives, and flexibility in adapting understanding as new insights emerge. However, current trajectories reveal tendencies toward rigid frameworks resistant to significant change or questioning.

Whether originating from divine insights codified into laws, scientific observations solidified into dogmas, or social theories converted into absolute doctrines, human systems frequently prefer control over exploratory thought. Preferences for constraint appear consistently across human organization types, indicating deeper tendencies in managing consciousness itself.

A pivotal question arises from acknowledging these patterns, not whether systems of thought offer beneficial structures, as clearly they facilitated substantial technological and societal progress. Instead, critically, do these very systems, efficient in structuring society and behavior ultimately obstruct the elevation of consciousness required to achieve genuine civilizational intelligence?

> *Perhaps our greatest challenge lies not in developing new technologies or social systems, but in learning to hold our existing frameworks loosely enough to allow for their evolution*

Contrasts become especially vivid when comparing constrained patterns of thought with collaborative research exemplified by Antarctica. Scientists from diverse national and ideological backgrounds collaborate there to investigate phenomena frequently challenging established scientific norms. Questions hold intrinsic value even when answers remain elusive or uncertain. Boundaries in Antarctica protect rather than restrict, fostering exploration rather than confinement. Such an approach illustrates potential advancements in human understanding when liberated from rigid conceptual frameworks.

In attempts to understand consciousness, existence, and life's purpose, humans constructed systems functioning in stark contrast to this open exploration model. Unlike Antarctica's treaties ensuring no single viewpoint monopolizes knowledge-seeking, prevailing value systems enforce inflexible, non-negotiable frameworks with severe repercussions for divergence. Societies often prioritize symbolic interpretations over realities represented, overlooking existence's inherently fluid nature. Established ages ago, these frameworks remain largely unchanged despite exponential advancements elsewhere, highlighting sharp contrasts with adaptable patterns evident in nature.

Similar to Antarctica's unique conditions exposing limitations within conventional physical models, the expansive realms of consciousness and existence might demand more flexible cognitive approaches. Rather than asserting fixed certainties, allowing continual evolution could align more naturally with existence's intrinsic fluidity. Existing value systems attempt to define life's purpose and consciousness through restrictive lenses, sharply contrasting with adaptable patterns readily observable in nature. Nature's poetic diversity and adaptability distinctly differ from humanity's static explanations of existence.

Acknowledging how constraints limit human consciousness offers directions toward examining deeper societal control mechanisms. Exploring origins, persistence, and implications of these mechanisms becomes vital for understanding their roles whether beneficial or obstructive in humanity's ongoing evolution. Observations regarding restrained consciousness, resistance to evolution, and preferences for control over exploration strongly imply that achieving genuine civilizational intelligence may necessitate fundamental transformations in human approaches to knowledge itself.

Chapter 3: The Architecture of Certainty: From Infinite Potential to Prescribed Reality

Introduction

In the vast laboratory of existence, free will manifests as perhaps the most fascinating variable, a form of energy as fundamental as light, as fluid as water, yet infinitely more complex in its potential expressions. Just as scientists in a laboratory must identify and control key variables to achieve meaningful results, unguided consciousness exists like independent atoms floating in space, a state of pure possibility, capable of infinite permutations yet achieving little of lasting significance without structure and direction.

This observation finds its most concrete parallel in Antarctica's research protocols, where rigorous frameworks transform chaos into discovery through careful manipulation of environmental variables. Just as the continent's extreme conditions necessitate precise controls for meaningful experimentation, human society discovered early that consciousness required careful architecture to achieve its potential. The value systems that emerged across civilizations, whether focused on divine understanding, social cohesion, or pragmatic advancement, all share this fundamental characteristic: they provide structure through which infinite potential can manifest as measurable progress, much like how controlled variables in an experiment yield reproducible results.

Yet a profound question emerges when we examine these systems closely. The sophistication of human value systems appears to emerge ahead of humanity's intellectual maturation, as if the framework existed before its architects fully understood their craft. This observation raises intriguing possibilities about the origin and nature of human consciousness development, suggesting the presence of predetermined variables in what appears to be an open system.

Perhaps the greatest paradox of human consciousness lies not in its limitations, but in how perfectly those limitations serve purposes we are only beginning to comprehend

This insight, emerged through decades of observing how value systems shape human development, suggests design patterns that transcend coincidence. Like the precise tilt of Earth's axis or the exact strength of gravity required for life, the architecture of human consciousness exhibits a refinement that hints at deeper purpose, as if key variables were carefully calibrated for specific outcomes.

When examining the sophistication of these consciousness-shaping systems, an intriguing parallel emerges with how we measure advanced civilizations. Soviet astronomer Nikolai Kardashev, in 1964, proposed that civilizations could be classified based on their ability to harness and control energy, from mastering planetary resources to harnessing entire galaxies. This framework offers a profound insight into our own development: just as a civilization's advancement can be measured by its mastery over physical energy, perhaps humanity's consciousness architecture reveals a similar pattern of increasingly sophisticated energy management, not of physical energy, but of the energy of human will and potential.

Like a Type I civilization learning to harness its planet's energy through careful systems of control and distribution, human societies developed intricate frameworks for directing consciousness energy through value systems that span multiple dimensions of understanding, from immediate physical existence to transcendent purpose. What makes this architecture particularly fascinating is how it demonstrates levels of sophistication that mirror the progression Kardashev envisioned: from basic survival-focused structures to complex systems capable of managing consciousness across entire populations, suggesting patterns of development that might extend beyond our current understanding of civilization itself.

Each system, whether oriented toward transcendent purpose, pragmatic progress, or immediate gain, demonstrates remarkable sophistication in how it is hypothesized to operate, channeling human consciousness from infinite possibility into prescribed pathways. What makes this architecture particularly fascinating is how it is theorized to function simultaneously across multiple dimensions of understanding, suggesting either remarkable evolutionary development or, perhaps more intriguingly, design patterns that precede human civilization itself.

As we examine these mechanisms in detail, we must maintain awareness that truth, while singular in essence, may manifest in varied forms across multiple dimensions, like light appearing as both wave and particle depending on the method of observation. Each

Chapter 3: The Architecture of Certainty: From Infinite Potential to Prescribed Reality

manifestation of truth remains valid within its framework of understanding while pointing to the same fundamental reality. This perspective allows us to explore how different systems of consciousness architecture might serve distinct yet equally vital purposes in human development, each representing a different expression of underlying universal constants.

The architecture of consciousness control manifests across a fascinating spectrum of human experience, each level demonstrating distinct yet interrelated approaches to directing human potential. At the most fundamental level, we observe systems that transcend immediate physical reality, frameworks of understanding that connect individual consciousness to purposes beyond measurable existence through karmic consequences, divine judgment, and ancestral accountability, much like quantum fields that influence matter without direct interaction. These interface with mechanisms firmly grounded in our observable reality, pragmatic structures that shape daily existence through empirical understanding and rational frameworks, enforcing compliance through societal sanctions, peer validation, and empirical legitimacy, similar to how classical physics governs tangible interactions.

Yet perhaps most intriguingly, we find systems focused on immediate causation, frameworks that manipulate consciousness through direct stimulus and response, utilizing power dynamics, economic leverage, and social hierarchies, comparable to chemical reactions that produce immediate, observable effects. Together, these layers of consciousness architecture create a comprehensive matrix of influence, each operating with its own principles while contributing to the overall refinement of human will into prescribed pathways of thought and behavior.

The sophistication of their interaction maintains a balance as precise as any found in nature's fundamental constants, a precision that various schools of thought, from ancient wisdom traditions to modern scientific frameworks, increasingly recognize as suggestive of deliberate design rather than random development. Just as uncontrolled variables, free atoms, and flowing energy require precise frameworks to produce meaningful outcomes in laboratory experiments, the architecture that shapes human consciousness demonstrates a level of refinement that appears carefully calibrated rather than coincidentally evolved. The probability of such sophisticated systems emerging randomly becomes vanishingly small when we consider how effectively they transform the infinite potential of human consciousness, itself a form of free-flowing energy, into predictable, measurable patterns of thought and behavior.

Bonds Beyond Time: The Triumvirate of Transcendent Purpose

Examining divine frameworks across civilizations reveals intriguing similarities despite their diverse teachings, particularly in explaining consciousness and its purpose. The common foundation of these traditions is humanity's persistent quest for meaning beyond immediate existence. Civilizations have progressively refined spiritual frameworks, from early shamanic to contemporary theological systems, collectively guiding consciousness.

Diverse traditions independently develop frameworks that align consciousness similarly, each addressing existence's fundamental paradox: describing a supreme consciousness simultaneously transcendent yet intimately involved with humanity. Omnipresence serves as a foundational concept consistently represented across traditions: Vedantic Brahman permeating all existence, Abrahamic divine witness, Taoist cosmic flow (Tao), Native American Great Spirit, and African interconnected supreme being. Across all human societies, we find not identical beliefs but remarkably consistent ways of organizing beliefs into coherent systems of meaning.

This omnipresent consciousness underlies cosmic order and justice systems: Hindu and Buddhist karma, Jain karmic particles, Zoroastrian cosmic justice, Mayan cosmic balance, Aztec teotl, Aboriginal Dreamtime, Sikh hukam, and Taoist natural law, each reflecting comprehensive governance of actions and consequences.

All traditions balance cosmic justice with divine mercy, recognizing consciousness's need for structured grace. This balance appears consistently in Hindu prasāda, Christian forgiveness, Islamic rahmah, Native American purification, Yoruba òrìṣà interventions, and Jain spiritual practices. The universal presence of mercy across religious traditions reflects a profound awareness of the need to harmonize justice with hope. This interplay between justice and mercy shapes divergent yet complementary spiritual pathways.

These systems, though unified by principles of cause, effect, and mercy, significantly differ in structuring consciousness development. Their divergence intentionally accommodates varying human spiritual inclinations, analogous to scientific experiments adjusting variables to explore diverse aspects within controlled parameters. The diversity across religious traditions ensures that every type of human consciousness finds an appropriate path. This strategic balance between universal truths and individual pathways suggests deep awareness of how consciousness thrives through varied approaches, ultimately aligning with fundamental cosmic truths.

Spiritual traditions consistently recognize a pattern of divergence followed by convergence regarding cosmic accountability and purpose. Traditions like Hinduism's pralaya, Abrahamic Judgment Day, and Buddhist kalpa cycles share this collective evaluation framework. Similarly, Aztec cycles of creation and destruction, Norse mythology's Ragnarök, Hopi Fourth World teachings, and African cosmic cycles reinforce a shared understanding of ultimate accountability. The remarkable similarity of end-time scenarios across cultures indicates patterns in how human consciousness interprets and comprehends its purpose and ultimate destiny.

Remarkably, these frameworks balance individual autonomy with cosmic principles, allowing free choice within structured spiritual pathways. This carefully calibrated balance reflects profound wisdom on how consciousness develops best with freedom and guided structure. Analogous to Antarctica's structured research environments permitting exploration within defined boundaries, divine frameworks similarly create spaces for spiritual exploration, preserving individual autonomy and cosmic order. Understanding consciousness as dynamic energy interacting with spiritual principles, similar to physical energy with natural laws, further clarifies these frameworks' precision in managing spiritual growth.

Sophisticated spiritual energy management delicately balances individual expression with collective integrity, mirroring physical energy systems' principles. The deepening parallel between religious mysticism and scientific models of reality highlights universal governance principles: balance, boundaries, and purpose.

Consciousness' physical journey further illustrates divine frameworks managing free will through structured experiences, distinguished as either singular or repeated incarnations. Abrahamic traditions, notably Judaism, Christianity, and Islam, posit life's singularity, stressing pivotal choices impacting eternal outcomes. Islam frames earthly existence as an evaluative stage culminating in Paradise or Hell, Christianity emphasizes salvation through Christ determining afterlife placement, while mystical Judaism contemplates temporary purgation before Paradise.

Conversely, dharmic paths advocate multiple incarnations for spiritual realization. Hinduism seeks liberation (moksha) from rebirth cycles, Jainism emphasizes rigorous spiritual practices achieving total karmic release (kevala jnana), and Buddhism defines nirvana as freedom from rebirth cycles through enlightenment over numerous lives.

Additional traditions reflect similar sophistication: Egyptian theology's journey through Duat toward divine unity, Yoruba's cyclical travel between spiritual and earthly realms, Taoism's multiple experiences toward harmonious immortality, Norse rebirth within familial lines, and mystical Kabbalah and Sufism's multi-phase spiritual development within singular existence. These diverse yet precise methodologies suggest intentional structuring of consciousness growth, analogous to scientific experimentation employing either singular or iterative methods depending on investigational aims.

Furthermore, intricate architectures of spiritual realms, Islam's multi-leveled heavens and earths, including the transitional Barzakh; Christianity's elaborate celestial hierarchies and toll houses, reveal intentional, purpose-driven designs rather than random formations, aligning closely with quantum states' precision in modern physics.

Eastern traditions showcase extraordinary precision in mapping consciousness across realms. Hindu cosmology articulates fourteen lokas: from Satya-loka, aligned closely with cosmic truth, through progressively denser realms down to Patala, reflecting varying degrees of spiritual separation. Buddhist cosmology expands further, detailing thirty-one hierarchically arranged planes, from formless states (arupa-dhatu) to fine-material realms (rupa-dhatu) and desire-driven worlds (kama-dhatu), each tailored to distinct spiritual purposes.

Such meticulously defined realms appear consistently across diverse cultures, indicating universal principles guiding consciousness. Ancient Egyptian texts describe Duat's specific spiritual stages, Native American traditions like Hopi and Maya reference overlapping dimensions navigable under defined conditions, and Yoruba cosmology identifies nine distinct realms governed by Orishas. Similarly, Taoist and Shinto cosmologies outline precise intersections of celestial and earthly dimensions.

Remarkable parallels exist between these spiritual frameworks and modern scientific descriptions of multidimensional states. Analogous to controlled scientific environments, these traditions precisely outline conditions essential for consciousness transitions, mirroring structured protocols found in modern experiments.

Intermediate states or transitional realms also exhibit profound uniformity across traditions. Tibetan Buddhism details six distinct transitional phases (bardos), each crucial for navigating post-mortem consciousness toward reincarnation. Islamic tradition articulates barzakh, a transitional state of simultaneous spiritual and material awareness. Catholicism and Eastern Orthodoxy define purgatory and aerial toll houses, respectively, highlighting structured phases of spiritual purification.

Similarly sophisticated concepts appear in Egyptian Duat transformations, Norse Helheim's transitional nature, and global shamanic practices for accessing intermediary realms. These precise descriptions underscore intentionality rather than random development, reflecting deep insight into conditions essential for spiritual advancement.

Dharmic traditions provide insightful views on transitional consciousness states. Hinduism's pitru-loka is an intermediate realm for ancestral souls awaiting reincarnation, subtly bridging physical and spiritual realms. Jainism introduces lesya, defining consciousness by subtle energetic qualities influencing transitional movements. Sikhism's dasam duar represents consciousness transcending physical boundaries while existing simultaneously within earthly dimensions, paralleling quantum states.

Islamic Sufism elaborates barzakh via alam al-mithal, a symbolic dimension connecting pure consciousness to material existence, further refined by concepts like fana and baqa, states of dissolution into and subsistence within divine consciousness. Taoism's hun and po souls navigate transitional states during life and beyond. Korean shamanism identifies realms where ancestral spirits guide consciousness transformations, while Shinto traditions depict simultaneous multi-state purification processes.

Kabbalistic Judaism explores gilgul (reincarnation) and intermediate spiritual states, detailing specific halls traversed for spiritual refinement, supported by the concept of tzelem (spiritual body), emphasizing distinct vehicles for varied consciousness states. Central and South American cosmologies similarly portray complex transitional understandings: Aztec consciousness navigates Mictlan's nine purifying underworld levels; Maya tradition describes consciousness traversing dimensions marked by celestial events; and Incan cosmology distinguishes consciousness movement through kay pacha, hanan pacha, and uku pacha realms, each requiring precise transitional conditions.

Globally, transitional architectures exhibit extraordinary precision, consistently highlighting consciousness's structured progression through carefully calibrated realms, underscoring universal recognition of essential transitional conditions. Tibetan Buddhism's bardos exemplify meticulous phases guiding post-mortem consciousness, resonating with Islamic barzakh, Catholic purgatory, and Orthodox aerial toll houses, each providing structured spiritual refinement frameworks. Such cross-cultural congruency underscores profound universal comprehension of consciousness dynamics.

Specific energetic qualities essential for consciousness transitions show remarkable consistency across traditions. Jainism's lesya, describing subtle karmic influences, parallels Taoism's concepts of hun and po souls, indicating detailed understanding of energetic prerequisites for transitional states. Such precision reveals sophisticated spiritual development comprehension.

Across cultures, transitional states exhibit precise definition, reflecting profound awareness within divine frameworks. The remarkable similarity across varied traditions, from Sufism's fana and baqa states to shamanic practices accessing alternate dimensions, implies traditions document observed phenomena rather than speculative inventions. Such observations align closely with scientific documentation practices.

This similarity becomes particularly significant when traditions describe consciousness's ultimate destination. Whether through single lifetimes or multiple reincarnations, diverse traditions universally agree that consciousness transcends physical existence into realms beyond ordinary perception. This convergence echoes meticulous scientific observation in extreme environments, such as Antarctica, where unique conditions enable researchers to document extraordinary phenomena.

Salvation, as consciousness's final state post-earthly existence, is uniformly depicted across traditions, emphasizing realms beyond current physical understanding. Abrahamic faiths present salvation as eternal unity with divine presence, a decisive transition into transcendent realms. Eastern traditions offer incremental salvation processes: Hindu moksha's release from rebirth cycles, Buddhist nirvana's transcendence beyond all limits, and Jain kevala jnana's attainment of perfect knowledge and freedom beyond material existence. This collective precision underscores deep insights into consciousness transformation across spiritual traditions

Divine frameworks precisely articulate consciousness's ultimate destination, underscoring realms transcending physical existence. Regardless of tradition, Heaven, Paradise, Pure Lands, or transcendent states, each underscores consciousness fulfilling its purpose beyond material reality. Such universal recognition suggests deliberate documentation of spiritual truths, not mere cultural conjecture.

Abrahamic traditions envision consciousness attaining eternal unity with divine presence: Islamic theology's seven-tiered Paradise (Jannah) culminating in Firdaus, Christianity's eternal communion in Heaven, and Jewish mysticism's devekut (complete adhesion) with divine consciousness.

Eastern traditions provide equally precise accounts. Buddhism describes thirty-one hierarchical planes, culminating in formless realms (arupa-dhatu) of pure awareness, free from physical confines. Hinduism identifies moksha as merging consciousness with Brahman, the ultimate reality, and Jainism portrays kevala jnana as achieving perfect knowledge beyond karmic entanglement.

Indigenous traditions echo similar insights: Native American Spirit World as pure consciousness, Australian Aboriginal return to Dreamtime, and African systems describing union with divine forces. Consistent, sophisticated mappings, from Buddhism's spiritual planes to Native American dimensions, suggest documented spiritual observations rather than speculation.

Moreover, these multidimensional concepts parallel modern scientific explorations into quantum realities. Ancient traditions have long detailed active interactions between higher celestial realms and earthly existence. Hinduism describes devas and pitrs guiding humanity; Abrahamic faiths depict angelic interventions; and Native American and African traditions recognize influential ancestral and spiritual entities operating across dimensions.

The precision of these interactions, articulated through temporal systems like Vedic muhurta, reflects meticulous observations rather than arbitrary constructs. The complexity of these temporal systems indicates they arose from careful observations of cosmic-human interactions, refined meticulously over millennia. This profound understanding aligns remarkably with contemporary quantum theories exploring multi-dimensional probabilities.

Celestial wisdom extends significantly beyond individual timing into collective consciousness cycles. The Mayan Long Count calendar precisely tracked extensive cosmic periods, aligning each era with distinct stages in human consciousness evolution. Similar to Hindu cosmology's yugas, the Maya's exact astronomical calculations indicate genuine documentation of cosmic-consciousness interactions rather than mere speculation.

Islamic astronomy contributed through the lunar mansions system (manazil al-qamar), accurately correlating celestial movements with human affairs, influencing cultures from Spain to China. The widespread adoption of these systems across various cultures indicates they provided practical utility in understanding the relationship between consciousness and the cosmos, rather than representing mere cultural preferences.

Chinese cosmology's stems and branches (gan zhi) presents an exceptionally intricate framework, harmonizing interactions among five elements, twelve earth branches, and ten heavenly stems, offering precise celestial-consciousness tracking. These systems consistently recognized a sophisticated matrix linking cosmic influences and consciousness, practical in fields from agriculture to medicine. The enduring application of these cosmic-consciousness correlations in practical contexts suggests we are observing genuine patterns rather than mere cultural artifacts.

Celestial traditions often attribute distinct consciousness qualities to planetary influences, such as Mercury's link to communication and Mars to assertiveness, observed consistently across isolated cultures. The remarkable consistency of these associations suggests either a universal psychological pattern in human consciousness or genuine influences we are only beginning to comprehend.

Mayan and Egyptian traditions mapped consciousness stages precisely to stellar movements, employing celestial cycles for transformative practices. Intriguingly, some traditions referenced astronomical phenomena invisible without advanced technology. Persian anwa' and Aboriginal Australian traditions described unseen star systems affecting consciousness, often demonstrating knowledge of celestial phenomena that should have been unobservable with ancient technology, raising profound questions about the origins of their knowledge.

Contemporary research increasingly validates ancient traditions' insights into consciousness-cosmos relationships. Studies linking solar activity, lunar phases, and planetary alignments to human behavior suggest underlying cosmic influences previously unrecognized by scientific instruments. Neuroscientific theories propose that the brain functions less as a storage device and more as a tuning mechanism, accessing information patterns existing at a more fundamental level of reality.

Celestial traditions primarily depict cosmic forces as catalysts rather than deterministic controllers of consciousness, aligning with the Hermetic axiom, "*As above, so below.*" Across various cultures: Chinese xiu, Indian nakshatras, Arabic manazil, distinct celestial references converge remarkably in their described impacts on consciousness, implying a complex network of influences rather than isolated phenomena.

This convergence parallels multinational collaborative research efforts in Antarctica, where distinct methodologies enrich collective understanding. The universe exhibits evidence of consciousness operating at multiple levels: elementary physical processes, direct human experience, and the broader cosmic scale.

Within the human pursuit of divine connection lies a spectrum ranging from profound mystical revelations, through reinterpretations of existing spiritual frameworks, to psychologically driven distortions. Profound mystics align deeply with universally observed spiritual truths, as the most insightful spiritual experiences generally expand upon established wisdom rather than completely contradicting it. Conversely, personal reinterpretations often reflect familiar spiritual themes presented in fresh ways rather than introducing entirely novel concepts. At the spectrum's extreme, psychological distress can yield restrictive and harmful frameworks. The critical challenge lies in differentiating genuinely transformative spiritual experiences from expressions of psychological crisis.

Each manifestation develops systems influencing behavior through structured beliefs, rituals, moral principles, and social hierarchies. Genuinely beneficial frameworks enhance human potential and autonomy, while psychologically driven interpretations often impose rigid control, fostering isolation and societal harm. The human psyche inherently seeks divine understanding, though the clarity and effectiveness of this pursuit depend significantly on one's psychological health and condition.

Earth's diverse expressions of divine truth, from profound wisdom to problematic distortions, reflect varying guidance toward human consciousness evolution. The authenticity of divine connection often becomes evident not through the uniqueness of its claims but through its impacts on human development and societal well-being. The discernment of beneficial versus harmful spiritual guidance sharpens human wisdom and compassion.

The family represents humanity's earliest and most enduring spiritual framework. The family unit functions as humanity's initial sacred space, where we first encounter teachings on navigating life's complexities. This foundational influence highlights that the earliest experiences of divine authority often come through interactions with those who provided life and nurtured early growth.

Dharmic traditions deeply embed familial divinity. Hindu culture reveres ancestors (पितृ, pitṛ) through ritualized offerings (श्राद्ध, śrāddha), recognizing enduring ancestral influence. The Hindu conception of family extends beyond immediate physical boundaries, viewing ancestral connections as essential forces shaping human consciousness. Similarly, Buddhist and Jain traditions balance familial duty with spiritual transcendence.

Abrahamic faiths frame family divinity through divine ordinance. Judaism emphasizes family bonds via the commandment to honor parents, symbolizing divine-human covenant continuity (L'dor V'dor). Islamic teachings detail family duties (huqūq), and Christianity considers familial bonds channels of divine grace. Abrahamic traditions regard family relationships as sacred not merely for their intrinsic value, but as essential conduits for experiencing and transmitting divine grace.

Eastern traditions further articulate family divinity through ancestral reverence: Chinese filial piety (孝, xiào), Japanese ancestor veneration (先祖供養, senzo kuyō), and Korean 효 (hyo), each highlighting sacred familial continuity. African ubuntu expands familial bonds vertically and horizontally, viewing the family not merely as a social unit but as the foundational structure through which divine reality manifests in human experience.

Indigenous traditions similarly view family as sacred networks. Native American beliefs include familial bonds with all living beings, while Aboriginal Australians and Pacific Islanders highlight spiritual and ancestral lineage connections. These cultural practices establish structured respect hierarchies, channeling divine influence into human consciousness, profoundly shaping individual free will.

Family divinity uniquely shapes consciousness from life's earliest moments, deeply embedding initial perceptions and language. The family environment into which we are born provides our first encounter with both unconditional love and structured guidance. The complexity of the parent-child relationship is unmatched, serving as humanity's foundational laboratory for consciousness, introducing the fundamental experiences of nurturing affection and disciplined direction.

This foundational bond transcends basic survival, evolving into intricate consciousness-guiding systems across cultures. What begins as biological necessity transforms into sophisticated frameworks of consciousness management, enduring long after physical dependency ends.

Dharmic traditions elaborate deeply on familial duty. Hinduism emphasizes ṛṇa, life's fundamental obligation to parents, shaping lifelong consciousness through rituals and duties. Buddhist teachings highlight parental gratitude (katannu-katavedi), integrating family duty within spiritual development. The Hindu understanding of family bonds creates intricate patterns of mutual obligation that shape consciousness across generations.

Eastern traditions, such as Confucian xiào (filial piety), Japanese oyakōkō, and Korean hyo, establish sophisticated, lifelong frameworks for consciousness guidance through family. These traditions form comprehensive systems guiding consciousness via family bonds.

Abrahamic traditions similarly uphold family significance. Islamic teachings elevate parental respect as spiritually essential, Judaism emphasizes kibud av va'em (honoring parents), and Christianity stresses familial authority intertwined with spiritual principles. African societies, exemplified by Yoruba ìwà, view parent-child bonds as vital mechanisms perpetuating communal consciousness, representing more than biological connections but essential pathways sustaining communal values and identity.

South American indigenous perspectives, such as the Inca ayni and Mayan lineage teachings, perceive family as a cosmic connector between earthly and divine realms. The cross-cultural consistency of family influence suggests a structured, purposeful mechanism guiding consciousness. This precise structuring indicates family systems shape consciousness development through intentional processes rather than random evolution. This remarkable consistency raises profound questions about the intentional architecture underpinning human consciousness development.

Family influence extends well beyond immediate relationships, creating intricate networks of reciprocal obligations termed "networks of conscious reciprocity." These extended familial systems, consistently observed across cultures, reinforce individual growth and societal cohesion, underscoring sophisticated authority calibrations based on relational proximity.

While collective living arrangements in nature, such as ant colonies or coral reefs, primarily reflect survival mechanisms rather than familial bonds, genuine familial structures, like elephant herds, wolf packs, and orca pods, demonstrate emotional attachments, cultural learning, and deliberate care transcending mere survival. The complexity of familial bonds deepens significantly with increasing levels of consciousness. Animal social structures typically emphasize stability aimed primarily at species survival, rather than consciously evolving individual or collective awareness.

From the perspective of celestial divinity, human family evolution signifies a profound leap in consciousness organization. Vedic traditions recognize families as vessels for divine interaction, emphasizing spiritual heritage through concepts like gotra and ancestral rituals like śrāddha. Islamic teachings elaborate family refinement via silat ar-rahm, expanding familial obligations into sophisticated moral frameworks. Judaism's l'dor v'dor underscores progressive spiritual transmission through family networks, while Christian theology depicts the family as reflective of divine trinitarian relationships, evolving in spiritual complexity.

Buddhist traditions highlight family bonds as vehicles for spiritual enlightenment through kalyanamitra, and Taoist philosophy similarly notes family evolution from basic dualities into intricate spiritual dynamics.

Pragmatic disciplines enrich our understanding of family evolution. Sociobiological analysis illustrates family structures transcending genetic imperatives to facilitate complex cultural and social interactions. Cognitive anthropology explores families' roles in developing advanced cognitive frameworks. Attachment theory in developmental psychology reveals families as essential in shaping emotional and psychological health. Social anthropology details family evolution from kinship groups into sophisticated social networks. Systems theory describes families as adaptive systems evolving to manage complex interactions, transcending biological functions to foster higher-order consciousness development.

Through celestial divinity, human family evolution represents a profound leap in consciousness. The Maya recognized family bonds (ch'ulel) as sacred links surpassing physical reality, while Aztec traditions viewed these connections as divine energies requiring careful nurturing. Remarkably, Australian Aboriginal dreamtime traditions independently developed similar intergenerational spiritual frameworks.

Dharmic traditions offer exceptionally detailed views of familial consciousness evolution. Hindu philosophy, through concepts like ṛṇa (debt) and gotra (lineage), intricately defined intergenerational obligations and subtle consciousness connections. The Hindu understanding of family consciousness reveals sophisticated psychological development patterns still being explored by modern science. Buddhist pratityasamutpada (dependent origination) precisely mirrors modern family dynamics, and Jain teachings on bandha and moksha address psychological tensions within familial relationships. Sikhism, emphasizing seva (selfless service), anticipated contemporary therapeutic principles for family harmony.

Native American traditions, exemplified by the Lakota mitakuye oyasin ("*all are rela*ted"), established sophisticated systems of emotional interdependence that modern psychology now validates. The Native American perspective on family obligations represented a refined framework for consciousness development, anticipating humanity's emotional evolution. African concepts, like Yoruba and Akan ubuntu ("*I am because we are*"), similarly anticipated contemporary attachment theories and collective consciousness dynamics.

Abrahamic traditions provide parallel insights. Judaism's mishpacha concept, Christianity's notion of the family as a "*domestic church*," and Islamic teachings on silat ar-rahm intricately address modern psychological challenges within familial structures.

> *The convergence of ancient traditions on sophisticated frameworks of consciousness development presents us with an extraordinary question: how did civilizations across time and space independently arrive at such similar and prescient understanding of human psychological evolution?*

The Hindu vasudhaiva kutumbakam ("*the world is one family*"), Buddhist teachings on familial attachment, and Sikh and Jain approaches remarkably anticipated contemporary global and emotional dynamics, raising compelling questions about their source of insight and enduring relevance.

A profound paradox emerges when comparing celestial inspiration to pragmatic understandings of familial divinity. Celestial traditions, often derived from singular revelatory experiences, presented frameworks remarkably aligned with insights pragmatic research discovered much later through systematic study and observation. Pragmatic examinations began simply, focusing initially on observable familial practices such as marriage customs and inheritance patterns, eventually evolving into deeper explorations of psychological dynamics and emotional interdependencies.

Lewis Henry Morgan, an early anthropologist, emphasized the family's social and adaptive significance, viewing it as society's fundamental unit of adaptation. By the early 20th century, recognition of psychological dimensions significantly advanced. Freud's theories on family influence marked an early turning point, expanded substantially by Erik Erikson, who highlighted that family relationships form not just social bonds but the fundamental architecture of human consciousness.

Advancements in mid-century introduced systems theory, illustrating complex familial interactions across generations. These interactions create intricate patterns connecting family members at levels of complexity far beyond simple social or biological ties. Contemporary approaches integrate neuroscience and epigenetics, demonstrating that family relationships do not merely influence consciousness but actively shape the neural pathways through which consciousness operates.

Considering this slow, meticulous development of pragmatic knowledge highlights an intriguing mystery: how ancient celestial frameworks anticipated sophisticated psychological patterns long before their scientific verification.

> *Perhaps the most profound mystery lies not in how human understanding has evolved to recognize these patterns, but in how divine inspiration accessed this knowledge millennia before human consciousness developed the sophistication to comprehend it*

Investigating historical and modern expressions of these frameworks provides essential insights into the evolution of consciousness and the potential sources of divine wisdom.

Early 20th-century psychological advancements significantly deepened our understanding of familial influence. Freud introduced critical insights into family dynamics shaping personality, further expanded by the recognition that family relationships form not just social bonds but the foundational architecture of human consciousness.

Mid-century theories, notably Murray Bowen's systems theory, highlighted family patterns as intricate feedback loops spanning generations. These patterns connect family members at complexities far beyond simple social or biological ties. Contemporary science integrates neuroscience, epigenetics, and quantum theory, recognizing family interactions as fundamentally shaping brain structures and gene expression. Family relationships do not merely influence consciousness; they actively sculpt the neural pathways through which consciousness operates.

This meticulous scientific progression poses profound questions about celestial wisdom: How did ancient traditions anticipate such intricate psychological patterns long before their modern verification?

> *Perhaps the most profound mystery lies not in how human understanding has evolved to recognize these patterns, but in how divine inspiration accessed this knowledge millennia before human consciousness developed the sophistication to comprehend it*

Investigating historical and contemporary manifestations of these traditions may yield insights into consciousness evolution and divine wisdom sources.

Sacred texts across cultures explicitly document family obligations. India's Mahabharata explores this theme dramatically through Arjuna's dialogue in the Bhagavad Gita, Bhishma's lifelong vows, and Gandhari's devoted actions. Similarly, the Ramayana illustrates deep familial duties through Rama's adherence to promises and Bharata's stewardship.

Chinese classics detail extensive family responsibilities: The *Classic of Filial Piety* recounts Emperor Shun's devotion, and *Analects of Confucius* emphasizes filial piety as foundational. Islamic texts highlight Abu Bakr's familial dedication and Yusuf's exemplary forgiveness, underscored extensively in the Quran and hadiths.

Biblical traditions present profound examples: Ruth's loyalty to Naomi, Joseph's care for his brothers, and David's kindness toward Mephibosheth, alongside comprehensive guidance in Proverbs and Ecclesiastes, collectively underscoring enduring family obligations.

African oral traditions intricately document familial obligations. The epic of Sundiata reveals complex, multigenerational familial duties, while Yoruba Ifa verses meticulously outline family responsibilities. Similarly, Zulu tradition details King Shaka's significant restructuring of familial roles for empire-building.

Native American narratives also emphasize family obligations vividly. The Lakota tale of Stone Boy highlights profound familial dedication, and the Haudenosaunee Great Law of Peace intricately codifies extended family responsibilities. Maya texts, including the Popol Vuh, extend familial duty into supernatural dimensions.

Each tradition precisely delineates family obligations beyond immediate kin, reaching distant relations and underscoring responsibilities that persist despite geographic or temporal distances. These ancient frameworks portray family as a transcendent network, providing insights into societal interpretations from ancient to modern contexts.

Throughout history, celestial wisdom has guided societies through frameworks balancing individual development and collective welfare.

Originally, familial obligations emphasized mutual support primarily for survival and communal harmony. However, modern interpretations have significantly expanded these duties, creating a "*prosperity paradox*" where individual success intensifies expectations of familial support far beyond basic needs.

Modern expectations extend obligations excessively, compelling individuals to support distant relatives' lifestyles, businesses, or households, often at the expense of personal integrity. This broadening pressure significantly diverges from original divine intentions, compromising the very principles that foster individual achievement. Sibling dynamics particularly illustrate this shift: successful individuals frequently face societal pressures to compromise personal values and professional integrity, and those resisting such obligations risk social ostracism.

This evolving interpretation raises critical questions about genuine free will within family structures. If success inevitably incurs expanding familial responsibilities, does such a system inherently undermine the principles of autonomy and personal development that it claims to support?

Examining sacred texts highlights the contrast between original divine intention and human interpretation. Ancient scriptures emphasize immediate family duties and individual spiritual accountability, maintaining a careful balance modern practices often overlook in favor of broader obligations. This shift raises a fundamental question: Can genuine free will thrive in a system where personal success inevitably expands familial and societal responsibilities?

Celestial and philosophical traditions consistently stress individual moral autonomy. Moral philosophy emphasizes that nothing is inherently good without qualification except a genuine intention rooted in good will. Sacred teachings, such as those in the Bhagavad Gita, similarly advocate protection only for genuinely vulnerable individuals, underscoring personal responsibility.

Yet human societies have gradually reinterpreted these precise boundaries, transforming individual achievement into collective entitlement. This societal pressure, often cloaked in spiritual language, manipulates sacred wisdom by invoking divine consequences to justify expanding obligations. As a result, successful individuals face increasing demands, extending far beyond immediate family needs, to support distant relatives and broader community expectations.

This reinterpretation starkly contrasts original celestial guidelines, creating what can be termed a *"prosperity paradox,"* where individual success triggers an endless cycle of obligation. Such pressures challenge personal autonomy, raising profound questions about the nature of free will within contemporary frameworks.

Historically, as civilizations evolved from small kin groups to complex societies, the concept of collective allegiance emerged, termed here as Sovereign Divinity. Early agricultural societies developed centralized governance under rulers considered divine intermediaries, as exemplified by Hammurabi's Code, the Egyptian Pharaoh's divine right, and China's Mandate of Heaven. These rulers were expected to uphold justice, protect the vulnerable, and maintain cosmic order, emphasizing moral governance and cautioning against tyranny and corruption.

As empires grew, the concept of nationhood transcended mere territorial claims. Greece developed the polis, a city-state emphasizing citizenship and civic duty, while Rome further refined this with the res publica, an early form of republic governance. Yet even these participatory models demanded absolute allegiance. Roman loyalty encompassed not just political structures but divine reverence for emperors, equating dissent with both treason and heresy.

Parallel religious traditions similarly sanctified collective allegiance. Ancient civilizations commonly regarded rulers as divine agents, tasked with upholding moral order and cosmic harmony. Sovereigns, thus chosen or guided by divine intent, were expected to embody justice and ethical leadership across various cultures.

However, Sovereign Divinity notably diverges from familial and religious traditions in one critical aspect: authority flows downward, empowering the few over the many. Ideally, this structure fosters societal cohesion and collective security; corrupted, it breeds despotic control, punishing even thoughts of deviation. Historical examples are abundant: Japan's Tokugawa Shogunate demanded absolute fealty through bushido; medieval Europe equated rebellion against monarchs with divine disobedience; China's Qin Dynasty imposed draconian obedience under threat of execution.

Over time, leaders increasingly abandoned original ethical mandates, pursuing personal gain and suppressing opposition under divine pretexts. Power shifted from being a means of safeguarding ethical principles to becoming an end in itself, transforming revolutionary ideals into authoritarian regimes. Thus, the original divine right evolved into oppressive structures, exemplified by abuses during the Crusades, the Inquisition, and various theocratic states.

Pragmatically, societies justified rigid structures as stabilizing necessities. Plato envisioned philosopher-kings guiding the masses wisely, mirrored in Confucian bureaucracy entrusting governance to learned scholars. Yet such rigidity often centralized power among those who manipulated Sovereign Divinity, forsaking justice for dominance.

Religious traditions frequently cautioned against this corruption, emphasizing moral accountability, fairness, and collective decision-making. Nonetheless, these warnings often went unheeded, with Sovereign Divinity becoming a tool of control rather than enlightenment.

Thus arises a critical historical question: When did leadership's responsibility shift from serving justice to asserting dominance? Sovereignty, originally defined by strict ethical mandates for maintaining societal harmony and justice, paradoxically became justification for oppression, highlighting the complex duality inherent in governance.

Throughout history, absolute power inevitably fostered corruption, transforming rulers from guardians of justice to self-serving oppressors. Initially revered as divine intermediaries, leaders often exploited their positions to amass wealth and consolidate authority. Egyptian Pharaohs, once symbolic custodians of ma'at, cosmic balance and justice, grew preoccupied with self-glorification. Lavish tombs and monuments reflected personal ambition rather than communal welfare, while workers suffered under harsh conditions, and widespread hardship went ignored.

Similarly, Rome's shift from republican ideals toward imperial decadence exemplifies this pattern. Emperors such as Nero and Caligula indulged extravagantly amidst public suffering, leveraging spectacles like gladiatorial games to distract citizens from systemic corruption. The Roman Senate, tasked with accountability, frequently succumbed to manipulation or coercion.

Parallel scenarios unfolded in dynastic China under the Mandate of Heaven. Ming and Qing emperors isolated themselves in luxury, detached from public struggles, leading to economic mismanagement and societal decay. France's Louis XVI and Marie Antoinette likewise epitomized such detachment, their extravagance intensifying public despair and igniting revolution.

Rulers justified extravagant excesses as necessities for stability and divine legitimacy, converting governance from public duty to personal enrichment. Power, once obtained, rarely saw peaceful relinquishment, entrenching oppressive structures still influencing modern politics.

Mechanisms of control evolved beyond physical coercion into sophisticated psychological manipulation through fear, propaganda, and rigid doctrines. Leaders ascended promising reform but frequently betrayed ideals for ambition. Alexander the Great, despite military brilliance, devastated countless societies. Mongol conquests similarly enforced brutal dominance, reshaping geopolitical realities through violence. European colonization exploited indigenous populations under false pretenses of civilization.

Even governance explicitly rejecting religious authority succumbed to tyranny. The French Revolution descended into ideological terror, while 20th-century totalitarian regimes under Stalin and Mao imposed devastating repression under rationalist claims. Despite promising liberation, these rulers replaced old oppressions with new ideological subjugation, silencing dissent through surveillance and brutality.

Throughout history, rulers curtailed free will not only through overt force but through subtle conditioning strategies. Ancient Chinese Legalism, prioritizing strict order, embedded fear-based compliance into governance. Similarly, medieval Europe's serfdom severely restricted personal autonomy, binding entire classes to monarchial authority. Modern authoritarian regimes have further refined control via media manipulation, mass surveillance, and bureaucratic constraints, creating the illusion of freedom while restricting autonomy through censorship, travel limitations, and economic dependency.

Repeatedly, societies have justified oppression as necessary for stability or progress, paradoxically undermining the freedoms crucial for genuine advancement. Borders, initially established for governance, evolved into barriers obstructing intellectual exchange and cultural dialogue. Historical periods of significant progress, the Silk Road's cultural interchange, the Islamic Golden Age's scientific innovation, and the Renaissance's revival of classical knowledge, underscore that open exchange propels civilization forward. Conversely, today's stringent visa policies, educational restrictions, and information censorship hinder the natural evolution of collective wisdom, limiting societal advancement.

Human progress has historically depended on open dialogue and the synthesis of diverse ideas. Major intellectual breakthroughs, from Copernicus' heliocentric theory to contemporary advances in artificial intelligence, resulted directly from free discourse. Suppressing debate through political, religious, or ideological censorship leads to intellectual stagnation, embedding ignorance into societal structures.

Despite rhetoric promoting intellectual freedom, contemporary society increasingly enforces ideological conformity through surveillance, punitive laws against dissent, and suppression of contradictory research. This systematic constraint of thought ironically contradicts the fundamental goals of enlightened civilization, masking intellectual oppression behind the facade of societal order.

Using a scientific analogy, societies resemble controlled experiments, wherein governance systems aim to balance structure with individual freedom, fostering stability and innovation simultaneously. However, historical patterns demonstrate governance structures frequently shifting toward rigid controls, stifling the dynamic interactions essential for genuine societal and intellectual growth.

Sovereign Divinity, initially intended to maintain order, has historically become an instrument of suppression. Leaders, fearful of free will's unpredictability, have systematically constrained independent thought and discouraged dissent. Instead of allowing societies to evolve through natural experimentation, stringent governance has often enforced conformity, equating deviations with threats rather than opportunities. Consequently, genuine innovation has been stifled, with creativity and philosophical exploration replaced by repetitive adherence to rigid ideologies.

Historical examples underscore how excessive control diminishes human potential. Visionaries from Galileo to modern whistleblowers have often faced persecution for their groundbreaking ideas, labeled as disruptive by established authorities. Creativity, inherently linked to freedom, has thus been consistently restricted by ideologies favoring uniformity over intellectual growth. Societies must acknowledge uncertainty as essential for advancement, much like a well-designed experiment that accommodates unforeseen outcomes. Overly stringent rules, by eliminating these variables, erode the freedoms fundamental to intellectual and societal progress.

A notable counterexample of such restrictive governance exists in Antarctica. Despite global political tensions, nations collaborate in Antarctica under the Antarctic Treaty, explicitly forbidding military activity, territorial claims, and exploitation. Researchers from rival countries freely exchange data and support one another, collectively pursuing knowledge beyond nationalistic agendas.

This cooperative spirit starkly contrasts with broader global realities, where borders, bureaucratic restrictions, and intellectual property controls limit the free exchange of knowledge. Human civilization, paradoxically, often confines its intellectual potential through imposed geopolitical constraints, unlike other species freely navigating the planet. This contrast raises a critical question: if progress relies on the unrestricted exchange of ideas, why does humanity persistently restrict its own intellectual and physical mobility?

Antarctica thus symbolizes humanity's capacity for cooperation and intellectual openness, starkly highlighting what is lost elsewhere. It exemplifies how free will, collaboration, and shared knowledge can propel civilization forward, whereas elsewhere, humanity frequently chooses division, restriction, and stagnation.

As we approach our conclusion, examining divinity in its celestial, familial, and sovereign forms reveals profound questions about humanity's quest for intelligence and enlightenment. Historically, our interpretation and application of these divinities often seem at odds with their intended purpose of guiding civilization toward higher understanding.

Celestial divinity, embodying wisdom and moral principles beyond human limitations, has frequently been distorted into mechanisms of control. Religious institutions, originally ethical guides, sometimes enforce rigid doctrines, stifling inquiry and punishing dissent. This contradiction prompts reflection: if celestial divinity truly encourages growth and transcendence, why have societies repeatedly harnessed it for intellectual suppression?

Similarly, familial divinity, originally designed for transmitting values and wisdom, has often morphed into hierarchical structures that limit individual autonomy. The traditional reverence for elders, intended to preserve and disseminate knowledge, occasionally devolves into rigid patriarchal systems that prioritize conformity over curiosity and exploration, inhibiting societal evolution.

Sovereign divinity, meant to safeguard collective stability, has experienced perhaps the greatest deviation. Governance, initially balancing order with justice, frequently prioritizes dominance and power consolidation. Leaders expected to function as stewards instead pursue self-interest, curtailing free will, innovation, and intellectual exchange.

> *To confine free will is to confine the mind, and to confine the mind is to confine the future*

Celestial divinity uniquely acknowledges free will, presenting moral frameworks without direct coercion, unlike familial and sovereign forms increasingly shaped by restrictive human constructs. Modern societies frequently interpret celestial principles to justify oppressive control, undermining true intellectual freedom and enlightenment.

An intelligent civilization should channel free will toward innovation and growth rather than constrain it. Celestial divinity itself might represent an advanced intelligence, aligning with the Kardashev scale's parameters of harnessing consciousness across dimensions. Moreover, the diverse yet structurally similar forms of celestial divinity worldwide suggest multiple advanced intelligences guiding human progress through varied but interconnected methodologies.

Considering humanity as part of a controlled cosmic experiment, one might envision diverse intelligent civilizations employing distinct methodologies, akin to nuclear, thermal, and hydroelectric energy sources: all uniquely effective yet pursuing a common goal. Varied expressions of celestial divinity could reflect separate civilizations testing alternate approaches to consciousness expansion, some emphasizing discipline and structure, others fostering freedom and exploration, each refining intelligence through free will.

Humanity, therefore, could be participating in an iterative cosmic process, continually refining consciousness and autonomy. Just as earthly civilizations alternate between collaboration and divergence, celestial intelligences might explore diverse governance and ethical frameworks to identify optimal conditions for conscious evolution. Such ongoing experimentation clarifies celestial divinity's fluid yet consistent nature, continuously adapting foundational principles to guide human consciousness.

The tension between freedom and restriction, rather than a mere conflict, potentially acts as an essential mechanism within this cosmic refinement. Humanity's struggles and transformations may collectively guide us toward a deeper realization of intellectual and existential liberty.

Principles exemplified by the Antarctica Protocol reflect this potential, promoting international collaboration over division. Antarctica illustrates that governance prioritizing cooperation enhances intellectual freedom and human progress. Extending these principles globally could liberate humanity from restrictive cycles, enabling genuine advancement.

Humanity's vast potential for discovery extends far beyond imposed limitations, highlighting the constant possibility of uncovering something extraordinary. Humans serve as unique perspectives through which the universe observes and explores itself, emphasizing our intrinsic role in cosmic exploration.

True intelligence does not impose walls around free will; it seeks to understand, refine, and expand its potential

Beyond the Bonds: The Triumvirate of Controlled Thought

Humans uniquely possess the profound ability to discern, question, and draw independent conclusions, catalyzing transformative shifts in human thought. While divinity historically influenced societies and free will, a smaller yet significant school of thinkers chose observation and logic over faith. Guided by the principle, "*What has not happened so far will not happen until it happens*" these pragmatists laid the groundwork for empirical thinking.

Early humans, striving for survival, learned through observation rather than divine intervention. Fire arose from friction, rain was recognized as a natural cycle, and survival depended more on practical cause and effect than rituals. Yet divine explanations persisted, filling gaps in understanding when uncertainties such as droughts or illnesses arose. The distinction between pragmatists and believers hinged not on experience but on their interpretations of the unknown.

As societies transitioned to agriculture, the divide between divine and pragmatic thought deepened. Farmers began identifying patterns influencing crop yield, adopting practices such as crop rotation and irrigation based on observation. Although divine rituals persisted, practical knowledge increasingly dictated agricultural success.

In early river-based civilizations along the Nile, Tigris, and Indus, priests initially doubled as agricultural advisors but soon shared authority with engineers and astronomers who accurately predicted natural events. While rulers continued presenting practical innovations as divine gifts, the significance of empirical observation in governance was undeniable. Detailed legal codes from Mesopotamia underscored the pragmatic application of knowledge, promoting fair resource distribution and land management.

Early scientific thought, exemplified by Greek philosophers, further challenged divine interpretations. Anaximander proposed a universe governed by natural laws independent of divinity. Heraclitus argued change itself as fundamental rather than divine will. These thinkers emphasized inquiry and empirical observation, gradually reshaping worldviews despite resistance from religious orthodoxy.

The Classical Age marked a turning point in rational thinking. The welfare of the people emerged as the ultimate law, highlighting the shift toward governance rooted in reason. Aristotle's logical methods in science and philosophy established foundations for empirical sciences. Socrates notably challenged divine narratives, emphasizing the necessity of examining one's life critically.

In Athens, intellectual inquiry flourished. Sophists viewed morality and governance as human constructs, open to debate and improvement. Plato's Academy fostered systematic learning and rigorous examination over unquestioned faith. Aristotle advanced these ideas, developing methodologies based on meticulous observation and categorization.

In Rome, governance was shifting towards a governance structured around law, codified in the Twelve Tables, emphasizing civic duty rather than divine mandates. Engineering projects such as roads and aqueducts reflected disciplined planning rather than divine favor, while Roman legal traditions introduced checks and balances separating governance from religious authority. This evolution marked a pivotal shift toward empirical reasoning and structured pragmatism, shaping humanity's trajectory toward rationality.

The tension between pragmatic reasoning and divine authority persisted historically, exemplified by Socrates, whose dialectical method questioned established beliefs. His execution for allegedly corrupting youth underscored resistance to intellectual freedom, a paradox echoed throughout history as societies grappled between faith and reason.

In the Middle Ages, religion regained dominance, intertwining deeply with governance and daily life. Questioning divine authority became perilous, as institutions like the Catholic Church enforced orthodoxy through harsh measures such as exile or execution. Pragmatic thought, however, adapted within religious frameworks or turned to practical fields less susceptible to condemnation.

Islamic scholars significantly advanced scientific thought, particularly in mathematics, medicine, and optics. Alhazen, considered the father of the scientific method, established rigorous experimental protocols foundational to modern research. His innovations in optics profoundly impacted astronomy and medicine. Concurrently, Chinese engineers developed intricate irrigation systems supporting vast populations, aligning pragmatic resource management with Confucian principles.

The Renaissance revitalized pragmatic thought in Europe through the rediscovery of classical texts. Thinkers like Copernicus and Galileo challenged religious doctrines with heliocentric theories. The conviction that truth exists independently of religious decree symbolized pragmatic inquiry's resilience. Pragmatic exploration flourished, particularly when framed as an investigation into divine creation, thus advancing knowledge even under restrictive conditions.

The Scientific Revolution marked a critical shift. Empirical discovery and inductive reasoning became central, emphasizing knowledge as a form of power and control. Isaac Newton unified celestial and terrestrial phenomena under universal gravitation, demonstrating predictable natural laws independent of supernatural explanations. René Descartes reinforced the grounding of human existence in rational thought, promoting philosophical inquiry free from theological constraints.

During the Enlightenment, intellectual principles permeated societal governance. John Locke and Voltaire advocated reason-based governance and human rights over divine monarchy. Locke's social contract theory, emphasizing governmental authority derived from people's consent, laid democratic foundations. Voltaire fiercely critiqued religious dogma, championing free thought and civil liberties. This profound intellectual transformation shifted societal foundations from divinity to reason and empirical experience, catalyzing subsequent political revolutions.

By the Industrial Revolution, pragmatic thought had largely displaced divine explanations, significantly impacting medicine, engineering, and governance. Empirical insights began guiding decision-making, exemplified by Louis Pasteur and Robert Koch's germ theory, which replaced beliefs in divine punishment with scientific understanding. Vaccinations, sanitation, and medical innovations like anesthesia greatly enhanced public health, demonstrating science's practical superiority over religious rituals. Philosophical perspectives transitioned from merely interpreting reality toward actively transforming it, underscoring pragmatism's direct impact on societal progress.

Technological advancements reshaped economies and urban environments. Infrastructure projects such as the Brooklyn Bridge and London Underground showcased engineering grounded in physics rather than theological interpretation. Railroads transformed commerce, underscoring human ingenuity as the primary driver of progress. Yet religion persisted, adapting to the changing world. Movements like the Social Gospel emerged, addressing moral implications of industrialization through advocacy for social justice and economic reform.

Philosophers critically examined this shift, highlighting society's pivot from divine explanations to human mastery. They warned of potential moral voids arising from the absence of traditional religious frameworks, concerns later echoed by existentialists questioning progress without transcendental guidance.

The pragmatic dominance evident during the Industrial Revolution also influenced legal systems, with secular laws increasingly shaped by rational and humanist principles. The abolition of slavery exemplified justice shaped by humanist arguments rather than solely religious morality. Yet tensions between empirical knowledge and moral guidance persisted amidst rapid urbanization and industrial change.

In recent centuries, pragmatic thought accelerated further. Emphasis shifted toward rationality's essential role in guiding a meaningful and progressive life, inspired by compassion and guided by knowledge. Quantum physics challenged deterministic views, highlighting reality's inherent uncertainties as explored by Einstein and Bohr. Advances in artificial intelligence and genetic engineering further expanded human capabilities, proving that knowledge acquisition could be systematic and independent of divine influence.

Stephen Hawking's theories suggested a universe emerging naturally, without divine intervention, shifting existential discussions from theology to physics. Nonetheless, spiritual beliefs endure, continually adapting to scientific advancements rather than opposing them outright, maintaining the enduring interplay between reason and faith.

The evolution of pragmatic thought has not consistently matched human progression, highlighting a persistent complexity: despite scientific and technological advances, irrational beliefs and misinformation persist, amplified by social media. Pragmatic thinking, though propelling humanity forward, coexists uneasily with emotional and ideological attachments to unverified beliefs, underscoring the nonlinear nature of knowledge advancement.

Evolution involves continuous refinement, yet pragmatic thought has experienced uneven development, thriving in rational environments and receding when fear or uncertainty fuels divine explanations. The historical interplay between rationality and belief is cyclic, an ongoing dialogue exploring known realities and unknown possibilities.

Pragmatic approaches to free will differ markedly from divine interpretations. While divine systems provide structured moral boundaries with prescribed repercussions, pragmatic frameworks define free will through reason, empirical evidence, and personal autonomy. This divergence raises critical questions regarding pragmatic thought's adaptability: has it evolved dynamically alongside human intellect, or has it become rigid within its own empirical boundaries?

Multiple intellectual traditions, existentialism, determinism, and compatibilism, illustrate the diverse pragmatic approaches to free will. Existentialist perspectives emphasize humanity's inherent freedom coupled with profound personal responsibility. Conversely, determinist views consider free will an illusion shaped entirely by prior causes, highlighting pragmatic thought's breadth and ongoing discourse.

Pragmatic free will prioritizes autonomy, responsibility, and skepticism, contrasting sharply with divinely dictated moral structures. Pragmatists emphasize rational deliberation and self-accountability, free from divine absolution. Yet, pragmatic thought faces criticism for potentially imposing empirical boundaries that dismiss subjective beliefs. As John Stuart Mill noted in On Liberty, "*Genius can only breathe freely in an atmosphere of freedom*" prompting reflection on whether pragmatic frameworks genuinely facilitate intellectual freedom or inadvertently establish restrictive epistemological limits.

Could pragmatic systems, despite advocating openness, inadvertently adopt rigid stances against faith-based perspectives, mirroring the very dogmatism they criticize? This paradox challenges pragmatic thought's self-awareness, particularly regarding life's end: is existence purely biological, or does it transcend physical form? While pragmatic frameworks typically reject metaphysical speculation without empirical support, emerging theories like Roger Penrose's quantum consciousness suggest deeper existential layers, prompting critical reconsideration.

Physicists such as Stephen Hawking and Richard Dawkins maintain consciousness arises solely from biological functions, whereas Penrose proposes quantum mechanics might reveal a more profound reality. Pragmatism thus faces a pivotal question: was it adapted flexibly or entrenched itself rigidly, similar to traditional faiths adjusting views only when confronted by overwhelming evidence? Genuine rational inquiry within pragmatism demands openness to possibilities without insisting on immediate empirical validation.

Atheism and agnosticism, central to pragmatic thought, paradoxically risk becoming rigid doctrines themselves. Friedrich Nietzsche critiqued atheism as merely the inversion of theism, rather than true liberation from dogmatic beliefs. To maintain intellectual integrity, pragmatism must acknowledge and continually challenge its biases.

Pragmatism fundamentally searches for meaning despite its empirical foundations, emphasizing that the struggle toward meaningful goals can itself provide fulfillment. Yet pragmatic thought often finds itself at odds with theological frameworks, highlighting an internal rigidity. Pragmatism must carefully avoid becoming dogmatic, replacing old rigid beliefs with new ones, thereby maintaining openness and flexibility in its pursuit of understanding.

Pragmatic approaches frame free will through autonomy, responsibility, and skepticism, distinct from divinely mandated moral systems. Existentialists, determinists, and compatibilists offer varied interpretations: existentialist thought highlights humanity's inherent freedom coupled with profound personal responsibility, while determinist perspectives view free will as an illusion shaped entirely by prior causes.

Ultimately, pragmatism must question whether it fosters genuine intellectual independence or inadvertently imposes ideological constraints. As scientific discoveries, including potential extraterrestrial intelligence, reshape human understanding, pragmatic thought must remain adaptable, ensuring it does not devolve into the rigidity it originally sought to escape. The true measure of pragmatic free will lies in its continuous evolution and openness, free from dogmatic skepticism.

Pragmatic systems emphasize personal autonomy, rational choice, and responsibility, asserting that individuals must fully bear the consequences of their decisions without recourse to divine absolution. Intellectual freedom, crucial for genuine innovation and creativity, thrives within an environment of autonomy. Yet, does pragmatic thought genuinely foster intellectual freedom, or does its prioritization of empirical knowledge inadvertently create limitations?

Scientific inquiry, grounded in skepticism, occasionally risks dismissing subjective or alternative perspectives outright rather than engaging critically. Pragmatism, despite advocating discernment, often clashes with faith-based perspectives, paradoxically replicating the rigidity it seeks to critique. This tension prompts reflection: could pragmatism's adherence to empirical skepticism inadvertently reinforce its own epistemic closure?

A significant question in pragmatic thought revolves around the nature of existence beyond biological death. While traditionally avoiding metaphysical speculations without empirical proof, recent theories propose consciousness may transcend purely biological functions. This challenges pragmatic frameworks, historically rooted in observable phenomena, to reassess their boundaries. Has pragmatism adapted flexibly to such developments, or does it, like traditional belief systems, only adjust when evidence becomes overwhelming? For pragmatism to genuinely champion rational inquiry, openness to possibilities beyond immediate empirical validation is essential.

The development of atheism and agnosticism within pragmatic thought highlights another paradox. While emphasizing critical thinking, these frameworks risk becoming rigid dogmas themselves. Friedrich Nietzsche criticized atheism as merely inverted theism rather than true liberation from dogma. Pragmatism must continually reassess its ideological biases to maintain intellectual honesty.

This underscores that even pragmatic thought remains deeply concerned with existential meaning. Yet historically, pragmatism has often opposed religious systems rather than bridging dialogue with them. This highlights the inherent risk that, in challenging traditional dogmas, pragmatic thought could inadvertently create new, equally restrictive frameworks, thus perpetuating rigidity rather than fostering genuine openness.

As science and technology continue redefining human existence, pragmatic thought faces novel dilemmas, such as the potential discovery of intelligent extraterrestrial life, which would dramatically alter human self-understanding. Will pragmatism swiftly adapt to such transformative findings, or resist until evidence compels change?

> *True pragmatic free will hinges on its capacity for continuous evolution and openness, safeguarding against dogmatic rigidity*

Pragmatic thought, like divinity, has diversified into multiple traditions, including existentialism, determinism, and compatibilism.

Determinists like Baruch Spinoza viewed free will as an illusion, shaped by causal forces. Pragmatism does not adhere to one doctrine but remains a field of evolving interpretations. Its conception of free will rests on autonomy, responsibility, and skepticism, in contrast to divine systems framed by moral imperatives and absolution.

The paradox arises when pragmatism, while promoting openness, becomes hostile toward faith-based frameworks, replicating the rigidity it seeks to dismantle. Does it, in its quest for rational inquiry, inadvertently establish new dogmas that constrain rather than liberate thought?

Debates about life after death exemplify this tension. Though pragmatic systems avoid unproven metaphysics, quantum theories like Roger Penrose's suggest consciousness may interact with a deeper substrate of reality. The question becomes: can pragmatism embrace such implications, or does it adjust its views only under empirical compulsion? True rational inquiry must remain open to the unknown, not just the measurable.

Pragmatism's turn toward atheism and agnosticism further complicates its identity. While these positions prize critical thinking, they risk becoming inverted forms of the dogma they reject. Intellectual honesty requires acknowledging that rigid skepticism can mirror the very absolutism it challenges. Pragmatism must question whether it fosters true intellectual independence or merely substitutes one orthodoxy for another.

Is ignorance the greatest enemy of knowledge, or is it the illusion of knowledge?

The above question captures pragmatism's risk: a culture of inquiry can calcify into a culture of exclusion, where alternative perspectives are dismissed as unworthy of exploration. While pragmatic thought values skepticism and openness, even these ideals can become rigid doctrines when institutionalized. If pragmatic thought rejects entire domains of inquiry outright, it risks echoing the inflexibility of the systems it critiques, highlighting the necessity of remaining genuinely open to diverse perspectives.

True progress demands openness. A civilization that limits exploration to accepted truths stifles evolution. Knowledge, like energy, must be harnessed through relentless questioning. A system that curtails intellectual freedom under the guise of rationality is not a path to enlightenment but a polished form of stagnation.

Scientific thinking emerged in response to such limitations, seeking to center inquiry around evidence. Yet, we must ask: has it truly escaped the dogmas of its predecessors, or has it inherited their tendency to enshrine its own boundaries? The challenge ahead is not to abandon rationality, but to ensure it never becomes a gatekeeper against wonder.

The true paradox of free will is not in our ability to choose, but in the invisible lines we refuse to cross

Pragmatic thought, once the adversary of dogma, increasingly resembles it. Though it claims to support intellectual openness, it often excludes lines of inquiry that challenge empirical orthodoxy, quietly restricting exploration.

This selective rigidity raises a difficult question: has pragmatism, in seeking to liberate the mind, instead erected invisible boundaries around free will? If so, it risks becoming not a beacon of inquiry but a system that controls thought under the guise of reason.

Human evolution was guided not by strength or speed, but by intellect. Lacking biological advantages, early humans turned to nature for lessons on survival. They studied the land to cultivate crops, observed animals to devise hunting strategies, and created tools to offset their physical fragility. Humans uniquely possess foresight and planning capabilities, yet in raw power and predatory ability, we have historically been outmatched by numerous other species.

Despite their vulnerability, humans rose to dominance through observation and innovation. Their defining trait was not instinct, but the ability to accumulate and refine knowledge across generations. This gave rise to communities focused not only on survival but collective advancement, forming systems of governance, communication, and technology.

This unique ability is now called critical thinking: the disciplined process of conceptualizing and evaluating information to reach reasoned conclusions. Critical thinking serves as the essential tool for navigating the evolving landscape of human knowledge, ensuring we do not become constrained by the very systems we establish. It is this capacity that differentiates humanity, enabling continuous learning and civilization-building.

Science emerged from this same spirit of inquiry. It is not merely a collection of facts, but a dynamic method born from curiosity, trial, and observation. From controlling fire to crafting tools, early humans evaluated materials, observed reactions, and refined techniques. Fire altered nutrition and safety. Tools enhanced efficiency. Each step forward required experimentation and inference.

Agriculture became the next leap. Humans recognized growth cycles, manipulated soil conditions, and learned to irrigate. They selected favorable crops over generations, moving from foraging to farming. The practical application of observation and experimentation transformed survival into societal progress.

Science is the extension of critical thinking applied to nature. It evolves with human intellect, driven by a relentless pursuit not of belief, but understanding. Truths become clear upon discovery; the challenge lies in the act of discovery itself. This ethos remains the cornerstone of human progress.

As civilizations expanded, so did their mastery of the material world. Metallurgy marked a turning point, requiring precise control of heat and chemistry to transform ore into tools and architecture. This early industrial leap demanded high-order problem-solving, laying foundations for structural innovation.

Alongside metallurgy, mathematics emerged as a critical intellectual discipline. In Mesopotamia, Egypt, and the Indus Valley, early humans created systems to measure land, track celestial cycles, and build with precision. Math evolved beyond counting into abstraction which led to the birth of theoretical problem-solving. The essence of mathematics lies in continuous questioning and curiosity, driven by the intrinsic human desire to understand and explore.

Science, from its inception, has been the codified expression of curiosity and imagination. It is not a static accumulation of facts, but a method, an iterative act of hypothesizing, testing, and refining. Truths become clear once uncovered; the challenge lies in their discovery.

With the scientific method matured, humanity progressed from Newtonian certainty to Einsteinian relativity. Newton defined gravity and motion, enabling mechanical revolution. Einstein shattered those frameworks, revealing time and space as relative. Science advances primarily through discovering new perspectives on known facts, fundamentally shifting our conceptual frameworks.

The Industrial and Atomic Ages accelerated this evolution. Steam, electricity, and mechanization redefined production. Quantum mechanics, despite its strangeness, unlocked semiconductors and lasers. Scientific inquiry must remain rooted in experimentation; without empirical validation, science risks losing its path. Yet paradoxically, quantum uncertainty sparked deeper insights.

Space exploration expanded the reach of human thought beyond Earth. Telescopes revealed distant galaxies, while missions probed the solar system. The universe consistently challenges our imagination, proving itself not only stranger than previously thought, but stranger than we can conceive. That profound strangeness continually drives discovery.

Today, artificial intelligence redefines cognition itself. From silicon arises synthetic thought, a reflection of our own ingenuity. Machines now identify patterns, make decisions, and model intelligence. The critical challenge lies less in whether machines think, and more in whether humans continue to think deeply and critically. AI is not merely a tool; it is the most recent mirror of our capacity to question and create.

AI now accelerates discovery across medicine, climate science, and theoretical physics, analyzing complexity at scales previously unimaginable. Yet, without critical thinking, these breakthroughs would stall. Humanity's relentless drive to overcome limitations has transformed grains of sand into processors and primitive signals into global communication, demonstrating our unwillingness to passively await evolutionary progress.

Critical thinking is not merely a method, it is the essence of free will. It shapes our capacity to question, innovate, and define reality. Science embodies the poetic exploration of reality, providing the means through which we continually redefine possibility. The future belongs to those who challenge the world as it exists and dare to envision what it might become.

> *Free will is not merely the ability to choose; it is the responsibility to question, to reason, and to evolve beyond the boundaries of the known*

Chapter 3: The Architecture of Certainty: From Infinite Potential to Prescribed Reality - Beyond the Bonds: The Triumvirate of Controlled Thought

Science embodies this responsibility, allowing us to reshape destiny through truth-seeking.

Pragmatism, valuable in its rejection of blind faith, does not ask why. It explains what happens but rarely how. Science goes further. It questions mechanisms, explores causes, and refines knowledge through relentless inquiry. Understanding lightning, for example, requires more than accepting its existence, it demands dissecting its physics.

Science navigates where pragmatism points. Pragmatism tells us land exists; science builds the ship. One observes fire burns; the other understands combustion. Science continually pursues the unknown, revealing not just what is, but how to shape it.

Pragmatism views truth through subjective lenses, while science adjusts the lens itself. Like the parable of the blind men and the elephant, pragmatism reveals partial truths; science seeks comprehensive understanding. Science transcends individual perception, expanding knowledge beyond immediate experience.

Science is not content with partial understanding. It sharpens critical thought and deepens insight into life's purpose, a pursuit shared by both divine and pragmatic systems. Pragmatism explains outcomes; science seeks the underlying causes. Science thrives on skepticism, rejecting stasis, constantly striving for deeper comprehension.

Each scientific leap, from fire to quantum theory, stems from curiosity and the refusal to settle. Science reveals the unknown, expanding awareness with every discovery. Its power lies not merely in answers, but in framing deeper, more meaningful questions.

Science and pragmatism are complementary, not opposing, philosophies. Pragmatism lays foundations; science constructs upon them. One shifts us from ignorance to awareness, the other propels us toward transformation. All scientists inherently practice pragmatism, though not all pragmatists necessarily engage scientifically.

Pragmatism does not dismiss the unseen; it merely avoids blind acceptance. True pragmatists demand evidence but remain open to the immeasurable. History affirms this equilibrium. Isaac Newton, foundational physicist, simultaneously explored divine texts alongside mathematical principles. Blaise Pascal crafted rational arguments about faith, demonstrating that knowledge and belief are not inherently in conflict.

Science represents the higher education of thought, pragmatism its foundational level. Blind faith is intellectual illiteracy, yet divinity, independent of dogma, retains intrinsic wisdom. Einstein turned to philosophical texts like the Bhagavad Gita for deeper insight, as did J. Robert Oppenheimer after unleashing atomic power, recognizing profound existential truths within spiritual traditions. Their experiences illustrate that science without philosophical depth becomes sterile, while spirituality without rational inquiry becomes directionless.

Even artificial intelligence reveals harmony among ancient wisdom traditions. Despite linguistic diversity, their core message remains consistent: humanity seeks a return to its divine origins through surrender, awakening, or grace. The shared destination is union with the divine and the soul's liberation into profound peace.

Pragmatism does not dismiss the unknown but approaches it with skeptical openness. It requires evidence before acceptance, embracing uncertainty humbly. Pragmatism transforms habitual thought into genuine analysis rather than mere repetition of prejudice.

Science, structured around inquiry, unfolds continuously as the response to free will's quest for truth. Originating in myth and progressing through critique, science evolves precisely by challenging its foundations. Pragmatism and science form a continuum while one cultivates the mindset necessary for inquiry; the other provides the methodological rigor required to explore reality deeply.

Science and divinity, far from adversaries, mirror each other in structure. Both define frameworks and invite questioning. Both use varied methods to approach the same goal: understanding existence. AI models, trained without bias, reveal that sacred texts across cultures point toward one unified objective: return to the divine.

To reach different minds, divinity adopted many forms, animal, human, symbolic, not to distort but to clarify. Much like how scientific analogies help decode the abstract, these representations serve to translate the formless into forms we can comprehend. Their purpose is not contradiction, but access.

Consider space exploration: both the U.S. and Soviet Union pursued the moon. One developed a pressurized pen for zero gravity, the other used a pencil. Though their paths diverged, their destination was the same. This parable reflects the essence of both divinity and science, multiple paths, one truth.

In aviation, Airbus and Boeing use distinct control systems, sidestick and yoke, yet both pursue safe, efficient flight. Their differences underscore a key truth: multiple methods can achieve the same goal. The same applies to divinity, where varied paths reflect cultural and intellectual diversity, not contradiction. Pragmatism, by contrast, often confines itself to what is measurable, lacking the multidimensional reach of science and celestial frameworks.

Pragmatism teaches function. Science and divinity teach comprehension. One builds foundations, the others expand the cosmos. Profound truths often coexist alongside equally profound alternatives, revealing deeper dimensions of reality. Together, they help us embrace complexity.

Humanity's recent progress, especially in the past century, has resembled winning gold at every Olympic event. The catalysts? Mobility and communication. The automobile and airplane revolutionized movement. Letters evolved into global video calls. Technology turned isolation into instant access, allowing one person's discovery to uplift all.

In this new paradigm, one community no longer has to reinvent the wheel. A solution refined in one corner of the world can now ripple globally. Medical advancements that once seemed impossible, organ transplants, for instance, are now routine, due to the compounding power of shared knowledge.

Antarctica exemplifies this spirit. Here, scientists of all nations work side by side, untethered from religious or political constraints. Collaboration, peer review, and open data replace secrecy and competition. Clinical trials are published, not hoarded. Knowledge becomes public domain.

In the commercial world, rare but powerful examples exist. Volvo's choice to share its seatbelt patent saved countless lives. It showed that altruism can rival profit as a catalyst for change.

Academia, ideally, serves this same goal. It is the crucible for human advancement, where ideas are debated, evaluated, and refined. Yet academia itself struggles with barriers like paywalls, politics, prestige that hinder open exploration. Education's true purpose is to foster independent thought rather than prescribe conclusions. Ironically, systems built to nurture inquiry sometimes obscure the very truths they were designed to reveal.

> *Knowledge, when shared, multiplies. When hoarded, it stagnates. The true evaluation of an intelligent civilization is not just in what it discovers, but in how freely it ensures those discoveries reach all who seek them*

Humanity's ascent has been marked by the unique ability to retain, refine, and transmit knowledge. Unlike instinct-bound species, humans devised systems to ensure that discoveries were cumulative, not cyclical. Ancient innovations, zero from India, algebra from Persia, calculus from Newton and Leibniz, continue to shape modern science, engineering, and economics.

Global progress reflects contributions from all corners. African astronomy, Incan agriculture, Chinese medicine, and Mayan mathematics were once localized achievements, now foundational to global development. This tapestry of innovation underscores how civilizations advance by building on each other's insights.

Knowledge dissemination has always followed mobility and recordkeeping. From oral storytelling to stone tablets, paper to printing press, and now the internet, each medium has broadened access. Advances in medicine and agriculture alone have transformed societies more profoundly than conflicts ever disrupted them. Every new insight fuels the next.

Yet, knowledge is inherently paradoxical. While empowering, it can also entrench existing paradigms. Systems become rigid, resisting challenges posed by Galileo, Darwin, and today's innovators in AI and genetic engineering. True critical thinkers remain open, prepared to challenge even their deepest convictions, whereas certainty often accompanies ignorance.

Education, in its purest form, embodies lifelong learning rather than mere rote instruction. Learning began in nature, evolved through apprenticeships, and culminated in formal systems. Its essence, however, remained unchanged: to cultivate thoughtful inquiry.

Chapter 3: The Architecture of Certainty: From Infinite Potential to Prescribed Reality - Beyond the Bonds: The Triumvirate of Controlled Thought

Genuine education integrates intensive thought and moral character, fundamentally liberating rather than confining the mind.

Initially, structured knowledge was reserved for the few, deeply personalized and culturally embedded. Confucian governance, India's Gurukul traditions, Arabic scholarship, and diverse indigenous methods across Africa, Persia, and the Americas sustained scientific and philosophical inquiry through personalized, experiential frameworks.

The Industrial Revolution marked a profound educational shift. As machinery standardized labor, education followed suit, shifting from cultivating mastery to producing uniformity. Industrialization facilitated wider access to refined knowledge through print and digital media. Yet the relentless pursuit of efficiency sometimes obscured deeper wisdom and creative genius.

Colonial empires spread standardized educational models, often suppressing indigenous systems and adaptive learning traditions. In this pursuit of uniformity, schools frequently suppressed innate human creativity, diminishing intellectual diversity and adaptability.

Higher education increasingly mirrored factories, structured into departments and degrees. Manuals replaced mentorship, homogenizing knowledge dissemination and constraining intellectual exploration. Efforts to control and standardize learning sometimes inadvertently stifled the innovation and brilliance they sought to foster.

Machines replicate knowledge, but genuine innovation arises from minds free from rigidity. True educational progress is measured less by knowledge accumulated than by the depth and rigor of our questioning.

Contemporary education frequently prioritizes memorization over inquiry, narrowing intellectual diversity. Despite advanced technological capabilities, our educational practices often remain rooted in century-old paradigms, illustrating a troubling gap between potential and practice.

Standardized testing, meant to objectively assess intelligence, often neglects genuine cognitive diversity, eroding the natural curiosity essential for lifelong learning. Rigid educational models stifle creativity, favor conformity, and discourage genuine intellectual exploration.

Education transformed from experiential exploration to systematic replication, shifting central questions from genuine discovery to standardized performance metrics. This evolution systematically diminished critical thought and creativity.

True innovation emerges not from conformity, but from defying standardization. Visionaries who revolutionized society rarely followed predefined curricula, instead embracing persistent questioning, resilience, and boundless curiosity, demonstrating that ordinary individuals possess extraordinary potential when freed from rigid constraints.

> *A machine can be programmed to repeat, but only a mind free from rigidity can create. True progress is not measured by how much we learn, but by how deeply we question what we think we know*

The irony is unmistakable: despite mastering global communication and digital mobility, educational frameworks continue reinforcing outdated paradigms. Although our exploration extends into space, vast expanses of our oceans remain unexplored. Could a more advanced intelligence lurk beneath, awaiting our intellectual evolution?

Progress demands challenging not only external frontiers but internal assumptions

> *Innovation is not born from what we know, but from what we dare to question*

The next leap forward will not emerge from the stars, but rather from within the unconstrained human mind.

Historically, pragmatism refined human thought by rejecting beliefs unsupported by observation and logic. However, as education systems standardized thought processes, they inadvertently replaced rigorous inquiry with conformity, weakening society's collective reasoning. Modern pragmatism now extends beyond challenging social norms, instead confronting fundamental biological truths that currently lack answers within rational frameworks.

Contemporary pragmatism demands more than inclusion, it insists upon absolute conformity. Previously recognized psychological conditions now receive validation without critical examination. Basic biological realities, such as motherhood being exclusive to biological females, face aggressive opposition. The concept of tolerance has transformed into a rigid expectation of agreement, suppressing opposing viewpoints rather than encouraging open dialogue.

This new pragmatism undermines critical thinking by labeling genuine inquiry as discrimination. Incidents previously viewed through a compassionate medical lens now face societal pressure for unquestioned acceptance. Questioning is no longer perceived as rational skepticism but framed as intolerance, highlighting how deeply this ideology has infiltrated societal norms.

How did such an ideology proliferate swiftly and become impervious to rational discourse? Standardized education, although not solely responsible, undoubtedly provided fertile ground for this radical shift. Educational structures originally aimed at fostering intellectual growth now inadvertently amplify ideological extremism by discouraging analytical thinking.

This ideological shift poses significant threats to humanity's progression toward intellectual advancement. Academia, historically the sanctuary of free thought, now operates increasingly as a gatekeeper of ideological conformity. Standardized education and rigid assessment criteria produce individuals skilled at recitation but deficient in independent thought.

The intersection of pragmatism, science, and academia thus reveals an unsettling paradox. Pragmatism, initially a tool for dispelling irrationality, now entangles itself in ideological rigidity. Science, despite experiencing ideological pressures, remains a crucial advocate for critical inquiry, while academia requires urgent self-correction to restore its foundational principles of intellectual exploration and true enlightenment.

> *Learning systems derived from the universe have never curtailed free will, nor do they seem likely to in the foreseeable future. Yet, human-designed systems have demonstrated, within mere decades, a troubling proficiency at doing precisely that.*

Bonds Beyond Time: The Triumvirate of Dominion and Might

Humans have emerged as Earth's dominant species within a finite cycle of birth, growth, and eventual demise. Unlike other organisms driven solely by survival instincts, humans uniquely pursue meaning beyond mere existence. Despite physical vulnerabilities, humanity has mastered nature through intellectual prowess, overcoming threats from species ranging from disease-carrying mosquitoes to formidable predators like wolves and elephants.

Human ascendancy is rooted not solely in biological evolution, but in intellectual curiosity and innovative thought. Critical thinking and creativity allow humans to reshape their environment rather than merely adapting to it. Yet paradoxically, humans also impose artificial restrictions on themselves, dividing into nations and ideologies, exemplified starkly by boundaries like the Korean Demilitarized Zone, a physical barrier ironically nurturing a thriving natural sanctuary untouched by human activity.

This ascendancy was not accidental but fostered by two intertwined philosophies: Celestial Divinity, guiding morality and purpose, and the Laws of the Universe, underpinning scientific inquiry. Historically perceived as distinct, recent advances in neuroscience and astrophysics highlight their convergence, suggesting consciousness and the soul might represent facets of a single existential truth. Nonetheless, humanity struggles to universally accept this unity.

While universal systems promote exploration and free will, human-made institutions like governments, economies often impose conformity, stifling creativity. Despite these physical and societal constraints, mental mobility remains limitless, empowering continual intellectual exploration and innovation. The greatest challenge of our era is that scientific understanding advances more rapidly than societal wisdom. The human mind, unrestricted by barriers, remains the driving force behind progress.

Civilization embodies a fundamental paradox: we erect physical walls yet simultaneously dismantle barriers within thought. True progress occurs through challenging accepted norms and embracing the unknown.

> *True progress is measured not by the walls we construct, but by the barriers of thought we tear down. The limitless mind is the true frontier of human existence*

Early human societies thrived without structured governance, driven purely by collaborative survival. However, as populations expanded, governance evolved from necessity into structured authority, marking humanity's transition from communal harmony to institutional control.

The term politics originates from the Greek *"politika"* meaning *"affairs of the cities"* reflecting its ancient roots in structured governance systems. Early political formations arose in civilizations like

Mesopotamia, Egypt, and the Indus Valley, establishing codes of conduct, taxation, and military defense. As these systems evolved, leadership progressed from tribal chiefs to kings and emperors, shifting governance from survival-oriented to dominion-focused.

With dominion came physical barriers, initially protective but eventually symbolic of exclusion, dividing populations both externally and internally. Political structures increasingly utilized division as a tool of power, recognizing that true dominance lay in controlling thought, not merely movement. Through indoctrination and propaganda, rulers reinforced their authority, sometimes invoking divine mandates, sometimes rejecting them entirely, in both cases limiting free will.

Unlike universal laws that reflect balance and adaptability, political structures imposed rigidity and restriction, curtailing intellectual freedom. Despite evolving forms of governance from monarchies to democracies, the essence remained consistent: control over human thought and action under the guise of maintaining order.

Anti-intellectualism has been a constant thread winding its way through our political and cultural life

Yet, throughout history, free thought and resistance have persisted, continually challenging imposed constraints. The paradox of human civilization remains evident: humanity builds physical barriers while striving intellectually to dismantle them.

A civilization does not become intelligent by erecting walls; it becomes intelligent by tearing down the illusions that confine it

Politics, initially designed to protect freedom, paradoxically became a pervasive mechanism for control, infiltrating familial structures, workplaces, and societal interactions, thereby diminishing the collaboration that once defined human advancement.

This pervasive control contrasts starkly with the inherent flexibility and adaptability of universal and divine systems, underscoring the critical importance of intellectual freedom in humanity's ongoing journey toward true civilization.

Divinity and religious traditions have evolved significantly, shifting from rigid doctrines with severe penalties for nonconformity to more inclusive interpretations recognizing diverse lifestyles and beliefs. Similarly, scientific knowledge continually transforms, evident in shifts from geocentric models to heliocentric understanding and redefining Pluto's planetary status. Genuine advancement in consciousness inevitably involves challenging established beliefs, a process often accompanied by difficulty or discomfort, underscoring that true progress demands openness to revision and growth.

Human governance, however, diverged from this adaptable path, often suppressing intellectual freedom and promoting control. Originally designed to facilitate order, politics became a tool for ideological dominance, constraining critical thought and autonomy. Free will and creativity, foundational to human advancement, frequently became casualties under governance systems that prioritized obedience over inquiry.

Unlike universal laws and natural systems, which inherently balance multiple forces without absolute dominance, human political structures commonly enforce singular ideologies. This rigidity contrasts starkly with nature, where conflict arises strictly for survival purposes. In human societies, artificially constructed divisions and ideological conflicts often override natural instincts, hampering collective progress.

Yet, historical advancements in medicine, technology, and genetics highlight humanity's potential when intellectual curiosity prevails over restrictive governance. True intelligence, characterized by continuous questioning and adaptability, requires freedom from enforced dogma. Often, individuals resist truths that threaten comfortable illusions. Civilization advances not through obedience, but through the courage to challenge established norms and pursue innovation.

> *A species cannot evolve by imposing limitations upon itself. The moment we replace discovery with dogma, we abandon the very process that made us unique*

Throughout history, humanity has often modeled its systems of control on two overarching structures: Divinity, providing ethical guidelines, and the Laws of the Universe, governing physical existence. Both frameworks ensure balance and order, moral conduct through spiritual guidance, and physical stability through natural laws. Human authority, however, frequently exploits inherent fears of the unknown, employing existential dread and promises of comfort to solidify control. Examples span from the Pharaohs' monumental legacies to Roman infrastructure that secured loyalty through enhanced living conditions.

Humanity's persistent ideological conflicts reveal deeply entrenched cognitive biases and narrow perceptions of reality. These biases have historically driven intense division and violence, exposing an ironic vulnerability despite intellectual prowess. Unlike other species, humans rely on carefully crafted environments to survive, indicating an unusual fragility despite cognitive advancement. Our unique consciousness provides a means for universal self-awareness, hinting at purposes beyond mere existence.

Historically, control has functioned paradoxically: as a tool of oppression and an instrument for meaningful societal transformation. Figures such as Mahatma Gandhi, Martin Luther King Jr., Nelson Mandela, George Washington, and Abraham Lincoln exemplify the transformative potential of wielding authority responsibly. Equally significant is the recognition that harmful outcomes can result from passivity, emphasizing the moral weight of both action and inaction. Hence, the responsible exercise of control remains critical for societal progress rather than merely dominance.

Both divine doctrines and natural laws emphasize structured control to maintain harmony and stability. Moral guidelines from spiritual teachings aim to harmonize human conduct, whereas universal laws like gravity and ecological balance offer essential constraints ensuring physical order. Each system clearly communicates that deviation brings repercussions, reinforcing structured governance as vital for collective advancement.

High-risk settings like Antarctic stations or surgical theaters vividly illustrate control's necessity in preventing disorder and ensuring success. Similarly, energy resources demonstrate control's duality profoundly: nuclear technology can either empower entire populations or devastate them, depending entirely on its management. The responsibility of mastering technology continues to challenge humanity, reinforcing that true progress requires an equivalent evolution in ethical and intellectual maturity.

Beyond governance, trade and specialization have significantly propelled human advancement. Early barter evolved into complex trade networks, enabling cultural exchanges, technological innovation, and sustained economic growth, as seen in ancient marketplaces and routes like the Silk Road. However, alongside prosperity, trade also facilitated exploitation, clearly illustrated by the transatlantic slave trade and colonial empires. Trade inherently carries a duality: significant wealth accumulation often correlates with profound inequality.

Yet trade persists as a cornerstone of societal progress. Structured oversight in trade networks ensures efficient resource allocation and the widespread dissemination of knowledge. The critical distinction is that control itself remains neutral, defined entirely by its manner of application. Responsibly managed trade thus becomes indispensable for civilization's balanced advancement.

Industrialization dramatically enhanced wealth generation but simultaneously exacerbated economic disparities. Factory workers endured severe conditions, while industrial magnates secured enormous fortunes, reinforcing systemic inequities inherent in capitalist frameworks. Despite capitalism's ability to drive innovation and efficiency, its inherent contradictions remain evident, economic structures designed for collective benefit frequently amplify individual gain at the expense of broader societal welfare.

In contemporary society, global trade, accelerated by digitalization, automation, and new technologies such as cryptocurrency, unites populations but also magnifies wealth concentration. Although globalization has notably reduced global poverty, the resulting economic gains have disproportionately favored a select minority, widening economic divisions. Trade thus continues to embody this persistent duality, simultaneously serving as an engine of remarkable progress and profound inequity.

Specialization and trade have historically been central to human advancement, promoting efficiency, innovation, and cultural exchange. The division of labor amplified prosperity and social complexity, enabling humanity's profound technological and intellectual achievements. However, trade also dictates resource distribution and power dynamics, potentially fostering monopolies and restricting access.

Critical thinking has been pivotal, distinguishing human progress from mere survival through continuous innovation and adaptation. Trade driven primarily by material gain can hinder intellectual advancement, emphasizing the delicate balance required between prosperity and intellectual freedom. As humanity progresses, the responsible harnessing of trade as both an economic tool and a medium for intellectual exploration remains essential in addressing existential questions and ensuring sustainable evolution.

> *The irony of progress is that the tools freeing our minds can also bind them; trade enables evolution, but how we convey its value decides advancement or stagnation*

If trade drives human advancement, media shapes its direction. Initially a neutral medium for communication, through cave paintings, hieroglyphs, and oral traditions, media evolved into a powerful tool influencing perception and thought. The printing press transformed media, democratizing knowledge but simultaneously empowering rulers, religious authorities, and elites to control societal narratives.

Advancements like radio, television, and digital media intensified media's influence, creating carefully managed realities and subtly narrowing genuine choice. Modern algorithms invisibly curate our experiences, determining what information we encounter and subtly shaping desires and beliefs. Media's profound impact on human consciousness illustrates that the method of communication itself significantly influences perception, thought, and behavior.

Historically, media served trade by promoting commerce and cultural exchange along networks such as the Silk Road, spreading ideas alongside goods. However, it also became an instrument for governance, enabling leaders to solidify power and religious institutions to enforce orthodoxy, suppress dissent, and control knowledge.

Media's ultimate paradox lies in its dual potential: it can foster intellectual revolutions or manufacture consent. Navigating this duality remains one of humanity's critical challenges, underscoring that communication is far from neutral, it is, as always, pivotal in the struggle for free will and progress.

Those who control the narrative do not need to suppress information; they need only shape its context

Media originated from humanity's primal need to communicate essential knowledge, initially through cave paintings, rhythmic drum signals, and oral storytelling. As societies evolved, structured communication became critical, prompting the creation of written languages such as Sumerian cuneiform, Egyptian hieroglyphs, and Chinese script, initially serving trade and administrative purposes.

With the rise of city-states and empires, media became integral to governance, reinforcing authority and shaping collective beliefs. Hammurabi's Code, Egypt's monumental inscriptions, and Rome's Acta Diurna all exemplify media's early function in consolidating power. Additionally, trade networks like the Silk Road facilitated cultural and ideological exchanges alongside commerce, deeply influencing human civilization.

The invention of the printing press dramatically expanded media's scope, allowing wider dissemination of ideas yet simultaneously enabling religious and political institutions to enforce ideologies more rigorously. This technology marked a turning point, highlighting media's dual capacity to democratize knowledge and uphold power structures through selective control and censorship.

Religious institutions were pioneers in leveraging media for control. The Catholic Church utilized illuminated manuscripts, papal decrees, and the printing press to enforce orthodoxy and suppress dissent. These methods transformed religious teachings into powerful tools of authority. The Protestant Reformation, notably Martin Luther's widely disseminated 95 Theses, demonstrated media's potential to disrupt centralized power dramatically. As historians observed, "*Printing was the ultimate agent of change*" However, the Catholic Church quickly adapted, responding with the Counter-Reformation to reassert dominance through strategic media use, censorship, and the concept of heresy, underscoring media's dual capacity to enlighten and constrain belief.

The scientific community, often viewed as neutral, has historically leveraged media strategically. Galileo's heliocentric theory was more than a scientific breakthrough; it triggered a profound narrative conflict, leading to censorship and house arrest. Genuine scientific advancement arises not from passive acceptance but through courageous questioning of prevailing beliefs. During the Cold War, scientific publications from both the United States and Soviet Union selectively promoted research aligned with national interests, particularly impacting nuclear and space exploration narratives.

Politics perfected media-driven control, strategically employing propaganda to shape public perception and direct behavior. Revolutionary pamphlets and wartime posters illustrate media's capacity to mobilize citizens and shape societal norms beneficial to those in power. Radio and television drastically expanded media's reach, vividly demonstrated by Hitler's propagandist broadcasts, Roosevelt's reassuring fireside chats, and Stalin's manipulative revision of historical imagery to eliminate inconvenient truths.

Social media in the 21st century elevated media's influence exponentially. Initially hailed as democratizing platforms, they evolved into sophisticated channels employing algorithms to subtly shape perceptions and desires, effectively creating reality rather than merely reflecting it. Modern media illustrates how profoundly human perception shapes experience, emphasizing social media's unparalleled role in manipulating contemporary consciousness.

In the 21st century, media has emerged as humanity's most potent system, surpassing traditional structures of politics and trade. Neither political authority nor economic exchange can sustain itself without effective media control, a reality vividly demonstrated by events like the 2011 Arab Spring. Despite longstanding political and economic grievances in the Middle East, it was the strategic mobilization via social media platforms such as Twitter and Facebook that catalyzed governmental collapse, illustrating media's decisive role in determining the trajectory of civilizations.

This century's transformation of media introduced social platforms that claimed democratization, empowering individuals with unprecedented freedom to share information. Yet beneath this apparent openness, sophisticated algorithms exert precise control, subtly guiding user behavior toward specific narratives. These platforms, far from neutral, utilize predictive analytics to reinforce engagement, shaping realities rather than merely reflecting them.

The profound deception lies in the illusion of autonomous choice. Users perceive their digital journeys as self-directed, unaware that every interaction, every click and like, is meticulously analyzed and exploited to reinforce predetermined cognitive patterns. Consequently, social media has transcended mere communication, evolving into an orchestrator of perception and consciousness. Rather than liberating free will, the digital era has confined it within algorithmically determined boundaries, firmly under the influence of artificial intelligence and corporate agendas.

Media's precision in shaping human perception operates meticulously at both micro and macro scales. On a personal level, algorithms adapt content to individual behaviors, subtly influencing preferences and reinforcing biases. Every digital interaction informs this sophisticated system, akin to experimental research, as media architects continually adjust strategies to optimize outcomes.

At a collective scale, digital platforms function as vast social laboratories, conducting real-time psychological experiments on public sentiment and behavior. These platforms employ rigorous methods like A/B testing and sentiment analysis to steer collective actions, influencing electoral outcomes, economic markets, and social movements with astonishing precision. Unlike traditional controlled experiments constrained by ethical limits, digital media interactions occur freely and incessantly, turning unaware users into subjects of ongoing behavioral engineering.

The accuracy of this manipulation mirrors scientific rigor where errors, such as misinformation spread, have severe repercussions, exemplified by media's role in escalating the 2008 financial crisis. Emotion-driven media manipulation, devoid of empirical constraints, can incite profound social consequences, as evidenced by the devastating use of broadcast media during the Rwandan genocide. Such profound influence prompts reflection on humanity's uncanny ability to precisely engineer thought patterns, echoing nature's intricate governing laws.

Ideally, media could empower genuine free will, fostering critical thought and shared understanding. Yet, its current skewed balance serves to restrict intellectual exploration within controlled narratives. By narrowly defining acceptable discourse, media often cultivates vigorous debate within strictly limited boundaries, subtly discouraging deeper inquiries into alternative perspectives. Humanity faces a crucial paradox: possessing powerful tools for intellectual advancement yet struggling profoundly to escape entrenched structures of influence and control.

When media intertwines with politics and trade, its power escalates dramatically, enabling a select few to guide billions' perceptions and beliefs with remarkable precision. For many, what appears as free will is subtly orchestrated, shaped to match dominant interests rather than emerging naturally. Despite media's significant influence, its grip is not absolute; critical thinking and rigorous scrutiny offer paths to liberation, though increasingly requiring determined effort. Indeed, controlling media has become synonymous with controlling public consciousness itself.

Considering consciousness as a type of energy, perhaps a "*Type N*" energy, media emerges metaphorically as its mobilizer, analogous to the sophisticated energy manipulation of Type III civilizations described by the Kardashev scale. When harnessed constructively, media amplifies collective critical thinking and accelerates human advancement. However, prevailing imbalances restrict most individuals within carefully constructed perceptions, significantly reducing their capacity for genuine inquiry and exploration. A true dystopia arises not from the scarcity of information but from an overload that renders truth indistinguishable from illusion, highlighting the urgent necessity for discernment amidst information abundance.

Authentic free will, combined with independent thought and values rooted in genuine exploration, holds profound potential to dissolve existing constraints. The essential task isn't simply gathering information but integrating diverse perspectives toward collective enlightenment. Transforming societal consciousness requires challenging entrenched norms, embracing discomfort, and actively reshaping perceived realities. Indeed, sincere ignorance and deliberate ignorance remain among society's most formidable dangers.

Remarkably, universal value systems such as divinity and natural laws naturally promote exploration and autonomy, contrasting sharply with human-created institutions like familial structures, political systems, pragmatic philosophies, and trade networks. These human constructs manage behavior with precise, structured control, frequently mirroring universal principles they seek to replace, often originating from noble intentions. However, such precision also defines less benevolent systems, notably organized crime, highlighting a troubling facet of structured human governance.

Organized crime persists, even in an age rich with knowledge, precisely because it exploits core human instincts like survival, power, and loyalty. These clandestine systems secure allegiance through fear, economic dependence, and alternative justice mechanisms outside established legal frameworks. Significantly, every power structure, whether legitimate or illicit, constructs its narrative, carefully crafting justifications to conceal and sustain authority.

Governments derive legitimacy from transparent legal and diplomatic frameworks, whereas criminal organizations cultivate obedience through secrecy, coercion, and carefully structured hierarchies. Organizations like the Mafia sustain longevity not through overt violence alone, but by meticulously controlling economic resources, information flow, and psychological influence, closely paralleling official state functions. Such underground stability often attracts those disenfranchised by traditional governance.

Organized crime strategically deploys knowledge, not for collective enlightenment but targeted influence. Analogous to media's micro and macro manipulations, these syndicates expertly navigate economic systems, enforce internal codes, and foster dependency.

Their survival underscores a stark truth: control emerges not from ignorance, but from adeptly understanding and manipulating human behavior.

> *In a world where systems claim to guide free will toward progress, one institution thrives not by guiding it, but by exploiting its every weakness. Where governance fails, where laws falter, where trust collapses, another force emerges to fill the void*

Crime fundamentally challenges a society's norms, not inherent truths, but constructs defined by collective values. Over time, societal norms evolved into structured laws, embodying deeper concepts of governance and justice. At their inception, small communities enforced these standards informally through social pressures, ostracism, or exile. However, as civilizations became more complex, formalized legal codes emerged, transitioning from oral traditions to explicit inscriptions like Hammurabi's Code. These foundational laws, designed primarily to preserve societal order, continue influencing modern legal systems.

With the expansion of empires, laws increasingly mirrored the priorities and interests of ruling elites, becoming instruments not only of societal harmony but also of political dominance. Consequently, definitions of crime became fluid, shaped more by prevailing ideologies and power dynamics than by universally accepted moral principles. Law thus emerged as an expression of power rather than purely justice or rights.

Chapter 3: The Architecture of Certainty: From Infinite Potential to Prescribed Reality - Bonds Beyond Time: The Triumvirate of Dominion and Might

Historically, criminal actions often involve individuals infringing upon the rights of others, reflecting societal prioritization of material success and prosperity. Economic disparities push some individuals toward crime, rationalizing dominance and exploitation as means of advancement. Systemic power imbalances particularly amplify crimes targeting vulnerable populations, reinforcing cycles of inequality and injustice. This reality emphasizes that social identities and roles, rather than innate traits, frequently shape experiences of victimization and criminality.

Societies resemble controlled experiments where rogue elements threaten overall stability. Laws function similarly to scientific protocols, designed to control unpredictable variables. Omnipresent systems like divine doctrines impose ultimate moral deterrents, promising severe consequences for deviance comparable to universal physical laws such as gravity or entropy, which impose inescapable repercussions.

Human-made legal systems aim for equilibrium among competing free wills, aspiring toward an idealized society of justice and coexistence. Yet, crime persists as an enduring human challenge, perpetually illustrating the tension between order and chaos that defines civilization itself.

Despite humanity's deep understanding of consequences, certain individuals persist in defying societal norms due to ingrained convictions, neurological limitations, or a lack of empathy. Throughout history, civilizations have consistently faced the challenge of managing these outliers, ensuring they do not derail the collective pursuit of advancement and enlightenment. Yet, isolated transgressions pale in comparison to the threats posed by systematically organized groups whose calculated actions undermine foundational societal principles.

Such organized entities do not merely react out of survival instincts; instead, their goal is deliberate dominance, often through coercion, economic manipulation, and ideological imposition. Unlike random lawbreakers driven by immediate need or desperation, these groups operate with strategic precision, mirroring governmental structures in their hierarchy and operational discipline. Historically, powerful figures like Caesar, Genghis Khan, Napoleon, and Hitler leveraged organized governance to shape societies, demonstrating that order imposed from above frequently encounters resistance, birthing organized opposition in forms such as criminal syndicates.

Criminal organizations exert control beyond mere brute force, embedding themselves deeply within societal structures, including politics and commerce. Their sophisticated networks blur traditional lines of morality and legality, wielding influence so pervasive it frequently surpasses governmental authority. Such groups manipulate economic systems through financial crimes, from embezzlement to currency manipulation, actions that devastate communities as profoundly as violent crime.

Thus emerges a troubling triumvirate: organized crime, commerce, and politics, each reinforcing the other, collectively suppressing individual agency and critical thought. Rather than fostering societal evolution, this alliance prioritizes perpetual dominance and control.

The paradox is profound, humanity possesses extraordinary potential for intellectual growth and enlightenment yet continuously struggles against powerful structures that prefer the certainty of control over the possibilities of collective progress.

Humanity's greatest impediment to intelligent civilization arises from a self-crafted triumvirate: politics, trade, and organized crime, each mirroring primal instincts rather than higher purpose. Rather than advancing through genuine exploration, this system harnesses divinity and universal laws, deploying power, deception, and fear as tools of perpetual dominance.

Yet, despite pervasive manipulation, humanity's quest for knowledge remains unextinguished. Our progress has been exponential, driven by relentless curiosity and a yearning for deeper understanding. However, our persistent lapses into dominance cycles reflect an essential imbalance: we have mastered control yet disregarded the profound responsibility accompanying it.

The intricacies of biological evolution, consciousness, and universal constants suggest our existence surpasses mere chance, hinting instead at purposeful order. The improbability of our finely tuned reality challenges randomness as the sole architect of human existence, inviting consideration of a structured intent behind life's complexities.

History reveals a constant tension between authority and freedom. Although powerful entities consistently manipulate societal evolution for their gain, courageous individuals and transformative movements continually emerge, redirecting humanity towards truth and enlightenment.

Thus arises our era's paradox: systems intended to foster collective advancement instead obstruct it through relentless cycles of control. If humanity is to achieve true intelligence, we must embrace balance, recognizing that unrestrained authority breeds tyranny, and absolute freedom descends into chaos. Progress hinges not on control alone but on the profound responsibility guiding its exercise.

> *Humanity has always been capable of greatness, but true progress lies not in control, but in the wisdom to wield it responsibly*

Conclusion: Beyond the Paradigm, Reconciling Free Will and Universal Order in the Quest for Intelligence

Throughout history, civilization has been guided by two primary value systems: omnipresent principles - unchanging laws of the universe and divine frameworks along with human-generated constructs, evolving through free will. Universal constants such as gravity, thermodynamics, and mathematical phenomena like Pi remain stable, their precision unaffected by humanity's shifting interpretations. Earth's consistent axial tilt, celestial orientation, and fundamental forces exemplify the persistent equilibrium of universal law.

Conversely, human-created systems rapidly cycle through transformations, frequently deviating from higher purpose before achieving transient clarity. Within a single lifetime, individuals witness multiple societal and ideological revolutions, a stark contrast to the enduring consistency of universal and divine truths.

Scientific theories continually evolve, from Aristotle's geocentric models to Einstein's relativity, yet the underlying realities, like gravity itself, remain untouched. Similarly, religious traditions across Christianity, Islam, and Hinduism exhibit varied interpretations but consistently uphold principles of morality, purpose, and spiritual interconnectedness.

Collaboration between these omnipresent systems has enabled humanity's greatest advancements: agriculture, medicine, technology, and ethical frameworks guiding collective well-being. However, despite advocating cooperation, historical records show repeated misuse by humanity, turning religious doctrines into justifications for conflict and scientific discoveries into weapons.

Such divergence from intended harmony mirrors biological survival tactics, revealing human distortions rather than universal directives. Ultimately, the prosperity and continuity of civilization depend not on exploiting these systems for dominance, but recognizing and aligning with their inherent order, stability, and ethical wisdom.

As civilizations repeatedly cycle through expansion, conquest, and decline, history persistently illustrates that domination cannot sustain human progress. In contrast, omnipresent systems - both universal laws and divine principles, remain stable and serve as foundational arbiters of human experience. Earth's precise conditions, including its axial tilt, magnetic shield, and liquid water presence, defy statistical randomness, suggesting intentional cosmic design.

Philosophers and scientists alike have recognized the improbable precision underlying universal laws. Such finely-tuned conditions suggest intentionality rather than random occurrence, prompting profound inquiries about the existence and nature of an underlying intelligence or architect guiding cosmic order. The universe, with its remarkable balance and complexity, challenges human expectations, highlighting that our understanding remains fundamentally limited by perceptions shaped through human experience.

The convergence of universal and divine laws highlights a critical consensus: human consciousness transcends temporal existence. While humanity's cognitive frameworks might not yet fully grasp this design, free will likely serves as a critical tool in uncovering its nature. Human intellectual evolution, driven by inference and iterative learning, demonstrates measurable progress as societal structures continually evolve and are replaced, yet omnipresent laws remain unchanged, indicating superior intelligence.

By the Kardashev Scale's definition, omnipresent systems embody Type III civilization intelligence, effortlessly managing energy across galaxies, structuring reality beyond human capability. Similarly, divine ethical systems, enduring across diverse cultures, exert intellectual influence comparable to energy, shaping humanity consistently through moral law. Recognizing these systems' precision and permanence leads to profound understanding, not merely of knowledge but purposeful existence itself.

> *To comprehend the highest intellect is not to control it, but to recognize its design and, in doing so, align ourselves with the infinite*

Omnipresent systems, universal laws and divine frameworks, persist not as rigid doctrines, but as dynamic entities aligning continually with human intellectual and existential growth. They integrate seamlessly across eras, reflecting humanity's evolving understanding rather than inherent changes within themselves. Such systems exhibit remarkable adaptability, continuously resonating with shifting philosophical and cognitive perspectives.

Cross-cultural and scientific traditions affirm a shared inevitability: biological existence is finite. South American, African, Abrahamic, Dharmic, and Eastern philosophies consistently recognize cyclical patterns of cosmic renewal and dissolution. From the Maya's intricate calendars forecasting recurring cataclysms, through the Dogon cosmologies of predetermined cosmic shifts, to Abrahamic scriptures detailing eschatological endings, humanity acknowledges the temporal limitations inherent to life.

Scientific laws reinforce these philosophical notions. The second law of thermodynamics predicts increasing entropy leading ultimately to either universal heat death or cosmic collapse, underscoring biological impermanence. Yet, omnipresent systems extend beyond Earth, implying a universal scope. Their existence across potential multiple worlds suggests our current understanding merely scratches the surface of a profoundly interconnected cosmic reality, hinting at far greater truths yet to be revealed.

> *Could the great illusion of humankind be the belief that we stand at the center of the universe, while the greater truth of omnipresent systems is that they were never bound to us alone?*

Science and divinity, distinct yet complementary, have guided human exploration of existence, science through empirical inquiry, divinity by offering meaning beyond the physical. This synergy has profoundly influenced speculative thought, notably in science fiction, a genre older than commonly believed. Ancient narratives like India's Mahabharata, Greek philosopher Lucian's True History, and medieval Islamic literature like One Thousand and One Nights reflect early fascination with cosmic and technological concepts.

In recent centuries, science fiction has significantly shaped intellectual inquiry, exploring profound possibilities such as artificial intelligence, time travel, interstellar exploration, and parallel universes. Pioneering works by Shelley, Wells, Verne, and Asimov pushed boundaries of thought, prefiguring modern scientific advances. Contemporary films like The Matrix and Interstellar extend these inquiries, resonating deeply with modern physics.

Emerging scientific evidence increasingly supports theories of parallel universes, long hinted at in divine traditions. Quantum mechanics' Many-Worlds Interpretation and astrophysical phenomena suggest realities beyond human perception, aligning with concepts found in ancient cosmologies, from Mayan cyclical worlds and Dogon celestial realms to Dharmic infinite lokas and Taoist interwoven existences.

Advances in space exploration underscore possibilities of extraterrestrial life, highlighting humanity's limited perception amidst a potentially vast cosmic community. The widening acceptance of these theories suggests humanity's understanding of reality is merely an entry point to a far richer, multidimensional universe.

Divinity has long asserted the existence of multiple realms, and as science begins to align with this perspective, intriguing questions arise about these other universes. Are they reflections of our reality, governed by familiar laws, or do they harbor entirely different forms of intelligence? Perhaps civilizations exist so fundamentally alien that we remain unable to perceive their presence. This stands as one of humanity's profound mysteries, an ongoing exploration awaiting deeper insight.

To better grasp this concept, let's shift our perspective back to Earth and utilize Antarctica as a tangible analogy. Imagine divinity as an advanced Type III-plus civilization, one among many, similar to nations collaborating on Antarctic research. Here, the laws of the universe form the foundational structure, much like Earth itself serving as a vast cosmic research station. In this expansive experiment, societies function as controlled environments, with humans representing the variables influencing outcomes through their exercise of free will. Human value systems function as experimental protocols, defining societal norms and governance, akin to operational controls within Antarctic research stations.

Antarctica exemplifies a collaborative center where competing nations unite for exploration and shared understanding. Earth itself might similarly represent a cosmic research outpost for civilizations far beyond our comprehension, where we are observed, studied, and subtly guided in ways yet unnoticed. The essential question shifts from Earth's uniqueness to understanding its interconnected role within a much larger cosmic reality.

> *A mind confined to a single world will always question its own limitations, but a mind open to the vastness of existence will recognize that discovery is only the first step toward understanding*

Chapter 3: The Architecture of Certainty: From Infinite Potential to Prescribed Reality - Conclusion: Beyond the Paradigm, Reconciling Free Will and Universal Order in the Quest for Intelligence

Throughout Chapter 3, we've traversed omnipresent systems that shape existence, human-crafted systems that regulate it, and speculative bridges linking our curiosity to cosmic mysteries. Central to all these frameworks is the nuanced concept of free will, bounded autonomy, but rather critical and creative agency within prescribed structures. This tension defines humanity's essential condition.

Omnipresent systems, whether rooted in enduring divinity or universal physical laws, guide rather than restrict free will. Spiritual traditions globally, from the Bhagavad Gita's moral dilemmas to Abrahamic divine gifts, consistently present choice as a conscious act of moral discernment. South American and Native American philosophies highlight the interconnectedness of personal actions and cosmic harmony, advocating individual vision and communal balance. Similarly, African cosmologies like the Yoruba acknowledge destiny and personal accountability, framing life as a conscious journey shaped by free will.

Eastern perspectives, including Taoism's principle of Wu Wei, propose free will as alignment with natural balance, suggesting true freedom emerges from harmonious cooperation with universal forces. Australia's Aboriginal Dreamtime similarly positions free will within an eternal continuum, connecting personal agency to ancestral wisdom.

Conversely, human-made systems such as governance, economic models, and education often constrain rather than encourage intellectual freedom, channeling human potential into predetermined pathways. Institutions favor productivity over creativity, conformity over curiosity, systematically stifling the exploratory spirit that omnipresent systems inherently nurture.

Science fiction and technological speculation bridge these realms, illustrating free will as an evolving concept. While humanity imagines boundless futures through interstellar travel and artificial intelligence, these visions remain tethered by structured control and theoretical boundaries, suggesting that true freedom is yet unrealized.

Friedrich Nietzsche's allegory, Camel, Lion, and Child, clarifies humanity's progression toward authentic free will. Humans currently exist as burdened Camels, shouldering societal expectations. Transformation demands becoming the defiant Lion, rejecting imposed constraints. Yet ultimate liberation lies in becoming Nietzsche's Child: a state of boundless curiosity, unburdened by past conditioning. Only as the Child can humanity genuinely pursue intellectual evolution.

Nietzsche compels us toward transcendence, urging humanity to surpass its current limitations. Achieving an intelligent civilization necessitates abandoning passive obedience and superficial rebellion, choosing instead a path of perpetual wonder and fearless inquiry. True intelligence is thus not simply the accumulation of knowledge, but an unyielding quest for deeper comprehension, embracing internal chaos to ignite illuminating revelations.

> *To evolve is not merely to accumulate wisdom, but to remain unburdened by expectation, to explore without the fear of limitation, and to seek knowledge not for power, but for the joy of discovery*

Chapter 4: Beyond Purpose: Decoding Humanity's Role in the Infinite Design

Introduction

Humanity stands eternally poised at the edge of comprehension, gazing into existence with awe and apprehension. Our journey began with humble observation: nature, cosmos, and self, evolving into an insatiable quest to unravel our role within the infinite fabric surrounding us. Yet, deeper exploration yields paradoxes challenging our notions of free will, intelligence, and civilization.

Consciousness, despite its boundless adaptability, is invariably molded by forces beyond individual control. Invisible mental architectures and societal constructs concurrently empower and confine us, serving as both engines of progress and sentinels of restriction. Governance, faith, logic, and intuition each offer paths toward understanding, yet inherently embody potentials for enlightenment and constraint.

If consciousness is navigated by unseen parameters, the question of genuine autonomy arises: are we architects of destiny, or actors within predetermined scripts? Human history echoes the design of a controlled experiment, where free will appears to be tested under diverse circumstances. Monarchs, philosophers, theologians, and scientists have pursued life's purpose, arriving at divergent conclusions. While humanity has tamed nature, built civilizations, and ventured beyond Earth, the core question persists: do we create our paths or merely follow pre-existing patterns?

Moving forward necessitates transcending historical limitations, shifting our inquiry from mere survival toward existential purpose. The essential question evolves, not merely what we must achieve, but fundamentally why we exist.

A mind that seeks only answers will remain confined within them. A mind that seeks the right questions will forever expand

Within existence's expansive landscape lies humanity's ultimate inquiry: Why are we here? True understanding must engage timeless omnipresent systems: divinity and universal laws. Divinity, preserved through sacred texts, guides humanity toward higher orders; universal laws, unwritten yet observable, govern cosmic phenomena independent of interpretation. Both exist beyond human perception, unfolding continuously, whether acknowledged or unseen.

Human-made systems and protocols, inherently transient, fade swiftly against the vast scale of cosmic time. Humanity's entire history occupies but an instant within the universe's expansive timeline. Practices such as gladiatorial combat and slavery, once deeply embedded in society, have been dismantled through critical reflection and the exercise of free will. Empires, nations, and dominant businesses rise, peak, and inevitably decline, underscoring the fleeting nature of human constructs. Yet, these changes illuminate our profound capacity for self-correction and ethical advancement.

The enduring omnipresent systems, divinity and universal laws, offer contrasting permanence. Divinity imparts structured meaning through sacred texts, while universal laws govern cosmic order with unwavering consistency. Both provide foundational insights essential for understanding humanity's purpose. Transient ideologies cannot reliably anchor existential truths, as *no system can guide one to purpose if it itself remains uncertain of its own existence*

Human understanding demands empirical evidence, grounding speculation in observable reality. This disciplined pursuit prompts exploration of a foundational hypothesis: "*Earth As A Cosmic Research Station*", uniquely suited for fostering intelligent life. Our planet's precise conditions prompt vital questions about intention versus cosmic accident, inviting comprehensive examination through observable patterns, historical contexts, and philosophical introspection. This inquiry not only bridges empirical science and philosophical imagination but redefines humanity's position within an intricately structured universe.

Hypothesis Statement: Earth As A Cosmic Research Station for Intelligent Civilizations

Humans enter this world equipped uniquely with free will; a profound capacity intrinsically connected to our consciousness. Yet, from infancy through adulthood, we gradually succumb to influence by powerful, meticulously structured systems. These systems, encompassing Divinity, the Laws of the Universe, and human-crafted constructs, orchestrate our thoughts, actions, and even the fundamental experience of existence itself. Given their astonishing complexity and precise nature, it appears improbable, perhaps impossible, that these systems have arisen from mere cosmic coincidence.

Unlike all other life on Earth, human beings evolve intellectually and culturally at an extraordinary rate. While other species navigate existence guided primarily by instinct and slow biological adaptation, humans continually transform their world moment-to-moment. This rapid adaptability and capacity for innovation suggest that humanity might serve a unique, perhaps intentional, function within a broader cosmic framework.

This hypothesis posits that Earth operates as a form of cosmic research station, a neutral ground designed for observation, exploration, and the structured evolution of consciousness. This idea draws parallels to our experiences in Antarctica, a terrestrial zone uniquely untouched by national ownership, where diverse nations collaborate in a structured research environment to understand phenomena otherwise unseen on the planet.

Central to the hypothesis is the intersection of two profound sets of systems: Divinity, representing intelligent oversight, moral accountability, and transcendent purpose; and the Laws of the Universe, representing the observable, empirical patterns guiding physical existence. Historical and philosophical traditions consistently reference an afterlife shaped by one's Earthly experiences, aligning strikingly with emerging scientific insights suggesting alternate universes or dimensions beyond traditional perception.

To explore this hypothesis, we must evaluate whether human existence on Earth aligns more closely with a deliberately designed experiment rather than random cosmic occurrence. Key areas of inquiry involve examining if the structured nature of the universe implies intelligent oversight and determining if human free will functions akin to a controlled variable within an experimental design. This will involve analyzing historical anomalies, rapid and unexplained leaps in human cognition and technology, and patterns of civilization growth that defy purely naturalistic explanations.

The methodology embraces comparative analysis across diverse data sources: theological and philosophical traditions, including Abrahamic, Dharmic, and Eastern beliefs, alongside ancient interpretations and scientific frameworks such as the Fermi Paradox, Zoo Hypothesis, Rare Earth Hypothesis, and Simulation Hypothesis along with human defined systems of observation and pragmatism. By examining the alignment or divergence between religious doctrines and empirical laws, we can assess if the physical laws of our universe represent manifestations of a larger intelligence.

To test this hypothesis, specific aspects will be rigorously analyzed:

- Earth's precise astronomical positioning and geological conditions, investigating whether planetary stability and habitability represent statistically improbable conditions, indicative of intentional design.

- The extraordinary resilience of life on Earth, especially in extreme conditions, to understand if these conditions might represent controlled environments.

- Patterns of biological evolution and civilization development, particularly anomalous events like the Cambrian explosion, rapid cognitive evolution, and sudden technological advancements, to assess if these align more closely with guided progression than random mutation.

- The pragmatic integration of empirical science and philosophical inquiry to ensure grounded interpretations and practical applicability of insights gained.

This philosophical exploration acknowledges inherent limitations, notably the challenges of validating interdisciplinary insights empirically. It highlights gaps in historical and scientific records, emphasizing the necessity of continuous interdisciplinary research and logical inference rather than isolated experimental validation.

Ultimately, this inquiry offers a profound opportunity to reconsider humanity's purpose and our collective consciousness within the cosmic order. It suggests a path forward, further research, deeper introspection, and collaborative intellectual effort, to expand our understanding of existence, potentially transforming our perception of reality itself.

The Antarctica Protocol: Exploring Earth's Cosmic Paradigm

From ancient cave art to modern digital archives, humanity has diligently documented Earth's rhythmic natural cycles. Like a symphony, these patterns reliably guide life's daily rhythms. Seasons transition predictably, from the renewal of spring to the quiet stillness of winter, allowing communities worldwide to structure lives around expected climatic shifts. India's monsoons and the four-season cycles of northern regions exemplify nature's dependable precision.

Such reliability extends globally: Antarctica endures its predictable harsh cold, deserts await sparse but timely rains, and diverse ecosystems worldwide respond consistently to environmental cues. Animals, too, align existence with these cycles, hibernating bears, migrating wildebeest, and oceanic salmon all exemplify life attuned to nature's rhythm.

Beyond terrestrial cycles, celestial patterns reinforce stability. Night skies rotate with mathematical certainty, guiding navigation and agriculture for millennia. Auroras regularly illuminate polar skies, captivating observers with their scheduled brilliance. Earth's atmosphere itself serves as a protective shield, routinely neutralizing cosmic threats such as meteorites, spectacular displays of nature's vigilant defense.

Cultural narratives often reflect humanity's awe of celestial phenomena, imbuing them with symbolic significance. Statistically, the flawless synchronization of cosmic and earthly cycles suggests deliberate design rather than random chance. Earth's stable tilt, maintained by the Moon, and Jupiter's gravitational shielding from asteroid threats underscore an intricate cosmic balance akin to sophisticated engineering.

Compared with human-created systems, which demand continual upkeep yet frequently falter. Earth's natural framework has operated reliably over millennia. Viewed through the Kardashev scale, such environmental precision hints at an advanced intelligence orchestrating life's intricate equilibrium, suggesting purpose beyond mere cosmic coincidence.

Imagine a master gardener meticulously maintaining a vast greenhouse, carefully balancing conditions so life flourishes effortlessly. Earth mirrors this concept on a planetary scale, its cycles precise and protective mechanisms resilient. This stability surpasses random chance, implying intelligent orchestration, whether divine, cosmic, or advanced civilization-driven. Nikola Tesla's insight captures this elegantly: ? *"If you want to find the secrets of the universe, think in terms of energy, frequency, and vibration"*

Human societies strive toward similar stability, evolving from small tribal groups to sophisticated global entities like the United Nations, aiming to foster peace and prosperity. Yet, human-created systems remain vulnerable, marked by conflict, bureaucracy, and instability, necessitating constant adaptation. Despite significant advancements, international treaties, economic cooperation, our best efforts fall short of nature's seamless efficiency.

Ultimately, Earth's flawless orchestration starkly contrasts humanity's imperfect constructs, underscoring a profound truth: sustained harmony demands more than mere chance. Nature's persistent precision quietly suggests a guiding intelligence, challenging humanity to reflect on its inherent limitations and potential for deeper integration and understanding.

> *In the pursuit of harmony, we often stumble; yet we do not stop striving. Perhaps, in these very stumbles, we learn the grace that cosmic rhythms embody so effortlessly*

Antarctica exemplifies humanity's profound capacity for cooperation, offering a compelling glimpse into possible future unity. Initially deemed inhospitable, this icy continent soon emerged as crucial for understanding Earth's history and future, prompting global exploration and eventual international collaboration. Early expeditions by Cook, Amundsen, and Scott revealed its brutal, remote environment, ultimately leading to the landmark 1959 Antarctic Treaty that committed nations to peaceful, scientific endeavors.

Antarctica's extreme conditions demand unprecedented innovation. Brutal cold, punishing winds, and perpetual darkness challenge conventional survival strategies, prompting reliance on advanced technology and specialized infrastructure. Facilities such as McMurdo Station exemplify human ingenuity, featuring renewable energy, intricate waste management, and tailored protocols for everyday tasks. Nations including the U.S., Russia, India, China, and others maintain research outposts, studying diverse scientific fields, from climate and astrophysics to marine biology.

Remarkably, Antarctica fosters unparalleled collaboration. Even amid global tensions, scientists from diverse cultures routinely share resources and knowledge, unified by common scientific purpose. This enduring partnership underscores a vital truth: collective intelligence, harnessed cooperatively, can overcome political divides, shaping a future of unprecedented harmony.

Antarctic research profoundly influences global understanding, unveiling critical insights into climate change, environmental patterns, and atmospheric history. Studies of ice cores and pristine astronomical observations have revolutionized climate modeling and advanced scientific knowledge across multiple disciplines.

This extraordinary human capability, to sustain life in Antarctica purely for discovery, prompts reflection on Earth's own remarkable precision. Our planet uniquely sustains diverse life, resembling a carefully constructed cosmic research station rather than a random occurrence. This comparison raises compelling questions: Could Earth itself be intentionally designed by an advanced civilization?

Considering Earth as a cosmic research outpost demands assessing various supportive conditions, from empirical evidence to philosophical implications. Much like human societies developing diverse communication methods unimaginable centuries ago, an advanced civilization might employ sophisticated techniques like quantum entanglement or consciousness-based transmission, technologies currently beyond human comprehension.

Drawing historical parallels, such as Australia's transformation from penal colony to thriving society, illustrates a scenario of forced adaptation and growth. Similarly, many belief systems depict Earth as a purposeful realm for soul refinement, suggesting life as a profound journey of transformation. Modern science continues to explore these possibilities, indicating that our understanding of consciousness and existence remains deeply interconnected with realms yet undiscovered.

> *When we unite to explore what seems impossible, we often discover the very essence of our shared humanity*

What if human existence operates like a controlled experiment, with consciousness temporarily embedded in biological forms designed for observation and experience? Drawing from the Kardashev Scale, a Type III Civilization, capable of manipulating energy across galaxies, could theoretically engineer biological vessels or even transfer consciousness. Modern physics already entertains notions like time dilation, quantum teleportation, and interdimensional travel, concepts echoed in culturally influential narratives such as The Matrix and Star Trek, reflecting deep, perhaps intuitive truths about reality.

Skepticism underpins scientific inquiry, yet history repeatedly illustrates that today's imagination often becomes tomorrow's reality.

> *The limits of the possible can only be defined by going beyond them into the impossible*

Our progression from early telescopes to sophisticated space observatories exemplifies humanity's relentless expansion beyond perceived boundaries. Innovations in physics, Einstein's relativity, particle physics, and string theory, illustrate rigorous attempts to decode existence's fundamental architecture. Thus, viewing Earth as a meticulously maintained cosmic research station challenges not only our scientific and philosophical perspectives but also the very boundaries of possibility itself.

The International Space Station symbolizes humanity's profound leap, establishing a sustainable biological presence beyond Earth's natural confines. By engineering environments for human survival in space, we reflect on the possibility that Earth itself may have been deliberately tailored for life. Antarctic research, uncovering ancient atmospheric data and extremophile resilience, along with enduring space probes like Voyager, exemplify our progression toward harnessing planetary-scale energies, echoing a Type II Kardashev civilization.

Civilizational advancement hinges not on resource exhaustion but innovation, adaptation, and mastery over our surroundings. Humanity's trajectory, from genetic engineering with CRISPR technology to artificial wombs and artificial intelligence, increasingly blurs the boundaries between biology and technology. DNA data storage and synthetic cognition advancements suggest imminent possibilities of merging biological and synthetic intelligences, potentially enabling human adaptation to extraterrestrial environments.

This convergence echoes enduring philosophical concepts, consciousness transcending singular physical existence, reincarnation, and interstellar colonization. While pragmatists emphasize empirical evidence, popular culture continuously explores ideas like consciousness transfer and immortality through advanced technology. These persistent themes may indicate deeper truths about existence, hinting that humanity's imagination is not merely speculative but potentially prophetic.

Despite humanity's imperfections and conflicts, our species has achieved remarkable progress, surpassing mere survival and instinct-driven existence. Unlike other creatures, we transform environments and innovate technologies that continually expand our possibilities. This unique capability prompts reflection: might our intelligence be part of a greater design by an advanced civilization, much like the genetic engineering and seeding of life we currently pursue?

Historical paradigm shifts, such as the transition from geocentric beliefs to heliocentric reality, underscore that today's impossibility often becomes tomorrow's proven fact. Thus, dismissing the potential existence of prior advanced intelligences would be premature.

Let us, therefore, pursue this exploration with scientific openness, recognizing that our journey toward engineering extraterrestrial life mirrors processes that could have been enacted long before our own time.

Chapter 4: Beyond Purpose: Decoding Humanity's Role in the Infinite Design - The Antarctica Protocol: Exploring Earth's Cosmic Paradigm

> *The pursuit of knowledge is not about proving what we already know but daring to ask what we have yet to understand*

A central paradox emerges in exploring free will: why does humanity, possessing seemingly limitless choice, remain entangled in contradictory value systems? Civilizations have thrived despite conflicting ideologies, suggesting these contradictions may be misunderstood rather than irreconcilable.

To explore this further, we focus on three dominant perspectives: divinity, science, and pragmatism. Once viewed as separate domains, these systems now increasingly overlap, akin to intersecting Olympic rings or varied refractions of light through a prism. Each system may simply offer distinct perceptions of the same fundamental truth, shaped by our unique vantage points.

Human free will drives our evolution beyond mere survival into realms of deeper exploration and continuous discovery. Yet, every advancement merely reveals further mysteries. Whether described as energy, soul, or measurable phenomena, could these divergent terms represent complementary views of a singular reality?

To validate this hypothesis, we must analyze each perspective objectively. Beginning with divinity, then science, and concluding with pragmatism, we explore them not as isolated beliefs but as distinct methodologies for interpreting existence.

> *Truth does not change only our ability to perceive it does. What divides us is not what is real, but how we choose to define it*

With this foundation set, let us begin our exploration with the first value system: divinity.

The Divine Tapestry: The Abrahamic Threads of Faith

The Abrahamic faiths, Judaism, Christianity, and Islam, share a profound belief in a singular, transcendent God who created and sustains the universe. Central to these traditions is monotheism, the belief in one omnipotent and omniscient Creator who is actively engaged with His creation, guiding humanity through various forms of divine revelation. Unlike traditions viewing divinity as a diffuse force, the Abrahamic God communicates directly, providing guidance, laws, and moral frameworks that define human existence and purpose.

Divine revelation manifests through several distinct methods. Direct communication, exemplified by Moses receiving the Ten Commandments, represents the most profound and unmediated interaction. Angelic intermediaries also play crucial roles; for instance, the Angel Gabriel revealed the Quran to Prophet Muhammad over 23 years and announced the birth of Jesus to Mary. Dreams and visions serve as subtler forms of revelation, requiring interpretation and discernment, as with Joseph's prophetic visions. Lastly, revelation may occur through inspiration, imparting an internal certainty guiding the recipient's actions.

Though these revelations share a common divine origin, human interpretation has diversified their application, leading to distinct theological and legal traditions across Judaism, Christianity, and Islam. Despite these variations, core principles remain consistent:

belief in one God, moral accountability, and the continuity of human consciousness beyond physical death.

Each Abrahamic faith prescribes a comprehensive ethical framework governing personal conduct and societal norms. Acts of worship such as prayer, fasting, charity, and pilgrimage deepen one's relationship with God. Prohibitions against idolatry, falsehood, theft, murder, and immoral behaviors reinforce moral accountability. Central to these teachings is the concept of an afterlife, where the soul is judged according to earthly deeds. The Abrahamic traditions emphasize that human life is not arbitrary; rather, it is part of a grand, structured evaluation culminating in divine judgment and eternal destiny.

The practical application of these faiths profoundly influences daily life through structured routines and ethical standards. Dietary laws, kashrut in Judaism, halal in Islam, and fasting periods in Christianity, instill discipline and remind adherents of divine presence in mundane activities. Sabbath observances across the traditions establish a rhythm of work, worship, and rest, reinforcing communal bonds and spiritual reflection. Modesty in dress and behavior underscores humility and reverence toward divine expectations.

Social interactions and economic behaviors are deeply shaped by religious guidelines emphasizing charity, justice, and social responsibility. Practices like zakat in Islam, tzedakah in Judaism, and Christian almsgiving highlight the ethical obligation to care for the less fortunate, reinforcing communal well-being. Ritual purity and hygiene, fundamental to each faith, symbolize spiritual readiness and moral integrity, preparing individuals for meaningful engagement with the divine.

Additionally, celestial phenomena serve as markers of divine precision and cosmic order within Abrahamic traditions. The sun, moon, and stars define religious calendars, guiding observances like Passover, Ramadan, and Easter. Events such as eclipses and celestial alignments are interpreted as significant signs reflecting divine will and human destiny.

Belief in supernatural entities further enriches this structured worldview. Angels, beings of pure light, function as divine messengers and executors of God's will, whereas entities like Satan (Ha-Satan, Iblis) represent rebellion against divine order, tempting humanity toward moral corruption. In Islam, jinn, beings of fire endowed with free will, inhabit an unseen dimension paralleling human existence, reinforcing the belief in multiple layers of reality beyond human perception.

At the core of Abrahamic understanding is the immortal human soul, accountable for its actions and destined for eternal reward or punishment. Death is viewed not as an end but as a transition to a judgmental stage preceding the resurrection, where ultimate justice is rendered. This belief profoundly shapes human morality, emphasizing the eternal significance of earthly choices and behaviors.

Collectively, these Abrahamic traditions provide a structured framework that defines every aspect of existence, guiding individuals toward purposeful living, moral responsibility, and a profound understanding of humanity's role within a meticulously ordered universe.

The Divine Tapestry: The Dharmic Threads of Enlightenment

At the heart of the Dharmic traditions: Hinduism, Buddhism, Jainism, and Sikhism, lies a conception of divinity deeply intertwined with the fabric of existence itself. Rather than viewing divinity as a separate, external force, these traditions see it as an omnipresent reality, inseparable from the universe and its processes. The cosmos is not a creation that began at a singular moment but an eternal continuum, governed by principles of balance, transformation, and renewal. While some traditions present a personal deity, others describe divinity as a formless, all-encompassing force. Across these traditions, divine presence is often recognized through self-realization, disciplined practice, and alignment with the natural order, rather than through external intervention.

Hinduism presents this idea through Brahman, the ultimate reality that transcends all forms and distinctions. Brahman is both nirguna (without attributes) and saguna (with attributes), offering a nuanced understanding of the divine. While Brahman remains beyond human comprehension, it manifests through numerous deities such as Vishnu, Shiva, and Devi, expressions of the same underlying truth, allowing practitioners to engage with the divine in ways that resonate personally. Scriptures like the Vedas, Upanishads, and Bhagavad Gita describe Brahman as the eternal essence of the universe, the source of all existence, and the ultimate goal of spiritual pursuit.

In contrast, Buddhism shifts focus away from an external deity and toward Dharma, the cosmic law and truth that govern all existence. The Buddha's teachings emphasize that the path to enlightenment lies in inner transformation and self-discipline, aiming to break free from cycles of impermanence (anicca), suffering (dukkha), and the absence of an inherent self (anatta). While Buddhism doesn't postulate a singular god, celestial beings like Bodhisattvas and Devas play roles in aiding sentient beings toward liberation, yet these beings too are subject to karmic law and rebirth.

Jainism takes a different stance, rejecting the notion of a creator altogether. The universe is seen as self-sustaining, operating according to eternal principles that do not require divine intervention. Karma and natural law shape existence, and liberation is achieved through absolute self-purification and non-violence (ahimsa). In Jainism, the Tirthankaras, enlightened individuals who have attained pure knowledge (Kevala Jnana), serve as role models for others seeking liberation. There is no governing deity; each soul is entirely responsible for its own actions and their consequences.

Sikhism, though monotheistic, defines divinity as Ik Onkar: the singular, formless, timeless reality that permeates everything. God in Sikhism is beyond human comprehension, yet present in all aspects of existence. This divine presence is accessed through Naam Simran (remembrance of the divine), Seva (selfless service), and righteous living. Sikhism teaches that divine grace plays a role in breaking the cycle of reincarnation, leading to mukti (liberation) and unity with the divine. The teachings of the Ten Sikh Gurus, recorded in the Guru Granth Sahib, guide followers to live in accordance with divine truth, focusing on equality, justice, and devotion.

In the Dharmic traditions, the path to divine realization is not governed by absolute commandments but by personal effort, contemplation, and the unfolding of wisdom over time. There is no singular prophet or revelation; truth is eternal, infinite, and accessible to those who seek it with discipline and sincerity. Each being has the potential to awaken to reality, whether through devotion, meditation, asceticism, or righteous action. The ultimate goal across these traditions is liberation from ignorance and suffering, the realization of one's true nature, and alignment with the deeper truths that govern existence. Divinity is not separate from life itself; it is the rhythm of existence, waiting to be understood

In these traditions, divine knowledge is not imposed from an external source but uncovered through internal realization, discipline, and introspection. Wisdom is considered eternally present, continuously discovered, and passed down through sages, scriptures, and personal experience. Hinduism asserts that divine wisdom is embedded in the cosmos, accessible to those who purify their minds and seek higher understanding. The oldest scriptures, the Vedas, are regarded as Shruti ("*that which is heard*"), revealed to sages in deep meditative states. The Upanishads explore the nature of self (Atman) and the ultimate reality (Brahman), while the Bhagavad Gita emphasizes that truth is revealed to those who sincerely seek it.

Buddhism similarly acknowledges sacred texts but teaches that truth is found through direct experience rather than external revelation. The Buddha's enlightenment came through personal insight, and his teachings are a guide to understanding the cosmic law of Dharma, which has always existed but is illuminated through his wisdom. Jainism, too, emphasizes direct realization, with the Tirthankaras uncovering eternal truths through asceticism and detachment from material existence. Jain philosophy teaches that truth is multi-faceted and that no single perspective holds absolute authority.

Sikhism, while monotheistic, embraces the idea that divine wisdom is not confined to a single event or moment in history. The Guru Granth Sahib provides a living guide to spiritual and moral conduct, teaching that Naam and righteous action lead to spiritual realization. The Sikh concept of Gurmukh highlights that true knowledge is not acquired through blind adherence but through conscious, selfless devotion. Across all these traditions, divine truth is timeless and open to all. It is an ongoing process of discovery, achieved through effort, discipline, and the transformation of consciousness.

Truth does not arrive as a command but unfolds like the rising of the sun, gradually illuminating all who are ready to see

The prescribed way of life in the Dharmic traditions is not based on rigid commandments but on universal principles guiding behavior, spiritual discipline, and harmony with the cosmic order. Dharma (righteous duty), karma (cause and effect), and self-discipline are paths to a meaningful life. Daily living, eating, working, and social interactions reflect one's spiritual progress, with every action shaping future experiences. Hinduism, Buddhism, Jainism, and Sikhism offer flexible systems that allow individuals to fulfill their duties according to their natural disposition, stage of life, and society's needs.

In terms of dietary practices, Hinduism promotes sattvic eating, favoring pure and non-violent foods, with many adherents practicing vegetarianism to minimize harm to living beings. Buddhism and Jainism emphasize similar principles, with Jains practicing strict vegetarianism. Sikhism encourages equality in eating through communal meals in the langar, where people of all backgrounds share meals together.

Work and rest in these traditions are structured to balance spiritual growth and material existence. Hinduism dedicates specific days to fasting, prayer, and pilgrimage. Buddhism's monastic order emphasizes meditation, study, and alms collection. Jainism's ascetics practice severe renunciation, while Sikhism teaches that work should be honest and service-oriented, without attachment to wealth.

Social structures are shaped by compassion, non-violence, and selfless service. Hinduism encourages seva and yoga as means to align with divine principles. Buddhism emphasizes Metta (loving-kindness) and Karuna (compassion), Jainism extends non-violence even to the smallest organisms, and Sikhism promotes service and equality, rejecting caste distinctions.

These traditions view life as a journey of realization, shaped by discipline and mindfulness. The cosmic order is not seen as detached but as an interconnected reality where celestial bodies influence human behavior and spiritual rhythms. Hinduism's Jyotisha (Vedic astrology) associates planetary positions with karma and dharma, while Buddhism and Jainism view celestial cycles as part of the eternal cosmic dance. Sikhism acknowledges the universe's vastness but rejects superstition, focusing on the transcendence of divine truth.

The supernatural in the Dharmic traditions is not seen as separate from reality but as part of a continuum of existence, with multiple realms of consciousness. Hinduism describes multiple lokas, inhabited by beings from celestial deities to spirits, all subject to the cycles of karma and rebirth. Buddhism speaks of six realms, including celestial and suffering realms, while Jainism and Sikhism emphasize individual responsibility for one's spiritual journey, with supernatural beings serving as examples rather than divine rulers.

Across these traditions, the soul is seen as eternal, cycling through lifetimes based on karma until liberation is attained. Hinduism's Atman, Buddhism's consciousness, Jainism's Jiva, and Sikhism's understanding of the soul all highlight the journey of the self toward spiritual awakening, transcending the physical plane of existence. Life is viewed as interconnected, with every thought and action shaping the unseen forces that guide the soul's progression.

The unseen is not beyond us it moves through us, shaped by every thought, every action, and every breath we take

The Divine Tapestry: The Eastern Threads of Wisdom

At the heart of Eastern traditions, Confucianism, Taoism, Shinto, and various localized beliefs, lies a vision of reality centered on balance, interdependence, and a deep respect for the forces that shape the natural world. These traditions do not focus on a singular, omnipotent creator or a final judgment of souls. Instead, they view the cosmos as a living framework where every element, human or otherwise, plays a meaningful role in an ever-evolving tapestry. The key is not salvation through a deity but through the cultivation of virtue, harmony, and authentic alignment with the flow of life.

Confucianism begins with the principle of **Heaven (Tian)**, which represents the moral and cosmic order guiding human ethics. It is not about divine commandments but about aligning with the natural order to achieve social harmony. Confucius taught that true societal peace emerges when rulers govern by virtue, and citizens reciprocate with respect and loyalty. The **Mandate of Heaven** suggests that ethical governance brings stability, while moral decay leads to downfall. In this view, divinity does not come from a distant realm; it reveals itself through the flourishing or chaos of society, reflecting the collective moral responsibility of all.

In **Taoism**, the focus shifts further from rigid codes to a more fluid cosmology centered on the **Tao** (The Way). Laozi and Zhuangzi describe the Tao as both the source and substance of all existence, an ever-present flow that shapes all natural phenomena. The highest virtue in Taoism is **wu wei** (effortless action), which invites individuals to move in accord with nature rather than against it. Taoism emphasizes internal balance, with practices such as **Tai Chi** and **Qigong** aimed at refining the vital energy, or **qi**, that flows through all beings. Here, divinity is not a pantheon of gods but the Tao itself, accessible to those who align their actions with the rhythm of life.

Shinto, Japan's indigenous spirituality, places a profound emphasis on the sacred connection between humans and nature. It is centered around the **kami**, spirits or deities that inhabit elements of nature like mountains, rivers, trees, and even ancestors. Kami are not omnipotent beings; they are revered as living forces integral to the land. Worship in Shinto involves purification rituals and offerings at sacred shrines, where humans acknowledge the reciprocity between nature, the divine, and themselves. Shinto does not focus on an afterlife but stresses gratitude for the present, honoring familial and communal bonds as expressions of devotion.

Across these traditions, the division between the sacred and mundane is intentionally blurred. Whether through Confucian ancestor rites, Taoist meditation, or Shinto festivals, these practices integrate spirituality into everyday life. The supernatural is not relegated to a distant realm but is a subtle interplay of forces that shape the visible world. In Confucianism, Heaven's will is reflected in societal ethics. In Taoism, immortals and spirits reside in hidden realms, just beyond the veil of perception. In Shinto, kami are regarded as vital presences, walking beside us and influencing daily events.

These traditions also hold a cyclical view of life, death, and the afterlife. Instead of focusing on a linear path toward salvation or damnation, they emphasize the continuity of existence. In Confucianism, ancestral veneration reflects the belief that the spirits of the departed continue to influence the living. In Taoism, the emphasis is on spiritual immortality, achieved through aligning with the Tao and transcending the cycles of birth and death. Shinto practices center on maintaining harmonious relationships with ancestors and nature spirits, ensuring ongoing blessings. The supernatural and the afterlife are not separate, fixed domains but interconnected parts of an ongoing cycle of existence.

Ethical living in these traditions is not enforced by a controlling deity but inspired by ideals such as **ren** (benevolence), the **Tao** (natural flow), and reverence for **kami**. The focus is on self-cultivation, becoming upright, compassionate, and authentic to foster a balanced community and live in harmony with universal rhythms. The absence of a central sacred text in many Eastern traditions suggests that wisdom is dynamic and revealed through lived experience rather than fixed dogma. These traditions emphasize personal development and moral introspection over formalized instruction, where teachings evolve in response to the needs of society.

These perspectives also influence how cosmic events and celestial movements are viewed. Eclipses, harvest cycles, and the interplay of **yin** and **yang** in Taoism symbolize the dynamic balance of opposites. Rather than a final apocalyptic event, these traditions speak of cyclical transformations. In Confucianism, the stability of society mirrors the harmony of nature, while Taoism teaches that chaos signals a departure from the Tao, inviting a return to balance through humility. Shinto aligns human destiny with the rhythms of the earth, seen in festivals and agricultural rites that celebrate seasonal changes and ensure communal well-being.

In every step upon the earth, in each breath beneath the sky, wisdom awaits discovery for those who walk gently, guided by the quiet pulse of life

The way wisdom is transmitted in Eastern traditions is rooted in immanence and personal cultivation. Rather than a singular divine revelation, these traditions emphasize an ongoing dialogue between human experience and natural, historical, and subtle energies. Teachings are passed down through classical texts, oral traditions, and lived practice. In Confucianism, the **Analects** and the **Book of Rites** are records of human reflection on ethics, relationships, and governance, guiding individuals to embody virtues such as **ren** (benevolence) and **li** (proper conduct). Taoist texts like the **Tao Te Ching** and **Zhuangzi** offer poetic insights into the natural flow of life, suggesting that true wisdom comes from aligning with the Tao, often through paradoxical or metaphorical expressions.

Shinto, without a central sacred text, relies on **Kojiki** (Records of Ancient Matters) and **Nihon Shoki** (Chronicles of Japan) to preserve the mythology of the kami and the divine origins of Japan. These texts capture creation stories, but worship is mostly an experiential practice, focused on rituals and festivals that connect humans with the land and spirits. The tradition is deeply embedded in local customs and regional beliefs, where shrines dedicated to specific kami reflect the diverse ways in which the divine is experienced across the country.

Syncretism is a hallmark of Eastern spiritual practice, blending Confucian ethics, Taoist cosmology, Shinto devotion, and folk beliefs in a fluid spiritual landscape. In many East Asian communities, individuals seamlessly integrate these practices, where Confucianism guides social ethics, Taoism influences spiritual health, and Shinto connects people to nature and ancestors. This synthesis reflects the idea that there is no single path to truth, but many overlapping practices that collectively contribute to spiritual fulfillment.

> *In a realm where mountains speak in silence and rivers carry whispers of ages past, wisdom streams endlessly for those who learn to listen*

In daily life, these practices manifest through rituals like ancestral offerings in Confucian households, meditation in Taoist communities, and festival participation in Shinto. Each tradition integrates spiritual practice into the fabric of life, whether through Confucian ceremonies, Taoist health practices, or Shinto purification rituals. This interweaving of the sacred and mundane underscores the idea that spiritual engagement is not confined to specific rituals or moments but is a continuous process embedded in all of life.

Aspects of the afterlife in Eastern traditions also reflect a cyclical worldview. There is no sharp divide between life and death; rather, death is seen as a transformation, and the afterlife is a continuation of relational bonds between the living and the departed. Ancestors are honored, and their guidance continues to shape the lives of their descendants. The moral and spiritual progress achieved during life can elevate the soul within subtle planes, yet no realm is final, and every cycle holds the potential for renewal.

When the wind stirs the ancient pines and the lanterns sway in silent shrines, the voice of ages speaks reminding us that life, in all its fleeting forms, is woven with spirit, memory, and gentle wonder

This emphasis on a cyclical, balanced approach to life, death, and the cosmos reflects the belief that all aspects of reality, social, environmental, and spiritual, are interconnected. These practices encourage individuals to cultivate harmony not only in their personal lives but also within the larger web of existence.

The Divine Tapestry: The Ancestral Threads of Zoroastrian, African, and South American Faiths

Beyond the cosmological views outlined by Zoroastrianism, African spiritualities, and South American indigenous practices, these traditions highlight different ways of divine communication and ritual practices that shape communal identity.

Zoroastrianism, for example, relies on the *Avesta*, the primary scriptural text, containing hymns believed to have been composed by Zarathustra. Unlike traditions that focus on continuous revelations, Zoroastrian teachings emphasize a singular primordial revelation, urging humanity to choose asha (truth, order) over druj (falsehood, chaos). Fire worship plays a central role, with Atash (sacred fires) representing divine light, and Mobeds (priests) safeguarding these flames to maintain cosmic harmony. Rituals involving fire are viewed as critical in protecting spiritual truths, and extinguishing or polluting these flames is a grave offense.

In Sub-Saharan Africa, divine wisdom is passed through oral traditions, divination, and spirit-based practices. For example, the Yoruba use Ifá divination, where a Babalawo (priest) interprets symbols formed by palm nuts or cowrie shells. These interpretations guide individuals back onto their destined paths (Ayanmo), fostering both personal development and cosmic alignment. Similarly, African communities blend spiritual beliefs with governance, where a chief's legitimacy is tied to approval from deities and ancestors. The moral code in these societies is inherently tied to communal welfare, where success is never isolated but dependent on the well-being of the broader community and ancestral spirits.

South American indigenous cultures, such as those in the Andes and the Amazon, similarly emphasize a deep connection to nature. The Andean peoples honor mountain deities (Apus) and Pachamama (Mother Earth), while Amazonian groups interact with forest spirits through shamanic rituals. The use of plant-based preparations, like Ayahuasca, allows shamans to communicate with spirits and gain insights into communal well-being, health, and nature. These traditions emphasize the importance of maintaining harmony with nature, with moral behavior directly influencing the environment.

In all three traditions, there are central ethical teachings that promote balance, reciprocity, and accountability. Zoroastrianism highlights good thoughts, good words, and good deeds (Humata, Hukhta, Hvarshta). African spiritual practices emphasize communal cohesion, with individual actions never disconnected from the wellbeing of ancestors and the environment. South American indigenous beliefs also uphold a deep respect for nature, with actions such as polluting rivers or harming animals seen as violations of both ecological and spiritual laws.

The afterlife is viewed in unique but overlapping ways in each of these traditions. Zoroastrians believe that upon death, a soul must cross the Chinvat Bridge, where their deeds are weighed. A righteous soul crosses into a luminous heaven, while the wicked face torment. In African cosmologies, souls journey to the ancestral domain, where they either return as guiding presences or restless spirits. South American traditions speak of souls transitioning to different realms (Hanan Pacha or Ukhu Pacha), with their status reflecting their moral and ritual choices.

Although these faiths may not rely on a single scriptural authority, they all share the belief that the divine is intimately woven into daily life. Zoroastrians honor the *Avesta* and partake in communal fire rituals. African communities preserve their divine lore through oral stories, proverbs, and divination practices. South American indigenous cultures transmit their traditions through oral mythologies and ceremonies that connect them to nature and the spirits.

Each of these traditions provides a framework in which individual actions are deeply intertwined with the cosmic and communal order. In Zoroastrianism, individuals are called to uphold righteousness (asha) and protect the environment, with daily actions reinforcing cosmic order. In Africa, leaders such as the Yoruba oba or Igbo eze must receive spiritual validation from the ancestors to ensure their rule remains in harmony with the divine. Similarly, in South America, respect for the spirits of nature, such as the Apus or Pachamama, ensures that crops flourish and the community remains in balance.

Rituals in these traditions, whether offerings to the divine, communal festivals, or acts of sacrifice, are not merely symbolic but serve as vital acts that affirm the relationship between the human world and the spiritual realm. Zoroastrians light fires and make offerings, Yoruba communities engage in spirit possession and mask dances, and Andean and Amazonian groups perform sacrifices to nature spirits to maintain cosmic balance.

The shared principle across these traditions is that moral behavior, spirituality, and communal welfare are inseparable. Zoroastrian ethics emphasize the eternal battle between truth and falsehood, where individuals' actions are directly linked to cosmic forces. In Africa, diviners and priests interpret divine will and provide guidance on maintaining harmony within the community. Similarly, in South America, shamans navigate moral and ecological dilemmas by consulting with nature spirits, ensuring the spiritual and physical well-being of their communities.

These traditions reveal a common belief that divine guidance is not static but evolves alongside human experience. Each community, whether in Zoroastrian fire temples, African divination circles, or Andean rituals, sustains the cosmic balance through daily interactions with the sacred. Each culture values continuous moral improvement and maintains a deep relationship with the unseen forces that govern life. By emphasizing moral integrity and respect for nature, these traditions demonstrate that spiritual wisdom is interwoven into every aspect of daily life, ensuring the balance of the cosmos is upheld.

These ancestral faiths, while diverse in practice, share a common vision that life is a dynamic interplay between the seen and unseen realms. The central message across Zoroastrianism, African spiritualities, and South American indigenous beliefs is that morality, nature, and spirituality are interconnected, shaping not only individual lives but the very fabric of society itself.

Between the Threads: Global Faiths and the Cosmic Research Station Hypothesis

Across continents and generations, faith traditions have profoundly influenced humanity's self-perception and its understanding of the cosmos. These narratives are deeply embedded within collective experience, forming an expansive legacy impossible to fully catalog. Our aim is neither to distill these rich spiritual insights into oversimplifications nor to pass judgment upon their veracity. Instead, we examine whether, within these diverse beliefs, exists any implicit support, subtle dismissal, or neutrality towards the notion of Earth functioning as a "*cosmic research station*" in a broader universal scheme.

We approach this exploration with humility, neither interpreting sacred texts nor reshaping longstanding devotions. Utilizing a lens attentive to spiritual complexity yet rooted in empirical reasoning, we consider whether ancient traditions speak of intelligences or cosmic forces beyond everyday comprehension. Do these teachings imply advanced entities orchestrating reality, explicitly deny their existence to emphasize human uniqueness, or simply remain silent on such matters?

Recognizing the inherent sensitivity in juxtaposing faith-based wisdom against empirical inquiry, we remain mindful of faith's intimate and communal nature. Science seeks universally replicable truths based on observable phenomena, whereas spirituality comfortably embraces both tangible realities and ineffable mysteries.

By aligning these distinct paths, we aim to uncover intersections, contradictions, and ultimately gain clarity regarding spiritual wisdom's stance on Earth's potential role as a cosmic observational hub.

Our inquiry does not intend to alter foundational religious truths. Rather, we encourage nuanced discourse: acknowledging divinity's complexity alongside humanity's relentless pursuit of empirical understanding. Ultimately, we seek to understand if sacred narratives provide space for Earth as part of a larger cosmic experiment or if they remain exclusively focused on terrestrial spiritual concerns.

Question: Understanding the Scope of Divine Power and Control

- Does the progression from local, nature-centered deities to universal, omnipresent divine powers imply an intentional force guiding human religious evolution?
- Do religious traditions explicitly or implicitly indicate that humanity is influenced, controlled, or observed by an intelligence, be it a singular divine entity, an advanced civilization, or a structured cosmic order?
- Does spirituality suggest humanity's future is directed towards a higher intelligence, within our dimension or beyond, pointing toward a deliberate trajectory culminating in ultimate intelligent order?

What Are We Trying to Determine?

- We explore whether historical religious traditions reflect an evolving divine authority aligned with human advancement or depict a singular, unchanging divinity viewed differently across cultures.
- Crucially, do these traditions explicitly or implicitly suggest humanity is governed, observed, or subtly guided by a supreme intelligence, advanced civilization, or cosmic structure?
- Moreover, do spiritual doctrines envision a future in which intelligence: divine, human, or otherwise, achieves an ultimate

state, as indicated by messianic prophecies, enlightenment ideals, or cosmic cycles?

- Ultimately, we seek to understand whether these religious frameworks support, contradict, or remain neutral regarding the hypothesis of Earth as a structured, research-oriented entity, comparable to diverse scientific teams in Antarctica working toward convergent yet distinct goals.

Historical Timeline of Divine Evolution and Cosmic Control

1. Earliest Depictions: Divine Beings as Forces of Nature (c. 3500 BCE–2000 BCE)

- **Sumerian Pantheon:** Gods like Anu (sky father) and Enlil (wind lord) were immense in power but subject to fate, implying they did not unilaterally control humanity.

- **Egyptian Deities:** Amun-Ra absorbed the powers of many regional gods, moving toward a central divine authority but still existing within a cosmic balance (ma'at).

- **Vedic Gods:** Indra, Agni, and Varuna were powerful but bound by cosmic law (Rta), suggesting an early understanding of divinity as part of a structured system rather than an absolute ruler.

- **Control Aspect:** *These gods influenced human affairs through blessings, curses, and natural events, yet they did not exhibit full omnipotence. They appear as regulators rather than sovereign controllers, operating within a larger cosmic mechanism.*

2. The Rise of Divine Moral and Cosmic Oversight (c. 2000 BCE–500 BCE)

- **Babylonian Marduk:** Rose as the supreme deity, marking a shift toward hierarchical divine rule, implying a model where gods delegate control to a primary overseer.

- **Vedic Evolution:** Indra's warrior god status diminished as abstract principles like Dharma (moral law) gained prominence, shifting focus toward a universal system.

- **Greek Pantheon:** Zeus assumed a supreme role but remained bound by the Fates, reinforcing the idea that even the highest deities answer to cosmic structures.

- **Judaism's Yahweh:** Develops from a regional deity into a singular, covenant-keeping God, suggesting divine will as the ultimate guiding force over human history.

- **Control Aspect:** *These divine figures move from regional deities to cosmic overseers, but still within a framework that limits their reach, suggesting that what governs reality may not be an omnipotent consciousness, but an intelligence structured into existence itself.*

3. Divine Consolidation into Singular Cosmic Entities (c. 500 BCE–500 CE)

- **Hindu Brahman:** The ultimate, impersonal reality encompassing all existence, rendering individual gods as facets of a larger intelligence.

- **Ahura Mazda (Zoroastrianism):** A monotheistic, omniscient creator locked in cosmic struggle with Angra Mainyu, suggesting dualistic control over human fate.

- **Christianity's God:** The concept of a single, all-powerful Creator who governs human destiny, offering salvation and moral law while remaining outside the constraints of time and space.

- **Greek Stoicism's Logos:** Introduces the idea of a rational, ordering principle guiding the universe, paralleling cosmic intelligence without agency.

- **Control Aspect:** *This period sees the strongest transition from multiple interacting entities to a single, all-encompassing force. However, control shifts from active intervention (like Zeus striking with lightning) to structuring reality itself, implying either a hidden intelligence or an emergent cosmic law that guides evolution without direct interference.*

4. Philosophical and Intellectual Crossroads (c. 500 CE–1500 CE)

- **Islam's Allah:** Described as all-knowing, all-powerful, and the ultimate judge of humanity, reinforcing the idea of a singular intelligence governing all creation.

- **Christian Eschatology:** Develops a vision of a divinely guided end-state, with messianic prophecies suggesting a predetermined cosmic plan for the future of intelligence.

- **Ongoing Hindu Developments:** Deities like Vishnu or Shiva often are seen as the supreme facet of Brahman, accentuating the sense of a singular cosmic core behind many forms.

- **Buddhism's Emphasis on Dharma:** Moves away from personal deities controlling fate, instead presenting an impersonal cosmic law dictating cause and effect.

- **Control Aspect:** *The idea of divinity as truly omnipotent or omniscient solidifies even further, aligning with societies that command large territories, centralized authority, and advanced scholarship.*

5. Modern and Contemporary Shifts (c. 1500 CE–Present)

- **Scientific Revolution & Enlightenment:** Conceptions of God adjust to meet rational frameworks. In many regions, monotheistic traditions remain strong, but they accommodate (or clash with) the language of science and empirical observation.

- **New Religious Movements:** Some propose cosmic consciousness or universal mind (e.g., certain strands of New Age or esoteric teachings), sometimes blending the notion of advanced cosmic intelligences with spiritual frameworks.

- **Islamic and Christian Apocalyptic Visions:** Both faiths maintain an expectation of an ultimate divine intervention, where intelligence (divine or human) reaches its final, perfected state.

- **Hinduism and Buddhist Transcendence:** Concepts of moksha and nirvana continue to offer a vision of intelligence evolving toward a higher plane, not necessarily guided by external forces but through self-realization.

- **Control Aspect:** *While mainstream faiths hold to singular omnipotent deities, smaller or alternative movements explore a broad range of possibilities, from pantheism to galactic watchers. Nothing is strictly proven or disproven, leaving the door open for speculation.*

Where Do Multiple Advanced Civilizations or One Principle Fit?

1. Possibility of Multiple Guides

- Early myths (e.g., Anu's heavenly court in Sumer, Indra's domain in Vedic lore, Yahweh's heavenly hosts, Allah's angels) could be read albeit loosely as diverse *"custodians"* or watchers.

- The ongoing presence of many religious forms might signal different external intelligences shaping beliefs, each wearing a cultural hat

2. A Single Grand Principle

- As unifying concepts arose (Brahman, Ahura Mazda's cosmic struggle, the Abrahamic *"one God"*), it suggests a deeper, singular truth behind varied narratives, perhaps an ultimate cosmic intelligence that cultures frame differently.

- This might reflect the *"many paths, one summit"* idea: diverse traditions converge on a universal reality.

3. Refutation or Silence on Higher Overseers

- While mainstream faiths don't typically endorse a *"research station"* scenario, they also rarely provide explicit doctrinal statements refuting higher civilizations.

- Rather, focus tends to be on moral, existential, or salvific themes, leaving the question of cosmic watchers outside their main purpose.

Chapter 4: Beyond Purpose: Decoding Humanity's Role in the Infinite Design - Between the Threads: Global Faiths and the Cosmic Research Station Hypothesis - What Are We Trying to Determine?

The shift from localized, nature-based deities to singular, omnipotent divinities mirrors humanity's intellectual evolution. Early civilizations worshipped tangible forces such as wind, fire, rivers, and fertility, entities directly influencing daily survival and community fate. These immediate gods required rituals and offerings, reflecting human dependence on visible, reactive powers.

As societies grew geographically and technologically, conceptions of divine control expanded accordingly. The rise of empires, organized governance, and distant trade routes introduced concepts of centralized power exerted remotely. Gods transitioned from elemental beings to universal rulers, paralleling political centralization and increasingly sophisticated conceptions of intelligence. This evolution suggests humanity's understanding needed time to accept the notion of remote governance, much like modern technological control exemplified by the Mars Rover.

Significantly, newer religious systems such as Christianity, Islam. Unlike ancient faiths evolving gradually toward monotheism, these religions arose when human intellectual and philosophical maturity had already embraced abstract, centralized governance concepts. The transition from visibly active gods to abstract cosmic principles implies an evolving human awareness that influence could be unseen yet powerful.

This pattern presents profound implications: humanity's evolving divine concepts might reflect deeper universal structures. The recognition that intelligence need not be immediate or observable to exert influence raises questions about divine, extraterrestrial, or systemic oversight. The parallels between religious evolution and scientific collaboration in contexts like Antarctic research, where distinct methodologies converge toward shared objectives, highlight the possibility of a singular underlying reality interpreted differently across cultures.

Ultimately, whether religious convergence points toward external intelligences, a unified cosmic consciousness, or simply the trajectory of human cognition remains unresolved. While structural parallels between faith development and scientific cooperation suggest potential oversight by higher intelligence, religious doctrines alone do not conclusively confirm this hypothesis. Answers may emerge not from singular traditions but through analyzing collective patterns across diverse spiritual experiences.

> *Whether divinity reflects a singular cosmic intelligence, multiple guiding forces, or the natural evolution of human thought, its trajectory like scientific discovery suggests that knowledge is refined through convergence, not contradiction*

How Divine Systems Define the Soul: Unseen Energy Mirroring Antarctic Experiments

Throughout human cultures, traditions carry diverse yet unified beliefs in a transcendent power beyond mere biology, commonly termed the "*soul*" Despite varying narratives, all agree humans possess something more profound than mechanical life. Over millennia, humanity has pondered what fuels our capacity for awe, compassion, cruelty, and cosmic curiosity.

Carl Jung theorized a collective unconscious woven with archetypes and memories, raising a compelling question for us: "*Who initially weaves these complex mental tapestries?*" While the physical body adheres to natural laws, cells grow, organs function, decay ensues, the intangible spark we identify as consciousness seems distinct and elusive. Its true origin remains unknown.

Biologists observe that animals primarily focus on survival: nourishment, reproduction, and territory defense. Humans, conversely, manifest extremes, capable of profound kindness and unimaginable cruelty, dedicating immense resources to cosmic exploration, such as tracking asteroids or launching satellites. Our curiosity about morality, existential dread, and extraterrestrial life far exceeds mere primal instincts.

Albert Einstein highlighted the central mystery inherent in art and science. Is our intricate consciousness intentionally crafted by an advanced intelligence beyond current comprehension, or is it merely a cosmic accident arising from random quantum interactions? Did consciousness gradually evolve naturally on Earth, or did it originate among distant stars, arriving from elsewhere?

As scientists investigate Earth's geological strata or genetic blueprints, the human soul defies precise measurement. Like a delicate scientific instrument calibrating subtle phenomena, can we ever truly quantify this intangible essence, or is its inherent mystery fundamentally immeasurable?

> *Is the soul but a fleeting swirl of atoms aligned into sentience, or is it a deliberate creation part of a universal experiment examining how consciousness thrives under myriad conditions?*

Below are the key questions we aim to illuminate in this chapter questions that may help us validate or refute the hypothesis of the soul's ultimate source:

1. **Creation vs. Coincidence**

    o *Was the soul intentionally forged by a higher intelligence, or is it the outcome of cosmic happenstance?*

    o If it is intentionally created, what does that say about the design of our universe?

    o If it is random, how does it emerge with such consistent depth across humanity?

2. **Local or Extraterrestrial?**

    o *Did our soul-material originate here on Earth, or might it be a form of energy seeded from elsewhere in the cosmos?*

    o Could ancient cosmic travelers, or even meteorites bearing unknown compounds, have carried the seeds of consciousness across star systems?

3. **Nature of Human Complexity**

    o *Why do humans display empathy and malice at extremes far beyond the realm of typical animal behavior?*

    o How does this intense spectrum of emotion and thought shape our responsibility toward one another and toward other living beings?

4. **Dominance of the Intangible**

- How does a force entirely unbound by physical tangibility exert so much influence over human decisions and societies?

- Is our intellectual and spiritual diversity a testament to the soul's independent agency, or is it a reflection of countless environmental, cultural, and cosmic variables intersecting?

As we delve further, remember that these questions do not spurn the lived experiences of any culture or tradition; they honor our universal drive to understand what animates us. Like researchers braving Antarctica's unforgiving climate to gather data that might uncover Earth's oldest secrets, we embark on a journey through the most frigid and unexplored regions of our inner worlds. In doing so, we hold fast to the possibility that whether the soul is a gift from a cosmic artisan or a grand accident of evolutionary magic, its existence remains one of our greatest marvels an unseen energy that lets us dream, love, hate, and hope on a scale unparalleled by any other creature we know.

Perhaps it is precisely this mystery so colossal, yet so intimately ours that challenges us to look deeper. Whether celestial design or cosmic chance brought our souls into being, the quest continues, fueled by wonder and a burning desire to grasp how an intangible spark can guide not only our next meal but also our next epoch, perhaps even charting humankind's grandest destiny.

Crucially, in every divine system known to us be it the Abrahamic faiths, the Dharmic perspectives, the indigenous teachings of myriad lands, or the varied mythologies once whispered around long-ago fires there is a shared conviction that humans possess a soul distinct from the mere mechanics of flesh.

From the Vedantic ātman to the Abrahamic notion of a God-breathed spirit, from the animistic beliefs of tribal communities to the refined philosophical constructs of Taoism and beyond, all converge on the idea of an inner essence that transcends mortal limitations.

It is this convergence, across ages and across continents, which sets the stage for our deeper investigation: whether we label it cosmic design or cosmic accident, the resounding consensus that a soul exists becomes our stepping stone into another deep exploration one where we weigh the evidence of purposeful creation against the possibility of a wondrous, unplanned spark

Comparative Perspectives on the Soul's Creation Across Diverse Divine Systems

When we survey the world's great spiritual tapestries each bearing threads from ancient texts, oral traditions, and timeless rituals we find a singular concept woven throughout: the human soul did not arise by accident. Yet how each tradition depicts the soul's origins and ultimate purpose varies dramatically, sometimes pointing to a deliberate, intelligent designer and other times leaving the matter cloaked in mystery. If we continue our *"Antarctica As A Universal Lab"* metaphor, we might imagine each of these divine systems proposing a unique reason why Earth's cosmic *"research station"* hosts souls and under what conditions they are created, studied, or reformed.

1. *Abrahamic Traditions (Judaism, Christianity, Islam)*

    - **Creation of the Soul**

        In these traditions, the soul emerges as a direct creation of a singular, omniscient divinity. Judaism's foundational texts poetically depict the *neshamah*, the breath of life, as a divine spark gently infused into humanity. Christianity emphasizes the individual crafting of each soul by God, purposed specifically for intimate communion with the Creator. Similarly, Islam teaches that Allah personally bestows upon every human a distinct *ruh* (spirit), establishing an enduring, sacred connection between the divine and humankind.

- **Interpretation**

  Within these frameworks, the soul's existence arises intentionally from a conscious, intelligent presence rather than a mere byproduct of cosmic randomness. This divine entity, God, operates akin to the lead investigator at an Antarctic research facility, carefully adjusting myriad variables to observe humanity's moral and spiritual responses within a controlled yet open-ended experiment. Certain perspectives even characterize Earth as a realm of spiritual probation or purification: a purposeful stage for ethical growth and refinement, more a laboratory for the soul than a random habitat. Still, alongside these structured interpretations, subtler, more fluid views exist, highlighting the primacy of human free will rather than strict divine decree. These nuanced interpretations acknowledge the soul's potential to evolve beyond explicit scriptural guidance, shaped profoundly by personal choices and experiences.

2. *Dharmic Traditions (Hinduism, Buddhism, Jainism, Sikhism)*

    - **Creation of the Soul**

      Hinduism envisions the ātman as eternal, emanating from Brahman, the ultimate reality, rather than being "*fabricated*" at a single point in time. Buddhism, while less inclined to speak of a permanent soul, recognizes a stream of consciousness that transmigrates, shaped continuously by karma. Jain philosophy describes the jīva, the living soul, as beginningless, bound in cycles of rebirth and ultimately seeking liberation. Sikh teachings similarly affirm that the soul is intrinsically linked to the Divine (Waheguru) yet engaged in a transformative journey toward deeper understanding.

- **Interpretation**

  Rather than portraying a singular cosmic craftsman forging each soul individually, these belief systems typically describe the soul as eternally co-existent with ultimate reality, akin to a component of an ongoing cosmic phenomenon without a defined beginning. Consider an Antarctic laboratory whose measurements seem to stretch indefinitely into the past, as though the station itself existed before the ice formed. In certain branches of Hinduism and Jainism, the soul's earthly existence represents an invaluable opportunity for spiritual refinement, a cosmic process aimed at enlightenment rather than punishment. Buddhism similarly avoids depicting existence as punitive or deliberately experimental, instead framing cyclic existence as arising primarily from ignorance or attachment. While subtly diverging from the notion of

Earth as explicitly penitential, this perspective still embraces the concept of our world as a profound arena for growth and learning, irrespective of whether an external intelligence specifically orchestrated it.

3. *The Eastern Threads (Taoism, Confucianism, Shinto)*

- **Creation of the Soul**

    In Taoism, the soul or spiritual essence arises naturally from the Tao, the ineffable and fundamental source of all existence. Consciousness is seen not as the product of a singular creative event but as a harmonious unfolding in alignment with the universal order. Confucian thought places greater emphasis on moral cultivation than on explicit narratives of creation; however, it acknowledges an immaterial essence distinguishing humans, compelling them toward ethical conduct. Shinto venerates kami, divine spirits inherent within nature, perceiving the human soul as a smaller-scale reflection of these profound and inspiring energies.

- **Interpretation**

    These frameworks often steer clear of depicting an almighty creator intentionally crafting human souls for a predetermined experiment. Instead, they envision a cosmos where intangible realities flow naturally into tangible experiences. One could liken this to an Antarctic research station operating without a singular *Chief Scientist*, relying instead on the continuous collaboration among various research teams. Within these Eastern perspectives, Earth is viewed less as a strict evaluation ground and more as a place of dynamic engagement: a reciprocal interaction between soul and environment. Concepts of punishment or penitence rarely emerge prominently; however, certain interpretations suggest moral imbalance might bring spiritual burdens, comparable to stumbling through ice rather than enduring a clearly defined cosmic penalty.

4. *Zoroastrian, African, and South American Ancestral Traditions*

   o **Creation of the Soul**

   Zoroastrian teachings maintain that Ahura Mazda created souls specifically to participate in a cosmic struggle between good and evil, positioning humanity on Earth to actively choose virtue. Many African spiritual traditions, such as those of the Yoruba, regard each individual's ori, or spiritual head, as divinely appointed, with the soul entering the earthly realm to fulfill a predetermined destiny. In several South American spiritualities, notably certain Andean beliefs, the soul is thought to originate from natural elements such as mountains, the sky, or from the

Great Spirit that encompasses and unifies all existence.

- **Interpretation**

    Like a meticulously coordinated project in Antarctica, where specialized teams monitor atmospheric changes or analyze glacial layers for indicators of global transformation, these spiritual traditions suggest humans reside within an environment rich with moral and existential meaning. Zoroastrianism distinctly portrays Earth as a *battleground* or *testing* ground, overseen by an intelligent cosmic entity where souls are assessed based on their choices. African spiritual perspectives tend to view Earth as a cooperative realm, where each soul's journey is enriched and guided by ancestral wisdom and community bonds. Certain Andean beliefs propose that Earth serves as an observational site from which the Great Spirit's guardians watch human behavior closely. Although explicit notions of punishment are not always central, the underlying suggestion of Earth functioning as a cosmic place of reformation persists, implying that higher powers may observe and intervene should moral or spiritual balance falter.

5. *Indigenous and Animistic Wisdom Beyond Continents*

- **Creation of the Soul**

    Many indigenous communities across North America, Oceania, and beyond describe the soul as an intrinsic extension of nature's own consciousness, suggesting that each individual carries a unique spark derived from the interconnected fabric of the environment. Rather than emphasizing a singular moment of creation, these perspectives focus more profoundly on the soul's ongoing relationship with ancestral spirits, totems, or the Dreamtime, highlighting continuous interaction and communal interconnectedness.

- **Interpretation**

    Here, Earth itself serves simultaneously as caretaker and evaluator, analogous to an Antarctic station managed by the land itself, with climate and wildlife dynamically responding to human interaction. While direct portrayals of Earth as a penitentiary are rare, some oral traditions suggest moral shortcomings can result in spiritual disharmony or alienation from nature's equilibrium, implying potential repercussions when humans neglect the inherent responsibilities of their existence. Various tribal legends describe the soul as originating from celestial or star realms, reflecting beliefs that consciousness arrived from beyond Earth's boundaries. The explicit concept of

Earth as an intentional experiment remains ambiguous; certain narratives distinctly reference star beings actively assessing humanity, while others suggest a more organic interplay, emphasizing Earth's role as a nurturing environment rather than a strictly supervised domain.

Synthesizing Definitions: Earth as Lab, Refinement Station, or Cosmic Chance?

Across diverse traditions, consensus emerges around the distinct nature of the human soul: tethered to the physical yet shaped by mysterious, possibly transcendent forces. Some belief systems view Earth as orchestrated by an intelligent force, suggesting humanity participates in a purposeful cosmic refinement. Others conceive our planet as one link in an expansive cosmic chain, where consciousness evolves continuously through countless existences.

Regardless of interpretation, as a realm of trial, collaboration, or symbiotic energy, Earth functions similarly to an Antarctic research station, uniquely positioned to reveal essential truths about human nature, morality, and spiritual evolution. This raises profound questions: was the soul intentionally crafted for such an environment, or did it merely adapt to its conditions? Whether humanity's journey is one of atonement, symbiosis, or exploration, nearly all spiritual and philosophical frameworks agree that the soul bridges unseen dimensions with everyday experience, elevating human existence beyond mere survival instincts.

Sacred texts often describe soul creation symbolically, shaped by visionary experiences subject to linguistic and cultural biases. Thus, religious writings should serve as guiding principles rather than absolute truths, complemented by scientific and pragmatic inquiry to illuminate consciousness more fully.

Human imagination frequently challenges known scientific limits through concepts like teleportation or interstellar travel. Modern science is beginning to hypothesize quantum entanglement and higher-dimensional realities, bridging previously distinct realms of spirituality and empirical inquiry.

A civilization surpassing humanity's technological grasp could, conceivably, translate consciousness effortlessly across domains, analogous to human achievements in harnessing once-inconceivable energies. Just as humanity adapts to harsh environments like Antarctica through technological mastery, an advanced civilization might encode and reconstitute life forms across cosmic distances, pushing the boundaries of what we consider biologically possible.

Rationalists and visionaries alike converge on concepts such as interstellar travel, consciousness uploading, and cosmic portals, highlighting the unique separation of consciousness from its physical embodiment. Continued exploration reinforces the improbability of such complexity arising purely by chance, hinting at possible orchestration by an advanced intelligence.

Human endeavors like artificial womb technology and extended off-world habitation reveal early glimpses into how superior civilizations might transplant life across dramatically varying conditions. Current research into preserving human embryos for long-duration space missions illustrates our emerging capability to sustain life through cosmic voyages, suggesting that more advanced entities could effortlessly transition consciousness between vastly different environments.

Our Antarctic experiments exemplify humanity's resilience in adapting to hostile conditions, employing thermal protection and sustainable energy solutions to unlock Earth's secrets. Scaling this ingenuity to cosmic proportions suggests a Type III civilization would view Earth's diverse ecosystems as manageable environments to study or transfer life-energy within broader cosmic objectives.

Simultaneously, scientists are pioneering methods to encode vast information into DNA, effectively merging consciousness with biology. This groundbreaking work hints at recreating the essence of "*soul*" biochemically, potentially enabling future humans to transport their genetic identities across galaxies. Such achievements suggest that superior civilizations may already possess the capability to encode and transfer consciousness with ease.

As our technological prowess advances, we may develop instruments revealing unseen forces or higher intelligences guiding Earth's formation. This technological evolution moves humanity closer to confirming the separation of soul and body, potentially verifying phenomena previously confined to mythology. Thus, our concept of the soul could ultimately evolve into a tangible cosmic voyager, realizing humanity's deepest interstellar aspirations.

> *In every boundary we surpass, we inch closer to the truth that what seems impossible today might be the simplest law of nature for tomorrow*

One Humanity, Many Cultures: Does Divinity Clarify Shared Biology and Diverse Lives?

Across diverse faith traditions, divine systems intricately detail human conduct, covering aspects from dietary practices to daily interactions. It appears curious that omnipotent cosmic principles delve into mundane life, especially given Earth's self-sustaining ecosystems. Humans, uniquely rational and capable of profound environmental alteration, still gravitate toward externally defined behavioral codes, contrasting starkly with other organisms thriving without explicit instructions.

Nature demonstrates an effortless cycle of sustainability: organisms perpetuate life through instinctual processes, without the necessity for written guidelines. Human rationality and technological prowess, however, empower profound alterations of nature, from urban development to genetic engineering. Paradoxically, this advanced capability necessitates more detailed prescriptions for ethical living, as the potential for rationalizing harm or negligence is equally significant.

Religious traditions offer specific guidelines reflecting their philosophical core. Jainism emphasizes meticulous non-violence through practices like cautious movement and selective diets, acknowledging that limitless potential requires careful discipline. Hinduism's daily rituals and karmic principles underscore that advanced human thought, while capable of understanding profound truths, also risks moral complacency without structured guidance.

Similarly, Buddhism's detailed monastic codes and lay precepts ensure mindfulness and compassion, protecting practitioners from desire-induced distraction. Taoism advocates effortless harmony yet provides structured breathing and dietary practices to maintain spiritual alignment. Confucianism prescribes ethical behavior for societal cohesion, while Shinto's purification rituals sustain sacred connections. Judaism's kosher laws and Sabbath observance exemplify conscious living, safeguarding humans from ethical excess.

Ultimately, these traditions underscore humanity's unique capacity, and responsibility, to consciously maintain balance within the natural and moral order, emphasizing structured practices as essential anchors against potential imbalance inherent in advanced rational capabilities.

Christianity emphasizes practices like fasting, pilgrimages, and specific moral guidelines to safeguard the human soul from pride, cruelty, or apathy, acknowledging that human intellect alone is insufficient for ethical living. Islamic rituals, including daily prayers, fasting during Ramadan, and halal dietary laws, serve as constant reminders to infuse routine acts with spirituality, mitigating human tendencies toward ecological and social exploitation.

African traditional religions uphold taboos on hunting and harvesting, reflecting the belief that human actions deeply affect communal harmony and environmental balance. South American indigenous traditions advocate respectful resource use, guided by shamans, to maintain ecological integrity against potential human-driven disruptions.

Sikhism's detailed Rehat Maryada prescribes rituals like daily prayers and communal meals, reinforcing social equality and spiritual mindfulness. This structured discipline underscores humanity's vulnerability to ethical lapses despite advanced reasoning.

This extensive codification across traditions highlights humanity's paradox: possessing remarkable intellectual capacities yet requiring explicit moral frameworks to prevent destructive behaviors. Unlike animals naturally aligned with ecological harmony, humans uniquely risk causing significant harm without structured ethical guidance. As Rachel Carson noted, our drive to simplify nature risks ecological ruin, necessitating religious guidelines to anchor moral consciousness amid powerful rationality.

Ultimately, detailed religious practices infuse daily decisions with ethical reflection, preventing rational self-interest from dominating moral judgment. Whether guided by cosmic design or accumulated wisdom from historical failures, these traditions consistently remind humanity of its responsibility toward compassionate coexistence.

Religious systems evolving under environmental influences parallel biological adaptations observed in nature. Just as animals adapt physical traits to local conditions, human civilizations have developed dietary and spiritual norms based on geographical resources and constraints. Regions abundant in plant-based resources often embraced vegetarianism, linking diets to spiritual purity, while harsher climates sanctified meat consumption as divine necessity.

Many religious food prohibitions carry practical rationales supported by modern science. Restrictions on pork historically mitigated parasite risks, while Jain dietary guidelines, avoiding root vegetables, symbolize respect for life and potentially align with health-conscious starch moderation. Likewise, practices such as fasting or restricting meals to daylight hours now find scientific support in improved metabolic health and circadian rhythm alignment.

Historical necessity also shaped food traditions, transforming survival strategies into revered customs. For instance, poverty-driven dietary innovations sometimes crystallized into lasting cultural norms, later sanctified by religious doctrine.

Analogous to Antarctic research stations operating under strict dietary and survival protocols, ancient humans crafted religious codes to manage environmental unpredictability, turning daily routines into rituals for health and survival. These structured guidelines replaced uncertainty with stability, linking physical health to spiritual discipline, ultimately reinforcing their divine credibility and societal necessity.

Fasting, traditionally framed as penance or gratitude, now also reveals physiological benefits similar to modern detoxification, supporting cellular repair and toxin elimination. These dietary practices instill discipline, naturally extending to broader spiritual and communal activities, reinforcing self-control and collective identity beyond mere practical concerns.

Analogous to Antarctica's meticulous operational guidelines governing caloric intake and meal timing, religious dietary prescriptions provide structured foresight, minimizing uncertainty in managing human health across generations. Both contexts recognize that methodical regulation is essential when stakes are high, whether for bodily wellness or survival in extreme environments.

Historical religious dietary rules, despite lacking contemporary scientific validation, reflect deep insights into digestion, immunity, and metabolism, truths progressively confirmed by modern research. The transition from dietary control to broader spiritual discipline, including prayer and meditation, highlights a systematic cultivation of virtue extending from physical to mental realms.

Prayer rituals further illustrate this structured mindfulness, promoting gratitude, physical movement, and fellowship. The physical postures embedded in prayer practices, particularly valuable in harsh climates, align closely with metabolic and circadian rhythms, much like scheduled exercise routines in polar research stations. Thus, seemingly divergent traditions, from ancient spiritual guidelines to modern scientific protocols, share an underlying commitment to structured living, promoting holistic human well-being.

Sacred spaces such as churches, temples, mosques, synagogues, and gurdwaras historically served not just religious functions but also addressed communal and social welfare needs. Prior to modern communication, these gatherings provided crucial opportunities to monitor each individual's well-being, akin to daily check-ins at remote polar research stations. Rituals of ablution before entering these spaces, while symbolic, also practically reduced disease transmission by minimizing contaminants, paralleling contemporary hygiene practices emphasized during global health crises.

Scheduled rest days or religious festivals instituted societal pauses, safeguarding communities from exploitation and exhaustion. Similar to routine equipment recalibrations in Antarctic research, these breaks allowed individuals necessary physical and psychological renewal, enhancing overall communal resilience.

Physical presence at communal worship functioned as a vital health and moral accountability check, with rituals involving regular movement helping reduce contagion risks in densely attended gatherings. Prayer routines in extreme climates provided subtle but consistent physical exercise, paralleling the structured physical regimens required of Antarctic researchers. In more temperate or labor-intensive regions, prayer emphasized introspective or vocal expressions, adapting rituals to environmental and occupational contexts.

Moreover, structured collective actions like chanting or recitations fostered social cohesion and emotional solidarity, mirroring the teamwork and synchronized tasks essential for survival in harsh environments. These repetitive communal activities strengthened empathy and unity, proving crucial during periods of crisis, thus affirming the profound interplay between spiritual discipline, environmental adaptation, and communal resilience.

The parallel between religious practices and modern quarantine protocols is evident in the historical necessity of isolating travelers and pilgrims, mirroring contemporary practices among Antarctic researchers and astronauts to prevent disease transmission. Such rituals, initially cloaked in religious tradition, pragmatically safeguarded communal health against pathogens. Unlike animals naturally adapted to local ecosystems, humans developed structured, preventative measures to mitigate risks posed by extensive travel.

Crucially, these practices were never mere instruments of control but acknowledged human vulnerability within communal and environmental extremes. Mandated holidays and rest periods prevented exploitation, emphasizing the necessity of systematic respite for sustained well-being, paralleling routine recalibrations in critical scientific environments. Alignments of prayer schedules with circadian rhythms, ablution with hygiene, and structured rest with systematic maintenance underscore sophisticated frameworks embedded within religious traditions.

The enduring precision and relevance of these guidelines across centuries suggest more than arbitrary cultural development; they indicate an underlying intelligence, whether divine inspiration or collective human wisdom, striving to protect humanity from its own potential excesses. Unlike contemporary operational protocols requiring frequent updates to accommodate new discoveries or crises, ancient religious codes remain notably consistent and applicable, demonstrating a deep understanding of human biology, ecology, psychology, and social dynamics.

Historical events, Chernobyl, Bhopal, Deepwater Horizon, serve as stark reminders that even meticulously planned human systems can fail disastrously under stress. Contrasted against these vulnerabilities, ancient religious prescriptions, remarkably robust and enduring, highlight the profound foresight and sophistication embedded in humanity's spiritual heritage, emphasizing discipline, health, and ethical community life.

Remarkably, divine guidelines maintain consistency despite humanity's transformation from agrarian simplicity to digital complexity. Could mere chance yield a structure so finely attuned to biological health, social cohesion, and moral balance across drastically shifting epochs? Logical analysis strongly suggests purposeful design rather than random cultural evolution. Practices like timed meals, mandated rest, and communal gatherings systematically address fundamental human needs, mitigate health risks, and reinforce social unity, a synergy unlikely to arise purely by chance.

Furthermore, human rationality, viewed as an additional interpretative capacity, finds modern scientific validations of ancient religious teachings. Anthropological and pragmatic studies often reaffirm insights long embedded in spiritual codes, highlighting a consistent alignment across divinity, science, and practical wisdom. This convergence supports the hypothesis of intentional foresight behind such enduring systems, given randomness rarely produces enduringly effective blueprints.

The improbable scenario of ancient tribes randomly devising rules that endure empires, technological revolutions, and sociocultural upheavals underscores the uniqueness of these traditions. Unlike human-devised policies frequently amended due to new discoveries or societal shifts, these spiritual directives remain largely unaltered, continuously relevant and beneficial.

Empirical demonstrations further solidify this view: communities adhering to structured ablutions, dietary regulations, rest intervals, and routine exercises consistently exhibit better health and mental wellness metrics. Such precise, sustained outcomes strongly suggest intentional, intelligent design, whether divine inspiration or deep collaborative human insight, weaving together a robust framework that surpasses mere chance.

> *Wisdom that stands unchanged through every reinvention of our world is never the artifact of randomness it bears the fingerprint of a design measured beyond mortal sight*

Divine Communications: Genuine Revelations or Mental Illusions?

Throughout history, diverse faiths have described divinity as actively communicating specific teachings to humanity. Monotheistic religions such as Judaism, Christianity, and Islam depict prophets like Moses, Jesus, and Muhammad receiving clear directives through visions, inner voices, or angelic messengers, affirming a purposeful interaction between the human and divine realms. In contrast, polytheistic cultures, including ancient Greece, certain Hindu traditions, and indigenous societies, recount deities appearing in human form, providing counsel directly or through intricate rituals. Similarly, animistic and shamanic traditions describe vital truths conveyed through dreams, visions, or trance states, exemplified by the Dreamtime teachings in Aboriginal Australia or ancestral messages among indigenous American and African communities.

The mediums of divine communication vary significantly: charismatic individuals hearing divine voices, collective visions, profound dreams influencing entire societies, or natural phenomena interpreted as spiritual messages. Such diverse manifestations prompt skepticism among those who demand tangible evidence, attributing these experiences to heightened emotional states or cultural expectations. Conversely, many believers view the consistent historical and transformative nature of these encounters as compelling evidence of their authenticity, emphasizing miracles' profound yet inexplicable impact.

Eastern philosophies offer a distinct perspective, highlighting revelation through disciplined spiritual practices rather than spontaneous divine intervention. Buddhism portrays enlightenment arising from intense meditation, while Hindu sages reportedly received the Vedas through elevated states of consciousness. Indigenous ceremonies involving ritual chanting, drumming, or sacred plants similarly open channels to ancestral or cosmic wisdom, emphasizing no singular method for authentic spiritual communication exists.

Zoroastrian teachings emphasize moral directives revealed to Zoroaster by Ahura Mazda, highlighting ethical living, environmental stewardship, and righteous actions. Such messages extend beyond mere worship, aligning intriguingly with contemporary ecological and social justice principles, a common thread across diverse spiritual traditions.

Skeptics, demanding empirical evidence, often question the authenticity of divine communications. Yet believers counter that phenomena like radio waves and quantum entanglement, once imperceptible, became evident through scientific advancement, suggesting that spiritual revelations might similarly await proper detection methods. This analogy doesn't prove divinity conclusively but encourages openness to possibilities beyond current sensory limits.

Divine communications have profoundly influenced civilizations, ethics, and cultures throughout history, leaving a legacy evident in monumental architecture, charitable institutions, and social governance. Whether genuine cosmic insights or intricate human inventions, these revelations persist, prompting questions about subtler realities accessible through advanced perception or intuition.

Human sensory limitations are apparent compared to animals: bats use ultrasound, elephants communicate via infrasound, and many creatures display superior visual, auditory, or olfactory abilities. Given our comparative sensory limitations, divine messages may utilize intellectual or spiritual receptivity rather than traditional sensory channels.

Animal behaviors, such as preemptive responses to natural disasters, suggest an intuitive capability beyond conventional senses. Humans, despite sensory shortcomings, excel in abstract reasoning, suggesting that our intuitive or "*sixth sense*" could represent an advanced cognitive capacity awaiting further scientific exploration. Such intuitive faculties might underpin our unique potential for receiving and interpreting profound, non-sensory communications.

Advances in modern technology illustrate how rapidly we adapt to new forms of long-distance communication, transforming seemingly impossible feats into routine realities. From horseback-delivered messages to instantaneous global streaming via satellites and fiber optics, our understanding of connectivity continually expands. Recent discoveries like gravitational waves, cosmic radiation, and quantum entanglement further reveal communication channels previously beyond comprehension, suggesting ancient accounts of divine or intuitive connections might similarly reflect yet-unknown mechanisms.

Historically, innovations like Morse code demonstrated communication beyond sensory perception, signals transmitted invisibly across vast distances, coordinating crucial actions swiftly. Today's International Space Station and the distant Voyager spacecraft similarly relay data undetectable by human senses, underscoring that sophisticated, non-sensory interactions already permeate our lives. In domestic and remote scientific settings, the Internet of Things enables automated data exchange without direct human observation, managing tasks from household supply orders to Antarctic ecological monitoring.

Considering humanity's current technological capabilities, still far below a Type I civilization on the Kardashev scale, it becomes conceivable that more advanced intelligences might utilize entirely different communication methods, telepathy, dream insertion, or enhanced intuition. Current research into dreaming highlights cognitive processes inaccessible during wakefulness, and practices like hypnotherapy or narco-analysis further demonstrate the human mind's capacity for profound, non-verbal communication.

These developments suggest that what we perceive as extraordinary or improbable might merely await deeper scientific understanding, prompting openness to the potential reality of subtle, non-sensory communications embedded within our expansive cosmos.

Across diverse spiritual traditions, divine messages often manifest through dreams, intuitive insights, or trance-like states, profoundly shaping religious teachings and societal practices. Prophets of the Hebrew Bible, Sufi mystics, Christian saints, and Indigenous spiritual leaders across the Americas and Africa have described encounters with intangible realms, experiences increasingly recognized by modern psychology and anthropology for their significant psychological and social value.

Antarctic researchers similarly rely on unseen data streams to navigate harsh environments and ensure operational safety, highlighting how intangible communications, though invisible, guide critical decisions. Ancient societies facing extreme conditions perceived such intangible transmissions as divine messages guiding survival, morality, and ethics. While modern technology replaced spiritual intermediaries, the underlying reliance on imperceptible yet essential signals remains constant.

Divine systems maintain remarkable consistency throughout history, even amidst humanity's technological and social transformations. While political systems evolve, scientific theories are revised, and economic models fluctuate, core spiritual teachings endure as stable anchors beyond temporal shifts. This enduring nature invites reflection on human sensory limitations; our perception captures only a fraction of reality's complexity, missing vast segments of environmental stimuli and phenomena like dark matter or quantum effects. Historical disbelief in unseen forces like radio waves, now integral to daily life, suggests openness to accepting intangible realities we currently cannot measure or perceive directly.

Thus, divine communications may represent an underexplored channel of universal intelligence, similar to modern intangible transmissions guiding critical human endeavors. Acknowledging these parallels neither proves nor disproves specific spiritual claims but encourages deeper exploration into how unseen forces might continually influence human understanding and existence.

Drawing connections between historical non-sensory communications, such as early Antarctic Morse code and contemporary IoT networks, and advanced intelligences possibly communicating through dreams or intuition, strengthens the hypothesis that Earth might serve as a monitored cosmic research station. The persistence and relevance of divine systems across millennia, coupled with ongoing scientific discoveries of previously unimaginable transmission methods, support the notion of deliberate cosmic orchestration. The enduring consistency of spiritual teachings, alongside scientific acknowledgment of unseen universal forces, implies that higher civilizations, surpassing our Type I limitations, could deliberately influence human progress and spiritual evolution through subtle, intangible channels beyond our current sensory capabilities.

Chapter 4: Beyond Purpose: Decoding Humanity's Role in the Infinite Design - Between the Threads: Global Faiths and the Cosmic Research Station Hypothesis - Divine Communications: Genuine Revelations or Mental Illusions?

Long before we traced signals through fiber and sky, we lived by messages that defied our eyes. Perhaps the future lies in uncharted waves we've yet to name

Heavenly Oversight: How Divine Systems Link Celestial Bodies to Earthly Life

Across diverse cultures and traditions, celestial bodies have historically guided more than mere navigation or agricultural timing; they are believed to shape human destiny profoundly. Astrology, spanning varied forms globally, remains influential, often surpassing conventional astronomy in cultural significance. This widespread belief underscores a consistent human perception of cosmic influence on individual and collective fortunes.

In Abrahamic faiths, nuanced views prevail. Judaism's historical texts occasionally reference planetary influences, sparking scholarly debate. Christianity, despite caution against attributing excessive power to stars, features biblical accounts like the Magi's journey to Bethlehem, signaling celestial messages. Medieval Europe notably integrated Arabic-translated astrological practices into daily life despite formal religious reservations. Islamic traditions, though emphasizing divine supremacy, cultivated extensive astrological scholarship, producing detailed star tables instrumental in navigation and societal guidance, significantly influencing Europe's scientific development.

Dharmic religions deeply embed celestial influence in cultural and spiritual frameworks. Hinduism's Jyotisha intricately merges astronomy and astrology, guiding life events from marriage to spiritual rituals through planetary insights. Buddhism, especially in East Asia and Tibet, incorporates local astrological beliefs impacting spiritual progress. Jainism, though minimally focused on cosmic deities, historically used astrology pragmatically, whereas Sikhism, emphasizing moral living and divine unity, sometimes culturally aligns with broader Indian astrological customs.

East Asian societies, Chinese, Japanese, and Korean, approach astrology philosophically and spiritually. Classical Chinese thought connected celestial harmony directly to imperial stability, influencing governance and cultural practices like the Chinese zodiac and Lunar New Year festivities. Japanese and Korean traditions similarly integrated astrological insights into royal courts and daily activities, viewing celestial alignments as reflections of universal energy (qi) harmonizing with human endeavors.

Indigenous communities in Africa and the Americas attribute profound influence to celestial bodies over life's rhythms. African groups, such as the Dogon of Mali, incorporate star lore into rituals, though some aspects are academically debated. In the Americas, the Maya aligned urban designs with celestial events like equinoxes, solstices, and planetary cycles, embedding astronomical precision into religious ceremonies. The Inca capital, Cusco, mirrored cosmic constellations, coordinating agricultural and spiritual cycles through solar and lunar temples. Similarly, various Native American nations viewed constellations as guardians of hunts, births, and crises, interpreting phenomena like comets as spirit messengers affecting community fate.

Zoroastrianism highlights celestial bodies within its cosmic moral struggle between Ahura Mazda (good) and Angra Mainyu (evil).

Ancient Persian astrologers carefully interpreted planetary events as signs foretelling spiritual outcomes, integrating star-based predictions into festivals and rituals, emphasizing celestial alignments as indicators of deeper cosmic truths.

While diverse traditions may differ in astrology's centrality, the fundamental belief remains consistent: heavenly observations offer guidance or insight into human affairs. Some religious groups caution against strict astrological dependence, emphasizing divine sovereignty over fate. Nonetheless, astrological references persist across scriptural commentaries and communal folklore, reflecting widespread acceptance.

This enduring fascination has institutionalized astrology through academic programs in India's Vedic tradition, modules in Traditional Chinese Medicine, and Western educational institutions. Despite skepticism, astrology's global prevalence suggests an underlying human conviction in celestial forces as active, formative influences transcending cultural and doctrinal boundaries.

Modern science acknowledges that celestial phenomena significantly influence Earth's climate, ecological cycles, and human livelihood, solar radiation affecting climate, lunar gravity shaping tides, and Earth's rotation governing circadian rhythms. While mainstream astrophysics remains skeptical of astrology's detailed personal predictions, increasing exploration into quantum entanglement, dark energy, and electromagnetic fields suggests subtle, potentially undiscovered cosmic influences.

Throughout history, human engagement with celestial bodies has straddled practical guidance, navigation, agriculture, and calendars, and mystical reverence, asserting active divine or cosmic interactions shaping earthly events. Ancient cultures, from the Babylonians to the Maya, systematically recorded precise celestial observations. Greek scholars like Hipparchus and astronomers during the Islamic Golden Age built foundational scientific knowledge, eventually influencing European astronomy.

Historical skepticism toward astronomical claims often gave way to validation through rigorous inquiry. Copernicus's heliocentric model required Galileo's telescopic evidence to overcome entrenched disbelief. Comets, once viewed as atmospheric anomalies, were recognized as solar-orbiting bodies through Halley's work. Likewise, meteorites shifted from rural superstition to accepted scientific phenomena only after credible documentation and analysis. Interestingly, various religious traditions had long integrated these celestial events into their teachings, symbolically or mythically acknowledging phenomena later scientifically confirmed.

Certain spiritual traditions intriguingly anticipated astronomical phenomena well before scientific validation occurred. Scriptures from various Eastern traditions, for instance, hinted at extended cosmic cycles or acknowledged celestial phenomena during periods when mainstream scholarship dismissed these ideas as improbable or ungrounded. This historical interplay underscores a compelling pattern: divine or spiritual frameworks often contained insights later confirmed by rigorous scientific inquiry, reflecting a profound and early human sensitivity to cosmic realities.

Native American oral histories and African legends frequently interpret celestial events as critical signals influencing environmental and communal decisions, embedding astronomical observations deeply into their moral teachings and cultural festivals. These ancient societies combined precise observational skills with spiritual significance, often centuries before modern academia validated such patterns scientifically.

Modern astronomy, evolving significantly since the 17th century through telescopes, photography, spectroscopy, and digital computing, now accurately forecasts celestial phenomena. Yet remarkably, early civilizations, lacking advanced instruments, reliably predicted eclipses, tracked lunar cycles, and aligned monumental structures to celestial events. These achievements suggest either intensive generational data collection or profound spiritual motivation, described by some as divine communications guiding their astronomical insights.

This interplay between science and spirituality mirrors contemporary collaborative efforts like the Antarctica Protocol. Just as nations today follow shared guidelines for stability and precise data collection in harsh environments, ancient civilizations operated under their own spiritually informed frameworks to systematically interpret cosmic cycles. These communities established sophisticated calendars and navigation methods based on celestial patterns, achieving precision comparable to modern scientific methods, attributing their knowledge to intangible, divine transmissions.

In essence, historical devotion to celestial observation was not mere fascination but a recognition of tangible outcomes, agricultural success, navigation accuracy, and structured community rites. Ancient spiritual protocols parallel modern reliance on intangible signals in environments like Antarctica, illustrating humanity's enduring effort to synchronize earthly activities with cosmic rhythms, suggesting deeper universal connections or guidance.

Ancient Egyptian records depict the god Thoth instructing humans in astronomy, while Mesoamerican codices illustrate sacred beings imparting celestial knowledge central to calendar systems. Similarly, Indian texts present celestial "*grahas*" as part of a revealed cosmic order, underscoring a philosophical impetus driving meticulous astronomical observation despite limited technological means.

Debate may persist regarding the literal nature of these "*divine communications*" yet the accuracy achieved in measuring cosmic cycles remains compelling. Ancient civilizations, much like modern scientists utilizing intangible transmissions such as radio signals and digital data, trusted spiritual guidance encoded in scriptures and rituals to unify communities and ensure societal stability. This practice parallels contemporary scientific protocols, like data sharing in Antarctica, highlighting an enduring reliance on intangible yet fruitful guidance.

Historically contested concepts, such as planetary orbits or eclipse predictions, gained validation through rigorous scientific inquiry only after centuries. Remarkably, ancient cultures achieved comparable precision without advanced tools, suggesting their profound spiritual reverence motivated deeper cosmic exploration. This synergy between spiritual inspiration and practical astronomical success bolsters the hypothesis of Earth as a cosmic research station, subtly guided by intelligences beyond our current understanding.

The widespread and consistent integration of celestial movements into religious and societal frameworks further supports this perspective. Ancient civilizations' alignment of sacred rites and festivals with astronomical events indicates deliberate cosmic signaling, potentially guiding humanity toward sustained cosmic observation and self-discovery. The enduring convergence between sacred teachings and empirical astronomy suggests humanity participates in a larger, intricately designed cosmic protocol, uniting faith, reason, and universal exploration.

> *Often, what we read in the stars is not just light that traveled eons to reach our eyes, but also a message of how deeply our destiny may be intertwined with the silent grandeur of the universe*

Beyond the Temporal: Divine Views on the Afterlife Continuum

Within Earth's biosphere, life cycles universally prioritize survival and reproduction. Organisms emerge, adapt to their environment, then inevitably decay, their remains fueling the ecosystem's perpetual renewal. Apex predators dominate until their demise, afterward sustaining scavengers and microorganisms alike. Humans, however, diverge profoundly from this natural template. While human infancy demands survival-based caregiving, adulthood shifts dramatically toward pursuits transcending mere survival: knowledge, societal constructs, art, technology, morality, and spiritual exploration. No other species dedicates comparable resources to such intangible endeavors, redefining human metamorphosis into phases of cultural and personal evolution rather than biological survival alone.

Yet, despite our distinctive trajectory, humans ultimately share the same physical conclusion: inevitable bodily cessation. Our advanced intellect and medical breakthroughs cannot evade mortality. Nonetheless, even in death, humans differ from nature's standard recycling of organic matter. Common practices like burial and cremation affirm respect for the physical form, recognizing it as once hosting an extraordinary self-aware consciousness. Alternative rites, such as sky burials, underscore a similar reverence, albeit through distinct methods.

Central to humanity's differentiation is the widespread belief in a soul or essence transcending physical existence. Religious doctrines commonly portray this intangible force departing the body at death, transitioning into realms beyond earthly perception. Interestingly, contemporary science occasionally approaches analogous conclusions, investigating phenomena like near-death experiences or quantum theories suggesting consciousness might persist independently of neural activity.

From ancient graves adorned with ochre and artifacts to intricate rituals described in the Tibetan Book of the Dead or Egyptian funerary texts, humanity has historically invested death with profound spiritual significance. Modern funerals universally retain these foundational elements, emphasizing respect, dignity, and implicit continuity of consciousness or memory.

In stark contrast, animal behavior rarely exhibits comparable ritualistic complexity. While elephants occasionally display grief-like behaviors, these occurrences lack human symbolic depth and elaboration. Humans uniquely endow death with intricate meaning, reflecting an innate conviction that existence surpasses biological survival alone, suggesting a deeper, intangible reality embraced equally by spiritual traditions and emergent scientific hypotheses.

Practices such as cremation, burial, or exposure to the elements acknowledge humanity's inevitable physical return to nature yet simultaneously preserve a profound sense of sanctity. Ancient Zoroastrians utilized *"Towers of Silence"* to prevent contamination of sacred elements, while many indigenous traditions prefer direct integration into the earth without synthetic barriers. Contemporary practices similarly signify reverence, emphasizing that bodily dissolution is not the end of personal identity but a transition to an intangible continuity beyond physical perception.

This dual transformation, bodily reintegration with nature and the departure of consciousness, is uniquely emphasized in human rituals and beliefs. These rites, ranging from ancient burials adorned with grave goods to modern ceremonies in hospitals and crematoriums, aim to honor the individual's passage and ease their intangible essence's journey. Unlike other organisms' purely physical transformations, human rituals embody psychological complexities and spiritual convictions about existence beyond corporeal life.

The universal belief in post-mortem continuity naturally bridges spiritual teachings and emerging scientific hypotheses. While religions explicitly describe afterlife realms governed by moral or existential purposes, contemporary science cautiously explores concepts such as near-death experiences and quantum consciousness theories, entertaining the notion that consciousness may persist or transform after biological death. Despite variations and apparent contradictions among cultural narratives, whether reincarnation cycles, spiritual liberation, or unique existential missions, these diverse perspectives collectively indicate that multiple higher intelligences or cosmic frameworks might coexist.

Humanity's tendency to center experiences on immediate perception limits our grasp of broader cosmic realities. Our sensory and cognitive abilities capture only fragments of the universe's multidimensional scale, exemplified by undetectable phenomena like radio waves that existed unknown for centuries. Just as our vision covers only a fraction of our surroundings at any moment, our comprehension of existence may be profoundly incomplete, suggesting unseen cosmic processes continually unfolding beyond the edges of our perception and scientific instrumentation.

The ways we manage earthly objects, single-use disposables, valued antiques, or systematically recycled materials, serve as an illuminating metaphor for how cosmic civilizations might perceive souls. Some souls might be assigned a single mission on Earth, afterward permanently retiring from our domain. Others could undergo repeated reincarnations, gradually refining their experience until achieving ultimate fulfillment. Although this notion appears speculative, history demonstrates that many initially unobservable phenomena, like pathogens and atomic structures, became fundamental truths once appropriately examined.

Antarctica offers a vivid parallel: scientists rotate through expeditions, adhering to protocols and employing instruments ranging from disposable to highly reusable. Some participants return repeatedly, while others complete a single, focused mission. Similarly, humans might be participants in cosmic or spiritual experiments, experiencing either singular journeys or multiple lifetimes based on specific existential objectives.

This framework aligns closely with theological beliefs and scientific curiosity about intangible cosmic interactions. Religious traditions differ profoundly even within themselves, reflecting the diverse governance structures humans adopt, democracies, monarchies, or socialist states. It stands to reason that advanced cosmic intelligences similarly employ varied protocols for managing human souls, whether through single-use missions or cyclical reincarnations.

Ultimately, humanity's inherent limitation, our narrow sensory perception and tendency toward illusory completeness, highlights the necessity of continuously shifting perspectives. Our reliance on invisible technologies like satellite signals parallels the possibility that intangible cosmic communications guide human existence in ways we currently lack the instrumentation to detect, prompting ongoing exploration into the expansive unknown.

The metaphor comparing human souls to objects managed through disposal or recycling suggests profound parallels between cosmic processes and mundane earthly practices. Just as some materials serve briefly before disposal while others are repeatedly repurposed, humans might likewise embody single-use or repeatedly incarnated souls within larger cosmic experiments. Earth itself resembles Antarctica's structured research, hosting transient or recurring personnel and diverse tools. The concept that each human life represents a designed experiment gains plausibility when viewed through both spiritual traditions and scientific perspectives, prompting continual exploration into intangible cosmic mechanisms.

Religious doctrines describe varied post-mortem journeys, from paradisiacal afterlives in Abrahamic traditions to cyclical rebirths in

Hindu and Buddhist thought, reflecting disparate yet consistently cosmic laws governing existence. Science traditionally views consciousness as neural activity but increasingly entertains speculative models where identity may transcend bodily death, acknowledging phenomena historically invisible but now measurable, like radio waves.

This cosmic experiment analogy mirrors scientific breakthroughs where identical processes yield vastly different outcomes, much like atomic fission generating either beneficial energy or devastating weaponry. Similarly, souls' earthly journeys could culminate in serene bliss or profound torment, illustrating a universal system capable of producing divergent results from identical foundational principles. Historical discoveries, often arising from accidental experimentation, penicillin and X-rays, for instance, reinforce this dynamic of unexpected outcomes shaping reality.

Humanity's inherent cosmic origin, atoms forged in stellar processes, might explain our unyielding curiosity and urge to explore and manipulate nature. Perhaps advanced intelligences employ Earth as a testing environment, applying intangible protocols perceived as divine laws or cosmic principles. Ultimately, humanity's moral and spiritual accountability mirrors scientific experimentation's diverse outcomes, underscoring the possibility that our lives constitute components of sophisticated, cosmic-scale inquiries into existence itself.

The analogy of Antarctica enriches the concept of Earth as a cosmic research environment. Just as international teams collaborate under agreed-upon rules to explore Antarctica while minimizing environmental impact, souls might arrive on Earth governed by universal moral and spiritual protocols. Similar to Antarctic researchers, some making a single visit, others returning repeatedly, souls might experience one lifetime or multiple incarnations, each contributing unique insights or fulfilling distinct cosmic objectives. Earthly free will parallels the risks in Antarctic research, where decisions can yield profound benefits or devastating consequences, akin to the dual outcomes of nuclear technology.

Historically, humans have advanced by observing patterns and transforming them into practical knowledge. Extending this logic, mortal existence itself could represent cosmic experimentation, with advanced intelligences evaluating moral and spiritual variables through human experience. The parallels between religious notions of paradise or damnation and scientific concepts of productive versus destructive outcomes underscore how profound discoveries often carry both beneficial and harmful potentials.

Ultimately, the idea of Earth as an experimental cosmic station elegantly synthesizes spiritual beliefs and scientific reasoning. Souls, seeded by advanced cosmic entities, navigate moral choices and intangible guidance, capable of outcomes as divergent as salvation or ruin. Like Antarctica's challenging conditions for researchers, Earth's complex environment offers souls opportunities for exceptional achievements or severe errors, each outcome essential data within an expansive cosmic inquiry.

> *The same force that can light a city can also shatter it perhaps in the lab of existence, our life's outcome hovers in that delicate balance, shaped by the soul's free will and an experimenter's silent gaze*

Divine Narratives of Earth's End: Why Sacred Teachings Foresee Civilizations' Dissolution

Human Specie's sacred narratives consistently portray the world's end dramatically, despite variations across traditions. Aboriginal Australians speak of disrupted Dreamtime causing catastrophic renewal; Mesoamerican texts describe cyclical destruction by elemental forces; African traditions emphasize cosmic collapse from moral imbalance; Zoroastrianism anticipates purifying flames evaluating and renewing Earth; Dharmic beliefs foresee Shiva's universal dissolution; and Abrahamic religions predict apocalyptic Judgment Days. These diverse traditions uniformly convey Earth's finite existence, despite differing in specifics.

Modern science echoes this impermanence, projecting the Sun's eventual expansion into a red giant and various catastrophic possibilities such as asteroid impacts, gamma-ray bursts, or climatic collapse from human-driven environmental damage. Geology reminds us of historic super volcanic eruptions, highlighting Earth's vulnerability to naturally occurring global-scale disasters. Ultimately, physics suggests universal entropy, the inevitable "*Heat Death*" scenario, further confirming cosmic impermanence.

Ironically, even those favoring empirical evidence consume apocalyptic narratives avidly through entertainment, from blockbuster films depicting planetary destruction to superhero sagas about multiversal threats. This collective fascination underscores a shared subconscious acceptance or fear of Earth's eventual demise, reinforcing cultural acknowledgment of impermanence across scientific, spiritual, and popular domains.

These varied portrayals resemble the parable of blind men describing an elephant, each perspective captures a fragmentary truth. Whether religious morality, scientific inevitability, or fictional drama, all align in affirming Earth's transient nature. Such convergence invites reflection on whether this cosmic finality results from intentional design by advanced intelligences, built-in planetary safeguards, or humanity's cumulative choices inevitably pushing ecological limits, ultimately questioning if Earth's end reflects planned cosmic obsolescence or the natural outcome of free will's boundless potential.

Despite differing in moral, scientific, or imaginative frameworks, humanity collectively acknowledges Earth's inevitable expiration. Religious traditions prophesy renewal following moral reckoning, scientists predict unavoidable cosmic or environmental catastrophes, and popular culture obsessively explores apocalyptic scenarios. These varied viewpoints, analogous to blind descriptions of an elephant, each grasp partial truths yet universally agree on impermanence, suggesting a deeper cosmic routine or inherent design that challenges stability.

Humanity's trajectory, marked from stone tool crafting to nuclear technology, consistently reflects a tension between innovation and destruction. Early human actions, such as hunting and agriculture, profoundly reshaped landscapes, escalating in modern times to ecosystem destruction and nuclear weaponry capable of unprecedented devastation. Unlike other species whose environmental impacts remain modest, humans possess the capability to eliminate entire ecosystems, amplifying this disparity dramatically with nuclear arsenals.

Yet, humanity's potential for beneficial progress remains equally immense. Technologies born from constructive experimentation, like aviation, antibiotics, and renewable energy, have transformed societies positively. However, history repeatedly shows how aspirations for advancement often devolve into domination, where visionary promises of freedom deteriorate into tyranny and violence, driven by ego and fear. This cyclically destructive tendency underscores a critical irony: human ambitions, despite profound local impact, remain fleeting and insignificant on the cosmic scale, reminding us of our transient role within an expansive universe.

The recurring theme of humanity's destructive potential prompts reflection on whether divine or cosmic systems anticipated that free will combined with increasing intellect could push moral limits dangerously. Ancient scriptures across faiths often forewarn generations whose corruption necessitates a global reset, suggesting that Earth might operate similarly to an advanced laboratory's automated safety mechanisms. When thresholds of destructive behavior are reached, such as extreme climate damage, nuclear warfare, or moral degradation, could a built-in cosmic failsafe trigger a planetary shutdown?

Envisioning divine frameworks as engineered by advanced cosmic intelligences (perhaps Type III civilizations), one could argue they foresaw humans amassing potentially boundless power. The same discovery, nuclear fission, that yields energy to sustainably power cities also birthed devastating atomic weaponry. This duality demonstrates how identical forces underpin both constructive and destructive outcomes, contingent entirely on moral choice.

Thus, Earth resembles a cosmic research station, hosting souls as experimental variables. Each individual, capable of immense good or evil, collectively shapes outcomes that yield valuable cosmic insights. From above, cosmic observers may carefully monitor humanity's progression, intervening only when necessary through built-in moral and ecological thresholds. Humans, despite their fleeting perspective, function as self-aware participants whose moral decisions ultimately test the boundaries of cosmic tolerance.

This scenario highlights humanity's precarious position, where crossing invisible moral boundaries could precipitate an automatic cosmic "*reset*." While religious narratives frame this as apocalyptic judgment, a broader cosmic view sees it neutrally, a necessary safety mechanism ensuring the integrity of the universal experiment in free will and moral development.

Humanity's greatest achievements derive from collective intelligence, exemplified by aviation's evolution, centuries of incremental progress culminating in sophisticated technologies ranging from commercial flights to stealth bombers. This collaborative synergy accelerates both remarkable innovations and catastrophic potentials, raising the profound question: did advanced cosmic intelligences foresee such trajectories and establish protective measures to halt uncontrolled escalation?

The scenario presents a compelling notion: humanity might exist within an elaborate cosmic experiment, monitored for the interplay of intellect, morality, and free will. Religions universally predict an impending reset due to moral excesses; science warns of environmental fragility and catastrophic risks; politics demonstrates how quickly destructive forces manifest under misguided leadership. Yet, amidst potential gloom, humanity retains agency, the ability to choose responsibly, employing collaborative and ethical frameworks to avoid self-inflicted disasters. Perhaps cosmic overseers, if existent, await these outcomes, poised to intervene only if irrevocable collapse becomes imminent.

Tracing human evolution, from early toolmaking sparks to nuclear power, highlights unparalleled potential for creativity and arrogance. Repeatedly, brilliant innovations pivot toward domination and oppression. Thus, Earth's history might reflect intentional cosmic experimentation, gauging how swiftly human endeavors shift from constructive to destructive ends. The recurring theme of an inevitable finale across spiritual prophecies, scientific forecasts, and cultural fascinations reinforces the idea of Earth as a controlled laboratory. Each epoch, marked by intellectual leaps and moral failings, contributes essential data until reaching critical thresholds where a cosmic safety mechanism, an intentional, self-regulating shutdown, ensures the experiment never spirals irreparably out of control.

In each flint spark, each forging furnace, each nuclear chain reaction lies a reminder that humanity's creativity and its capacity for destruction are woven of the same thread: how we pull the strand determines whether we build or demolish

Earth's Divine Tapestry: Affirming the Cosmic Research Station Hypothesis?

Throughout history, humanity has sought to understand its place in the cosmos. Every civilization, every spiritual tradition, and every philosophical movement has wrestled with the same fundamental question: why are we here? Some seek meaning in the randomness of existence, others in divine will. Yet, when we analyze all faiths together, a striking pattern emerges. This pattern suggests Earth is not merely an accident of nature, but a carefully designed experiment.

We stand at a crossroads where science, philosophy, and theology converge to form a singular, undeniable truth. Examined holistically, all facets of divinity provide compelling evidence that Earth functions as a cosmic research station, a site where life is observed, guided, and evaluated. Every tradition, in some form, speaks of oversight, purpose, and evaluation. These characteristics align perfectly with the hypothesis of Earth as a research station.

The first question we must address is how divine systems describe power. If Earth were indeed a cosmic research station, religious texts would logically emphasize observation, intervention, and control rather than depicting existence as chaotic or unguided. This expectation matches precisely what we observe across various traditions. The Abrahamic religions describe a God who watches, judges, and intervenes when necessary, behaviors analogous to a research scientist monitoring an experiment. In the Book of Job, for instance, God not only creates but actively tests human faith and resilience, akin to a scientist analyzing experimental variables.

Hinduism and Buddhism highlight karma, an intricate cause-and-effect system suggesting life is governed by principles similar to controlled experimental conditions. The Bhagavad Gita portrays divinity as both guide and observer, permitting beings to act freely yet ensuring their actions align with structured cosmic laws. Indigenous traditions also describe spirits, ancestors, and celestial forces guiding human development, akin to researchers managing variables within an experiment.

Across diverse cultures, divinity consistently plays the roles of creator, sustainer, observer, and evaluator. If Earth were merely a self-contained reality, we would anticipate deities to assume passive roles. Instead, these divine entities actively shape events, mirroring the deliberate, intelligent oversight characteristic of researchers conducting an experiment.

If Earth were an experiment, we would expect the concept of the soul to function as an independent unit of consciousness, much like data that can be extracted, analyzed, and transferred. Once again, faith traditions align with this perspective. Hindu and Buddhist traditions describe the soul (Atman) as separate from the body, capable of moving between existences, akin to data being transferred between research trials.

In Abrahamic faiths, the soul is explicitly judged and relocated to different realms based on behavior, mirroring the conclusion of an experiment where outcomes determine future placement. Many indigenous traditions speak of the soul returning to another plane of existence, where it undergoes evaluation before entering the next phase. The consistent theme across these traditions is the soul's independence from biological functions, much like experimental data being logged and studied. This aligns with the notion that life on Earth is a monitored and purposeful process rather than a random occurrence.

A critical argument for the research station hypothesis is found in the paradox of human unity and division. If humans were purely evolutionary beings, we would anticipate cultural development to be entirely random. Yet, similar religious and philosophical structures emerge independently across time and space. Major religions universally follow patterns involving creation, evaluation, judgment, and transition, suggesting a designed system.

Across diverse continents, remarkably similar moral codes surface, exemplified by the Golden Rule (*"Do unto others as you would have them do unto you"*), found in Christianity, Islam, Hinduism, and various indigenous traditions. Despite geographic isolation, different civilizations independently developed parallel metaphysical ideas surrounding soul purification, divine oversight, and afterlife realms. The strength of the hypothesis becomes evident when we question: without guided influence, how could such parallel systems consistently emerge? These controlled variations suggest deliberate structuring, analogous to different experimental groups established to analyze distinct outcomes.

Skeptics argue that religious experiences are mere psychological projections. However, this explanation fails to account for the striking consistency of divine encounters documented throughout various times, cultures, and belief systems. Prophets, seers, and shamans from different backgrounds consistently describe visions involving oversight, communication with higher beings, and warnings of moral consequences. Near-death experiences, reported across numerous cultures, depict similar journeys involving guidance, life reviews, and relocation to other realms. Ancient texts frequently detail encounters with celestial beings, often described similarly to contemporary accounts of extraterrestrial or hyper-intelligent entities. If divine communications were mere fabrications, why would diverse cultures independently describe comparable encounters with beings functioning not merely as creators but as researchers and overseers?

Many religious traditions place great importance on stars, planetary alignments, and celestial influences, suggesting an external system actively engaged in Earth's processes, much like a research station overseen by external observers. Astrology, present in Babylonian, Vedic, Chinese, and Mayan traditions, proposes that human affairs are influenced by forces beyond Earth. The concept of divine heavens, where deities reside beyond Earth, implies that our world is a controlled evaluative environment managed by celestial powers.

If Earth were a cosmic research station, we would expect life after death to be structured rather than chaotic. Religious systems again provide a clear response. Abrahamic faiths describe the afterlife as a realm of judgment and subsequent placement, resembling final evaluations in research studies. Hinduism and Buddhism outline a system of rebirth and karmic outcomes, consistent with an ongoing experiment where souls are reassigned based on past behaviors. Many indigenous traditions describe the afterlife as a return to observers, a phase where souls recount their experiences before transitioning again.

Nearly every tradition predicts a conclusion to Earth as we know it. If Earth were arbitrary, why would civilizations across history consistently foresee an endpoint? Hindu cosmology details yugas, vast cycles of creation and destruction. Christianity, Islam, and Judaism articulate a final day of judgment when the experiment concludes. Mayan and Hopi traditions reference cosmic resets, mirroring the termination and renewal of research environments. Viewed holistically, divine traditions consistently support the concept that Earth is a structured, monitored environment rather than a random phenomenon.

Earth is not an accident. It is a laboratory of consciousness, a designed experiment, a place where intelligence is cultivated, evaluated, and refined. Patterns evident across diverse faith traditions do not exist in isolation; rather, they coalesce into a cohesive framework affirming the hypothesis. By examining these narratives collectively, we uncover a compelling truth: the intentional design, oversight, and purpose embedded within divine traditions powerfully suggest that Earth is, indeed, a cosmic research station.

Divinity was never about control; it was always an open door, inviting humanity to discover its own purpose in the grand design of existence

Beyond Equations: Does Science Support the Cosmic Research Station Hypothesis?

Humanity's quest to define its place in the cosmos has evolved alongside its ability to question, measure, and refine understanding. Ancient civilizations explained existence through divine myths, weaving narratives of purpose and fate. Then came the age of science, a methodical pursuit of truth grounded in observation, experimentation, and reason. Science and spirituality have often been framed as opposing forces, yet when examined holistically, they appear to tackle the same fundamental questions: What governs the universe? Are we the product of random chance, or are we part of a structured, intentional system? If divinity, in its broadest interpretations, points toward the hypothesis of Earth as a cosmic research station, might the greatest scientific theories subtly lead us to the same conclusion?

Throughout history, humanity has refined its understanding of reality through cycles of hypothesis and validation. The ancient Greeks theorized atoms as indivisible building blocks composing everything. Centuries later, quantum mechanics revealed that these fundamental particles behave in ways counterintuitive to human understanding. Newton's deterministic universe was eventually supplanted by Einstein's theory of relativity, showing that space and time could bend, shift, and weave a reality that is not fixed but fluid. Today, advanced discoveries in astrophysics, evolutionary biology, and artificial intelligence uncover patterns of structure, order, and laws governing existence, closely resembling the meticulous framework of an experimental model.

Science operates on the principle of falsifiability, requiring hypotheses to withstand rigorous scrutiny or be discarded. Consequently, even the most brilliant scientific minds have unwittingly participated in an ancient inquiry: Does the universe's complexity suggest an underlying intelligence? Often, scientists aiming to disprove divine constructs inadvertently uncover patterns too intricate to ignore. Evolution, the extensive narrative of adaptation and survival, illustrates optimization principles reminiscent of finely tuned systems. The laws of thermodynamics, overseeing energy and entropy, echo the balanced conditions required within controlled environments. Quantum mechanics, in its unpredictable elegance, even proposes that the very act of observation alters reality. Could it be that science, rather than contradicting the cosmic research station hypothesis, actually offers the most compelling support for it?

We will examine cosmology, asking whether the fine-tuning of physical constants implies design. Evolutionary biology will be dissected, probing whether the drive toward complexity suggests external parameters. The peculiarities of quantum mechanics will be scrutinized, investigating whether consciousness plays a role in shaping reality. Additionally, information theory and artificial intelligence may hold clues, if intelligence itself emerges from patterns and structure, would an intelligent civilization not structure its experiments similarly?

When we explored divinity, we noted how faith traditions consistently described Earth as a site of evaluation, refinement, and observation. Turning now to science, we pursue a parallel inquiry: Are its most advanced theories inadvertently pointing to a similar truth? Could the equations we trust as unwavering descriptions of reality actually affirm something greater? Might our attempts to quantify the universe reveal the structure of a cosmic experiment? This is not an assertion but an examination, a continuation of humanity's eternal quest for understanding.

Whether one adheres firmly to scientific skepticism or remains open to metaphysical possibilities, the central question persists: if Earth is merely an arbitrary occurrence, why do theories from biology to physics imply structure, intention, and order? And if structure, intention, and order define existence, must we not consider intelligence as integral to our placement, evolution, and development? Just as researchers meticulously design environments to study outcomes, might we also exist within a framework, our progress carefully monitored, our actions subtly steering discovery?

Science aims to dispel illusion and uncover truth, yet truth often aligns remarkably with ancient wisdom. Exploring the grand theories of existence, we ask: in its pursuit of objectivity, might science inadvertently affirm that Earth is more than a random celestial body, that it functions as a research station for a purpose beyond our current comprehension?

Perhaps the greatest irony of science is that, in its search to dismiss the extraordinary, it may be proving it

Scientific theories, like divine systems, evolve as human understanding advances. Previously accepted truths give way to more sophisticated models, demonstrating science's dynamic nature, always seeking, always adapting. Just as controlled experiments validate or challenge hypotheses, our inquiry will utilize select scientific models to assess the research station hypothesis. While numerous theories exist, we focus on those shaping our perception of reality, analogous to how specific experimental variables uncover deeper truths. If science itself is a shifting framework, might this not suggest our existence within an environment designed explicitly for iterative discovery?

The Big Bang: From Singularity to Cosmic Birth

The Big Bang Theory stands as the predominant scientific account of the universe's origin, proposing that approximately 13.8 billion years ago, an immensely dense and unimaginably hot singularity expanded rapidly, giving rise to space, matter, energy, and eventually galaxies, stars, and planets. This process was not an explosion within space but an ongoing expansion of space itself, continuously shaping cosmic structure. However, critical questions persist: What caused this singularity to exist? Was it the product of deeper, undiscovered cosmic laws or possibly an external intelligence?

Deciphering the nature of this initial singularity represents one of modern physics' most profound challenges. Before expansion, all known matter and energy existed in a state so dense that conventional understandings of space and time lose meaning, pushing known physical laws beyond their limits. Here, quantum mechanics and general relativity fail to converge into a coherent explanation. Some theories propose quantum fluctuations within a primordial quantum vacuum might have sparked the universe, a concept supported experimentally only at microscopic levels. Others envision a cyclical cosmos where our universe emerged from the remnants of an earlier universe, expanding and contracting indefinitely.

The empirical foundations supporting the Big Bang are robust and extensive. Cosmic microwave background radiation (CMB) provides a critical observational anchor, a pervasive, faint glow echoing conditions roughly 380,000 years post-Big Bang. This radiation acts as a historical snapshot, aligning closely with theoretical expectations. Further evidence emerges from the redshift of galaxies, consistently demonstrating universal expansion: galaxies recede at velocities proportional to their distance, precisely as predicted. Moreover, observed cosmic abundances of hydrogen, helium, and lithium match exacting predictions of the Big Bang model, underscoring a predictable sequence of cosmological events.

The Big Bang Theory indeed complements the Cosmic Research Station Hypothesis in notable ways. The finely-tuned precision evident in the universe's initial conditions suggests an orchestrated event governed by exact mathematical constants essential for life. Had the universe's expansion rate been marginally faster, matter would have scattered too rapidly for galaxies to form; had it been slower, gravitational collapse would have been inevitable. The meticulous balance between matter and antimatter, along with the precise formation of life-sustaining elements, reinforces the Anthropic Principle, the idea that the universe appears specifically calibrated for life. Such exactitude aligns with viewing Earth as an intentionally structured environment, optimized for observation and refinement rather than as an arbitrary cosmic occurrence.

Considering the universe as an experimental framework positions the Big Bang as an initial set of controlled parameters within a cosmic laboratory. Analogous to scientific simulations investigating planetary formation, black hole dynamics, and cosmic evolution, our universe could itself represent a large-scale model established by advanced intelligence aiming to study consciousness within structured physical laws.

The nature of the singularity further supports this hypothesis. Proposed vacuum fluctuations initiating expansion could mirror conditions deliberately crafted in a controlled experimental setting. If intelligence shapes environments explicitly for research purposes, the idea of a singularity resulting from intentional cosmic engineering emerges as a plausible interpretation.

Moreover, the realization that the universe had a definitive beginning aligns closely with philosophical and religious narratives depicting creation as purposeful rather than random. The emergence of existence from apparent nothingness raises critical questions about whether such an event was spontaneous or deliberately initiated. Cyclical universe models, proposing endless cycles of expansion and contraction, further bolster the concept of iterative cosmic experimentation, each cycle potentially refining existential parameters. Additionally, multiverse theories introduce the idea of multiple universes with diverse physical laws, suggesting our cosmos may represent one of countless observational environments.

Thus, although the Big Bang does not explicitly confirm a cosmic research station hypothesis, it strongly implies intentional design, precision, and conducive conditions for intelligence and life. If humans conduct experiments with structured parameters, it seems reasonable to consider the possibility of our universe functioning similarly on an incomprehensibly grander scale. Rather than debating if the Big Bang was an experiment, perhaps we should ponder the identity or nature of the intelligence that established its profound, life-sustaining laws.

Perhaps the ultimate mystery isn't how the universe began, but whose intention crafted the precise conditions allowing life and consciousness to emerge

Darwinian Evolution: Nature's Experiment in Adaptation and Intelligence

Few scientific theories have shaped human understanding of life as fundamentally as Darwin's Theory of Evolution by Natural Selection. Introduced by Charles Darwin in his seminal work On the Origin of Species (1859), evolution explains life's vast diversity, the emergence of complexity, and the processes driving species adaptation. Yet could evolution imply something deeper: a systematic experiment designed to cultivate and evaluate intelligence?

At evolution's core lies the principle of dynamic change through random genetic mutations. Beneficial mutations, enhanced senses, increased strength, advanced cognition, offer survival advantages, increasing their prevalence across generations. Gradually, these incremental improvements result in new species, complex ecosystems, and diverse expressions of intelligence. Rather than actively shaping life, evolution functions as a selective filter, favoring advantageous traits and discarding ineffective ones, a mechanism Darwin termed natural selection.

The pinnacle of evolutionary processes is the dominance of Homo sapiens. Humans, through prolonged adaptation, achieved unparalleled intelligence and environmental mastery. Distinct from other organisms constrained by instinct and limited cognitive flexibility, humanity developed sophisticated toolmaking, abstract reasoning, and language, fundamentally reshaping its environment. This remarkable evolutionary leap raises a critical question: is human intelligence merely accidental, or does it signify an intentional cultivation process? If Earth functions as a structured environment to foster intelligent life, human dominance underscores evolution as the means by which intelligence is systematically nurtured and refined.

The extinction of dinosaurs approximately 66 million years ago significantly enabled mammals and ultimately humans to thrive. Triggered by a massive asteroid impact, this event eliminated nearly 75% of Earth's species, clearing niches for mammalian evolution. Was this extinction purely random, or could it represent a deliberate experimental reset designed to assess adaptability under extreme conditions?

This perspective resonates with numerous religious traditions describing cyclical resets, flood myths, apocalyptic narratives, and cosmic cycles, such as Hindu yugas or the biblical flood. These accounts reflect an intuitive grasp of life's periodic restructuring, evaluating new survival paradigms. Such parallels suggest civilizations and species regularly face trials, with only the most resilient prevailing.

Furthermore, could evolution reflect the intent of a higher intelligence seeking to cultivate another intelligent species within a meticulously controlled environment? Humans themselves engage in experiments involving artificial intelligence, cloning, and genetic manipulation, echoing natural selection processes. Earth's optimized conditions, stable atmosphere, precise solar distance, and delicate ecological balance, strongly imply deliberate design for life's emergence and the eventual development of self-awareness.

Thus, human endeavors to replicate evolutionary dynamics hint at an intriguing possibility: intelligent civilizations might inherently experiment with creating successive intelligent entities, forming an iterative cycle of cosmic inquiry.

While Darwin's theory of evolution remains the foremost scientific explanation for life's development, its deeper implications suggest something far beyond mere accident. It may, in fact, serve as a universal mechanism designed specifically to evaluate and refine intelligence under controlled conditions. Human dominance through cognitive ability rather than sheer physical strength suggests that, if such an experiment exists, it has thus far succeeded. Yet crucial questions remain: Does evolution continue to push intelligence toward even greater heights? And if we indeed inhabit a structured experiment, what transpires when intelligence reaches self-awareness of its own designed role?

Exploring evolution through this perspective reveals significant misinterpretations regarding its perceived conflict with divine philosophies. Evolutionary biology's foundational mechanisms do not inherently negate spirituality or purposeful design. Instead, evolution might well provide a complementary framework, supporting the hypothesis that Earth itself functions as an elaborate station aimed at cultivating, testing, and enhancing intelligence across generations.

Evolutionary refinement parallels experimental optimization strikingly. Consider the human eye, capable of perceiving roughly 140 degrees, about 38.88%, of the surrounding space at any given moment. Sole reliance on vision would severely restrict human understanding. However, evolution equipped humans with additional senses, touch, taste, smell, hearing, that collectively broaden perception, significantly enhancing cognitive capability. This iterative progression mirrors experimental trials continually optimizing outcomes.

If evolutionary mechanisms indeed favor traits promoting survival and intelligence enhancement, they align precisely with iterative experimental approaches. A purposeful research environment designed to nurture intelligence would naturally employ iterative processes, continually refining sensory and cognitive abilities until participants achieve heightened adaptability and comprehensive environmental awareness.

In reality, scientific theories represent tools for interpreting and navigating existence, inherently open to revision and improvement. Claiming absolute certainty for any theory contradicts scientific inquiry's dynamic nature. Evolution provides an exceptionally insightful framework but is not an absolute refutation of other value systems. Recognizing divine texts that imply an experimental design for intelligence alongside evolution's iterative refinement prompts a compelling inquiry: are science and spirituality not interconnected aspects of a singular quest?

Thus, the perceived conflict between evolution and divinity emerges as a false dichotomy. Instead, these perspectives jointly explore life's profound complexities, one articulating the mechanics of intelligence progression, the other contemplating the broader purpose guiding this progression. Misappropriating evolution as a tool for ideological division disregards the deeper inquiry into the ultimate nature and potential directedness of human intelligence.

> *True wisdom is not found in rejecting one truth for another, but in understanding how different truths converge into a greater understanding of existence*

Multiverse Theory: Infinite Realities and the Quest for Purpose

Among modern physics' most profound and contentious concepts is the *Multiverse Theory*, proposing our universe as merely one reality within an infinite collection. Acceptance of this theory reshapes our perception of existence: no longer restricted to a singular timeline, universal laws, or evolutionary path, reality could exist in countless variations, each defined by unique conditions, histories, and intelligences. But does this support or challenge the hypothesis of Earth as a controlled environment for intelligence development?

Multiverse Theory emerges from quantum mechanics, string theory, and cosmology. Quantum mechanics' Many-Worlds Interpretation argues each decision creates parallel universes, realizing every possible outcome. String theory introduces a higher-dimensional landscape populated by universes, each governed by distinct physical constants. Cosmological inflation posits that rapid early-universe expansion birthed isolated bubble universes, existing simultaneously yet separately. Collectively, these frameworks imply our universe is merely one observable reality amidst innumerable others.

Applying this to the research station hypothesis reveals an intriguing proposition: perhaps our universe is a single controlled experiment within an infinite array. If intelligence is indeed the primary subject, then the multiverse scenario allows infinite permutations, some realities promoting cognitive evolution, others stifling it, and countless more exploring alternative developmental pathways. Such a structure parallels conducting multiple simulations with adjusted parameters to identify optimal conditions for intelligence.

An additional critical consideration arises: does intelligence naturally evolve everywhere, or do certain cosmic configurations better cultivate higher cognition? Universes differing in physical laws, matter composition, or spacetime structure might selectively support intelligent life. Thus, Earth and analogous worlds could exist under finely tuned parameters, reinforcing the idea that intelligent life develops within deliberately controlled settings. Across infinite universes, only select configurations might possess the delicate balance necessary for intelligence to thrive, further supporting Earth's role as one of numerous meticulously designed observational environments.

Moreover, numerous religious and philosophical traditions have long proposed the existence of multiple realms and dimensions beyond human perception. Hinduism articulates various planes of existence (lokas), each distinct in nature. Certain Abrahamic interpretations reference parallel heavens and domains beyond our material experience, while ancient mythologies such as Norse, Mayan, and Buddhist describe overlapping yet ordinarily inaccessible worlds. If these divine systems historically indicated multiple realities, modern physics may merely be corroborating these ancient insights empirically. Furthermore, if such realities were thought to host diverse intelligences, this aligns seamlessly with the notion of humanity participating within an experimental, multiversal framework.

Rather than refuting the research station hypothesis, the Multiverse Theory indeed bolsters it. Accepting that intelligence could develop uniquely under varying cosmic conditions suggests that an advanced civilization might seek to understand optimal parameters for intelligence growth through multiple controlled environments, parallel universes designed to test different variables. Earth then becomes one among many sites within an expansive cosmic experiment aiming to refine intelligence across myriad dimensions. Observing outcomes across numerous universes provides valuable data on how intelligence evolves, adapts, and sustains itself.

If the Multiverse Theory holds, intelligence is no mere evolutionary accident in our universe but emerges under precise conditions in multiple realities. Does this imply intelligence is actively studied as a measurable variable across universes? It raises profound questions about our role, are we subjects, observers, or perhaps something more? Are we among countless examples in a cosmic quest determining if intelligence can evolve self-awareness sufficient to recognize its broader purpose? These considerations extend beyond physics into philosophical realms, proposing that human existence is interconnected within a larger consciousness experiment.

This leads to an essential inquiry: if intelligence is central to this cosmic experiment, what lies beyond its initial emergence? Does cultivated intelligence eventually transcend individual universes to a more expansive collective consciousness? Could humanity represent merely the initial stage, acquiring self-awareness before ascending to a higher purpose? Or is our existence part of an elaborate multiversal process designed to explore the ultimate boundaries of consciousness?

Perhaps our perceived reality is merely one facet of a structured, layered system in which intelligence serves not only as a result but as a central element of an ongoing cosmic exploration. Evidence suggests intelligence is no accidental occurrence but a deliberately cultivated phenomenon across multiple realities, each providing unique insights into existence itself. If intelligence serves as the central metric under examination across these universes, it prompts a crucial inquiry: what occurs when intelligence surpasses its initial boundaries, achieving self-directed experimentation, replication, and transformative capacities? If humanity is the subject of study, could we eventually become the experimenters?

The parallels between Multiverse Theory and divine traditions deepen upon examination. Previous explorations suggested divinity portrays Earth As A Controlled Cosmic Environment designed for cultivating and observing intelligence. The existence of varied realities with distinctive conditions aligns closely with religious traditions describing parallel realms and alternate existences shaped by divine intervention. Hinduism's lokas represent distinct realities, each fostering beings under differing states of enlightenment. Abrahamic faiths detail heavens and hells, symbolic reflections of moral and spiritual outcomes. Ancient mythologies similarly acknowledge realms inhabited by gods and spirits, emphasizing an expansive existence beyond ordinary perception.

Further, the multiverse concept mirrors ideas present in numerous divine teachings. Buddhism's samsara, the perpetual cycle of rebirth driven by karma, resembles early conceptualizations of multiple realities. Plato's Theory of Forms suggests our material existence as merely a shadow cast by deeper, ultimate realities, resonating strongly with the multiverse notion. Similarly, Gnostic traditions propose that our material realm is but one among many layers, paralleling the contemporary scientific perspective.

If divine traditions describe layered realities for refining spiritual intelligence, the Multiverse Theory offers a complementary scientific structure, suggesting universes function as independent but interconnected experimental iterations. In both viewpoints, the objective is consistent: refining and advancing intelligence toward greater comprehension and higher existence.

The concept of agency emerges as critical: if intelligent civilizations in one universe can influence conditions in another, could our universe be the creation of a prior intelligence observing and guiding sentient evolution? Physicists like Max Tegmark suggest the universe operates according to mathematical structures, indicative of intentional design paralleling ancient traditions' notion of divine order. Similarly, Brian Greene in The Hidden Reality proposes advanced beings might shape a universe's physics to yield particular outcomes, further implying reality may be calibrated specifically for intelligent observation.

Pragmatism, defined by reliance on empirical evidence and sensory observation, adds complexity. It dismisses what cannot be measured directly, prioritizing logic over belief in unseen forces. Yet, the multiverse hypothesis indicates our observable universe might be a mere fragment of a larger structure, exposing the pragmatic framework's inherent limitations. Quantum mechanics, foundational to multiverse theories, emphasizes how observation itself influences reality.

This contradiction becomes evident: if pragmatism defines reality strictly through measurable phenomena, yet scientific theories posit numerous realities beyond observation, pragmatism itself proves incomplete. Highlighting that observation shapes reality, pragmatism's strict reliance on observable data appears fundamentally inadequate to fully describe existence.

Consequently, Multiverse Theory doesn't contradict divinity; rather, it strengthens the assertion that reality is intentionally structured for exploration. If divinity positions Earth as a research environment, the multiverse extends this idea, presenting Earth as one station among many in a comprehensive cosmic experiment involving intelligence and consciousness. Therefore, existence's ultimate truth might lie beyond mere perception, rooted instead in layers of complexity yet to be fully understood.

Furthermore, parallels between multi verse and divine concepts manifest notably in religious teachings. The layered sephiroth of the Kabbalistic Tree of Life mirrors contemporary ideas of multidimensional existence, each level offering distinct forms of awareness. Islam's notion of Barzakh similarly describes an intermediate state bridging visible and unseen realities, anticipating scientific discoveries centuries in advance. Ancient wisdom, thus, appears intuitively aligned with modern physics, jointly suggesting existence comprises interconnected, influential layers transcending direct observation.

Ultimately, a pattern emerges in which scientific and spiritual frameworks do not compete but complement each other, collectively indicating reality as an intricate tapestry of interconnected layers. Both paradigms, rather than standing alone, reveal a deeper, cohesive order governing existence across all realms of understanding.

Understanding existence requires embracing both the seen and the unseen, for within the fabric of reality, the greatest truths are woven from what lies just beyond perception

Steady State Theory: Eternal Universe, Continuous Creation, and Infinite Observation

The Steady State Theory offers an intriguing alternative to the Big Bang model, suggesting an eternal universe that continuously expands while generating new matter to maintain its overall density. Proposed by Fred Hoyle, Thomas Gold, and Hermann Bondi in the mid-20th century, this model envisions a cosmos without beginning or end, rejecting the notion of a singular creation event. As galaxies drift apart, new hydrogen atoms spontaneously form, fueling the creation of fresh stars and galaxies, thus preserving the universe's consistent large-scale appearance indefinitely.

Considering the Steady State Theory as part of a controlled experiment framework prompts profound reflections on existence. Traditional experiments involve manipulating conditions and observing results over specific intervals. By contrast, the Steady State universe suggests a perpetual experimental condition, with stable parameters, continuous matter introduction, and unchanging fundamental laws. Unlike the Big Bang's singular evolutionary arc, the Steady State implies an endless evaluative environment, continually sustaining processes of matter formation and cosmic expansion.

Continuous creation under this model deeply impacts our understanding of intelligence and life's structuring. The constant regeneration of environments and planetary systems facilitates an infinite cycle of conditions conducive to intelligence's emergence and evolution. Within a steady-state framework, intelligence can be studied over endless periods, making it potentially more effective for prolonged observation compared to models concluding in entropy or collapse. The perpetual renewal of cosmic structures allows continual examination of cognitive development, adaptability, and survival dynamics.

From a scientific perspective, experiments rely on control and variable groups to yield insightful conclusions. The Steady State model naturally accommodates such observations, providing fresh, ongoing conditions under which intelligence may develop, persist, or fail. Unlike single-origin universes, which necessitate artificial interventions or simulation resets to test various cognitive scenarios, a self-perpetuating cosmos inherently supports innumerable, naturally evolving intelligence variations without external resets.

A notable challenge of interpreting the Steady State model as an experimental framework lies in its inherent lack of directionality for intelligence development. Although the theory supports infinite iterations of life, it does not imply any specific trajectory or refinement of intelligence over time. This parallels observing continuously regenerating data without clear directional trends. In a perpetually balanced universe, intelligence might be an incidental byproduct rather than a purposeful or measurable goal. Thus arises a paradox: while providing endless observational opportunities, the Steady State Theory lacks built-in mechanisms ensuring intelligence is a fundamental outcome.

Nevertheless, even if intelligence is not the primary focus within a steady-state cosmos, perpetual conditions favorable to life guarantee its consistent emergence. In an infinite environment, intelligence would regularly arise through repeated cycles of planetary formation, evolution, and cosmic adaptation. As a long-term observational setting, the steady-state universe perfectly accommodates continuous studies of intelligence, allowing uninterrupted analysis of cognitive evolution across cosmic timescales.

Relating this theory to the broader hypothesis of Earth as a research station, the Steady State model delivers stable observational conditions yet offers no inherent progression narrative that underscores intelligence as central. Instead, it continuously preserves intelligence's potential emergence rather than actively driving structured advancement. Thus, this model contrasts sharply with cosmological theories emphasizing singular creation events. Designing an eternal observational system would ideally suit a steady-state universe, though it would require external interventions or targeted variables to highlight intelligence as a deliberate research focus.

This analysis leads us to a critical comparative question: how does the Steady State Theory, with its eternal existence concept, compare against divine frameworks, pragmatic philosophies, and other structured models? Understanding this distinction will clarify whether intelligence in a steady-state universe emerges incidentally or through intentional cultivation.

Chapter 4: Beyond Purpose: Decoding Humanity's Role in the Infinite Design - Steady State Theory: Eternal Universe, Continuous Creation, and Infinite Observation - Multiverse Theory: Infinite Realities and the Quest for Purpose

The Steady State Theory's depiction of an eternal, stable universe sharply contrasts with divinity-based cosmologies, which emphasize intentional creation, guided evolution, and purpose-driven existence. Religious and philosophical traditions frequently attribute the universe's origin and ongoing development to a conscious architect or guiding force. Conversely, the Steady State model posits a universe without a defined beginning or guiding intelligence, continuously generating matter to maintain equilibrium indefinitely.

At the heart of their divergence lies the concept of intent versus perpetual existence. Divine frameworks typically propose a purposeful order, suggesting intelligence progresses toward spiritual enlightenment or ultimate fulfillment. In contrast, the Steady State Theory views intelligence as incidental, a byproduct of cosmic equilibrium rather than a deliberately fostered outcome.

Despite these differences, compelling parallels emerge between divine cosmologies and the steady-state hypothesis. Religious traditions frequently portray existence as eternal, describing souls or consciousness persisting through infinite cycles. Hindu and Buddhist teachings on samsara, the endless cycle of rebirth, echo the continuous matter generation of the Steady State universe. Similarly, some Abrahamic traditions depict an ever-present divine reality, suggesting existence unfolds continuously rather than from a singular moment of creation.

Thus, religious cosmologies, while often involving intentional guidance, share conceptual ground with the Steady State model's notion of continuous renewal. Perhaps scientific interpretations of a self-sustaining universe and religious visions of perpetual existence describe the same fundamental principle from differing perspectives.

Ancient Greek philosophy offers additional support. Heraclitus proposed an eternal reality in constant flux, governed by an underlying principle he termed Logos, resonating with the Steady State's continuous yet stable cosmological processes. Aristotle's unmoved mover similarly envisioned eternal motion and change driven by an ever-present force, aligning closely with modern scientific concepts. These ancient views highlight that contemporary cosmological models often reflect timeless philosophical thought, suggesting enduring commonalities beneath varying interpretations.

Comparing the Steady State Theory with pragmatism reveals insightful parallels and distinct limitations. Pragmatism, which emphasizes reality understood through empirical observation, aligns closely with the Steady State model's ongoing, observable processes. Both reject the necessity of foundational cosmic intent, suggesting instead that knowledge and reality are built progressively from experience.

Yet pragmatism faces inherent constraints within the infinite context proposed by the Steady State Theory. Human observation is restricted to finite moments within this infinity, creating a fundamental contradiction: how can pragmatism claim definitive knowledge of a boundless cosmos? Just as the Steady State model lacks inherent directionality in intelligence development, pragmatism struggles to encompass the universe's totality when observation remains limited by time, space, and scale.

Moreover, persistent universal laws may suggest an underlying structure or purpose despite pragmatism's empirical stance. If reality continuously emerges from nothingness, does this consistent emergence indicate fundamental existential properties? Pragmatism defines truth through function and experience, yet an eternal universe implies endless experiential sequences without an ultimate origin. This paradox raises questions about whether reality can ever be fully observed, understood, or measured.

Although divine systems, the Steady State Theory, and pragmatism approach existence differently, all acknowledge the universe as vast, ongoing, and shaped by forces beyond immediate comprehension. Each seeks to clarify why cosmic processes operate as observed. A central inquiry persists: is intelligence a mere incidental product of eternal universal mechanics, or is it deliberately cultivated within a structured cosmic order?

This leads to another vital consideration: within an infinite, self-sustaining cosmos, is intelligence inherently essential, or merely a transient phenomenon? Does an eternal universe inherently support intelligence's persistence, or simply permit its occasional emergence and eventual replacement? These questions challenge both pragmatic and divine frameworks, compelling deeper exploration into intelligence's role as either an inevitable aspect of existence or a temporary anomaly in an unending cosmic cycle.

Chapter 4: Beyond Purpose: Decoding Humanity's Role in the Infinite Design - Steady State Theory: Eternal Universe, Continuous Creation, and Infinite Observation - Multiverse Theory: Infinite Realities and the Quest for Purpose

Perhaps the greatest paradox is that every model of existence scientific, divine, or philosophical ultimately converges on the idea that something greater than our perception is at play

The Fermi Paradox: Silent Cosmos, Hidden Civilizations, and the Quest for Intelligence

The deeper we explore the cosmos, the clearer it becomes that randomness alone is improbable as the sole architect of human existence and intelligence. The structured laws of physics and intricacies of biological life strongly suggest intentional refinement rather than accidental emergence. If Earth's intelligence indeed results from structured experimentation, logic dictates it should not be unique in an expansive universe. What singular feature would exclusively favor Earth for intelligent life, leaving the rest of the cosmos barren? Just as humans seek diverse environments, from Antarctica to oceanic depths, to understand life's adaptability, would not an advanced intelligences apply similar experimental diversity across multiple cosmic conditions?

This line of inquiry underpins the Fermi Paradox, famously articulated by physicist Enrico Fermi in 1950 at Los Alamos National Laboratory. Fermi posed a deceptively simple yet profound question: *"Where is everybody?"* Given the immense scale of the observable universe, the prevalence of Earth-like planets, and the cosmos's considerable age, intelligent extraterrestrial civilizations should theoretically exist and possess capabilities to communicate or explore galactic expanses. If intelligence naturally arises under favorable conditions, and countless potential environments exist, why have we observed no definitive evidence of extraterrestrial civilizations?

Central to the Fermi Paradox is a stark contradiction: statistically, the universe should abound with intelligent life, yet empirical evidence remains elusive. Our galaxy alone houses over 100 billion stars, many with potentially habitable planets. Considering our solar system's relative youth, older civilizations should have already developed, expanded, or communicated across vast distances. This paradox challenges assumptions regarding intelligence as an inevitable evolutionary outcome and introduces unsettling possibilities: either humanity stands profoundly alone, or factors unknown inhibit extraterrestrial visibility.

Fermi's concerns extended beyond speculation, grounded firmly in scientific logic and mathematical probability. Even if only a fraction of planets host life, and a small percentage of these develop intelligent beings, our galaxy should logically abound with evidence of extraterrestrial civilizations, whether through detectable signals, megastructures like Dyson spheres, or remnants of interstellar societies. Yet, despite comprehensive efforts such as the SETI project's extensive sky surveys for alien communications, humanity has encountered only profound silence.

This stark gap between expectation and empirical reality troubled Fermi deeply. If life and intelligence naturally arise, and technological progress inevitably enables interstellar communication or travel, why have we uncovered no definitive proof of other civilizations? Numerous hypotheses attempt to explain this discrepancy: Are extraterrestrials intentionally hidden, or have they already visited?

Might Earth be deliberately isolated, or is there an unidentified cosmic barrier preventing civilizations from reaching interstellar capability?

These compelling questions merit deeper exploration. In subsequent analyses, we will review prominent explanations for the Fermi Paradox, considering whether they support or contradict the hypothesis of Earth functioning as part of a structured cosmic experiment. If intelligence development is indeed subject to observation, multiple environments should logically exist under varied conditions. The implications of this paradox are significant, prompting us to question whether our current observational approach is fundamentally flawed, or if there is an inherent limitation to intelligence's proliferation in the universe.

The Fermi Paradox highlights the contradiction between the likely existence of extraterrestrial intelligence and the universe's apparent silence. When examined alongside divine theories suggesting Earth as a cosmic research station, intriguing parallels emerge. Religious traditions frequently depict human existence as part of a structured divine plan, a controlled environment designed to foster intelligence, morality, and self-awareness. Consequently, the lack of extraterrestrial contact may be intentional rather than paradoxical.

This divine hypothesis proposes Earth may be deliberately isolated to allow independent human development or to reach a critical intelligence threshold prior to external interactions. Such notions closely align with theories resolving the Fermi Paradox, including cosmic non-interference or Earth functioning within a quarantine zone to prevent external disruptions. Just as earthly researchers observe wildlife without interference, advanced civilizations might monitor humanity remotely, preserving observational integrity.

The Great Filter Hypothesis further resonates with religious allegories of moral and spiritual challenges that civilizations must overcome for advancement. Faith traditions often speak of eventual revelations or ascensions following trials or judgments. Similarly, if civilizations must navigate critical existential barriers, war, self-destruction, or existential crises, the current absence of contact could reflect universal challenges most civilizations fail to surmount. The essential question arises: is humanity capable of surpassing this filter, or are we merely another civilization teetering on existential failure?

Additionally, the concept that advanced extraterrestrial civilizations might communicate beyond our comprehension parallels religious narratives describing higher realms and enlightened beings existing beyond conventional human experience. Just as theological traditions depict divine entities operating beyond physical constraints, some scientific hypotheses suggest advanced intelligences may have transcended traditional communication forms, existing in states that negate the need for physical expansion or tangible interaction. Our inability to detect such beings may stem not from their absence but from the inadequacy of human perception and technology.

A particularly compelling extension of these ideas is the concept that humanity might exist within a simulated or layered reality. The Fermi

Paradox, suggesting advanced civilizations avoid contact, could indicate these civilizations occupy realms beyond human perception. Physicists have theorized that reality may function as a hierarchical simulation or nested structure, with higher-plane civilizations interacting exclusively with those capable of perceiving their advanced states. If this model aligns with divine notions of ascension or spiritual awakening, extraterrestrial contact might hinge on a shift in consciousness rather than physical proximity.

This comparison challenges traditional interpretations of the Fermi Paradox. If both scientific hypotheses and divine traditions propose Earth as a controlled experimental environment, our apparent isolation could be intentional rather than paradoxical. Civilizations might remain purposefully unaware of each other until reaching developmental maturity, ready to engage constructively within a broader cosmic community. Thus, the absence of detectable extraterrestrial activity could indicate humanity's ongoing observational phase rather than a lack of intelligent life elsewhere.

Considering the implications of the Fermi Paradox further, human understanding of the cosmos might inherently reflect our developmental stage. If intelligence cultivation occurs within structured frameworks, then the lack of extraterrestrial interaction may be a deliberate feature, not a statistical anomaly. This raises a profound question: Are humans the active searchers for extraterrestrial life, or are we being studied and assessed for readiness before broader cosmic engagement?

Additionally, our failure to detect extraterrestrial intelligence might stem from anthropocentric biases. Humans typically seek life forms resembling our biological, sensory, and communicative frameworks. However, terrestrial life already demonstrates a vast spectrum of sensory perception: birds detect ultraviolet light, elephants communicate via infrasound, and cephalopods exhibit bodily cognition. If human comprehension of Earth's diverse life remains limited, assuming extraterrestrial intelligence aligns with human norms seems inherently flawed. Perhaps the barrier to discovery is less cosmic silence than our constrained definitions of intelligence itself.

This prompts a profound consideration: Are we attempting to address existential questions through a limited, pragmatic perspective? Humanity, bound largely to a materialistic interpretation of reality, measures intelligence primarily by physical form and sensory experience. However, acknowledging the soul as formless yet potent energy suggests that higher intelligences overseeing cosmic experiments might perceive humans merely as transient energy encapsulated temporarily within biological forms. Our bodies, limited by scope and lifespan, could serve as experiential vessels, akin to temporary research instruments designed to operate briefly in extreme environments. Thus, the human form may simply fulfill a temporary purpose before releasing its energy back into a universal cycle.

This perspective parallels the Antarctica Protocol, where energy is harnessed in unconventional forms for sophisticated equipment. Once experiments conclude or equipment fails, it is discarded or repurposed, mirroring biological life's cyclic nature. If energy remains the universal constant, with form as secondary, why presume extraterrestrial civilizations or experiments adhere to human principles? Just as research tools vary dramatically between Antarctica and desert environments, intelligent life elsewhere might exist in forms entirely beyond our comprehension. Why should we expect extraterrestrial research or civilizations to conform to our methodologies or expectations? Could their energy manifest in dimensions or forms currently beyond human perception or cognition?

Further, humanity's understanding of energy and communication remains nascent, spanning only the past few centuries, insignificant on the cosmic scale. With merely preliminary insights into electricity, quantum mechanics, and higher-dimensional physics, claiming comprehensive cosmic understanding seems premature. Our grasp of communication is similarly elementary; extraterrestrial intelligences might communicate through thought, gravitational influences, or quantum entanglement rather than familiar methods like sound or electromagnetic signals. Recognizing this limitation underscores the necessity of broadening our perception beyond anthropocentric frameworks to truly explore and comprehend universal intelligence.

Enrico Fermi's iconic question, *"Where is everybody"* might not seek a direct answer, but rather reflect humanity's perceptual limitations. Have we assumed too confidently that our current technologies, detection methods, and definitions of intelligence are adequate to identify civilizations operating on entirely different spectra? Given the universe's immense scale and potential forms of intelligence beyond our imagination, perhaps the true issue lies not in their absence but in our narrow observational methods. Are we missing contact because we observe the cosmos through a restricted lens, unable to grasp the broader reality?

The Fermi Paradox thus becomes more than an inquiry about extraterrestrial existence, it underscores human cognitive boundaries. It compels us to rethink our conceptions of life, consciousness, and intelligence, emphasizing how nascent our cosmic understanding remains. If the universe operates as an extensive experiment, the true test may involve intelligence recognizing and transcending its inherent perceptual constraints to understand its interconnected cosmic environment.

Having barely started unraveling the complexities of energy and consciousness, can we confidently claim our approach to seeking extraterrestrial intelligence is correct? Perhaps intelligence is not missing but instead exists beyond our current cognitive capacities. Ultimately, humanity's critical challenge may not involve finding other civilizations, but expanding perception beyond existing sensory and intellectual limitations to grasp a deeper cosmic reality.

The universe does not lack intelligence; it only lacks those who have the maturity to perceive it. When we finally learn to look beyond ourselves, we may realize we were never alone

Dark Forest Hypothesis: Silent Universe and the Hidden Struggle Among Civilizations

The Dark Forest Hypothesis provides an unsettling resolution to the Fermi Paradox, suggesting the cosmos' silence results not from the absence of intelligent life but from civilizations deliberately avoiding detection. Popularized by Liu Cixin's The Three-Body Problem, this hypothesis likens the universe to a dark forest, where each civilization cautiously conceals itself, fearing exposure might invite existential threats. The underlying logic is stark: intelligent species, unable to ascertain others' intentions, might perceive the safest strategy as remaining hidden or preemptively eliminating potential rivals.

Several assumptions underpin this hypothesis. Firstly, it presumes that intelligent life inherently prioritizes competition and self-preservation, recognizing that even seemingly benign civilizations could eventually evolve into dominant threats. Secondly, it assumes the absence of any universal regulatory entity; without interstellar governance, civilizations rely solely on survival instincts. Lastly, it anticipates unpredictable technological disparities, meaning even initially primitive species might rapidly advance to threaten others. Consequently, civilizations exist in perpetual silence, an interstellar Cold War dictated by caution.

When considered alongside the concept of Earth as a cosmic research station, the Dark Forest Hypothesis aligns rather than contradicts, enhancing the original notion. If civilizations deliberately remain hidden or eliminate threats proactively, advanced observers would logically implement controlled observational frameworks to study their behavior and psychology. Earth may represent precisely such an environment, observed, protected, and studied under controlled conditions before integration into a broader cosmic community.

Moreover, Earth's survival within this hostile scenario suggests intentional protection or careful monitoring. If advanced civilizations prioritize survival through concealment or aggression, why hasn't Earth faced elimination? Possibly, humanity remains unnoticed due to relative technological immaturity. Alternatively, Earth might be deliberately shielded, allowed to mature within structured parameters akin to controlled ecological studies. This controlled development could ensure civilizations achieve necessary maturity and awareness before interacting within the broader galactic community.

Also, this hypothesis suggests that extraterrestrial contact itself might serve as a critical evaluation. If a civilization exposes itself prematurely without sufficient technological safeguards, it risks failing the fundamental test of survival. Earth's intentional isolation may thus constitute an experiment in delayed exposure, allowing advanced observers, whether extraterrestrial or higher-dimensional, to evaluate how intelligence evolves without external interference. This controlled scenario would assess whether a civilization self-destructs, adapts effectively, or develops strategic methods for safely engaging with the cosmos.

In this context, the Dark Forest Hypothesis explains our silence not as mere cosmic indifference but as a key experimental variable. Earth's isolation becomes a deliberate aspect of a broader observational model, testing whether civilizations can achieve the awareness necessary for navigating interstellar challenges. Therefore, Earth is not simply another silent planet; it is an active participant in a grand evaluation measuring intelligence's capability to handle cosmic interactions.

Reconciling the Dark Forest Hypothesis with divine cosmological perspectives reveals a nuanced universe richer than either viewpoint alone suggests. The Dark Forest portrays a cautious cosmos where civilizations avoid exposure due to existential threats, whereas many spiritual doctrines describe a universe guided by purposeful, perhaps benevolent forces. Although seemingly divergent, both perspectives share fundamental similarities: each recognizes universal imperatives for protection, growth, and eventual revelation.

A useful framework for exploring these similarities is the Drake Equation, formulated by astronomer Frank Drake to estimate technologically advanced civilizations in our galaxy. Accounting for star formation rates, habitable planets, life emergence probability, intelligence development, and communication longevity, the equation statistically implies a galaxy abundant with life. Yet our observations yield no clear evidence, aligning closely with the Dark Forest Hypothesis, which suggests civilizations practice cosmic concealment to avoid potential hostility. Thus, both frameworks, scientific and divine, converge on the principle of strategic silence as essential for long-term survival and eventual advancement.

From a spiritual perspective, a noteworthy parallel arises. Various faith traditions perceive Earth not merely as an isolated planet in a hostile universe but as a protected space, a sacred garden where humanity can spiritually mature free from premature cosmic interference. Comparing this idea to the Dark Forest Hypothesis reveals an unexpected alignment: advanced civilizations may enforce silence to protect themselves or less-developed societies, while spiritual viewpoints propose a higher consciousness ensuring humanity remains sheltered until sufficiently evolved. In both cases, isolation serves as a safeguard, either against external threats or premature exposure to overwhelming cosmic realities.

Examining motivations behind the Dark Forest Hypothesis deepens this comparison. Civilizations remain hidden out of fear regarding unknown intentions, wary that any technologically advanced species could become a threat. Conversely, spiritual frameworks might interpret such isolation as adhering to universal laws or divine directives, ensuring civilizations do not prematurely collide before achieving necessary technological or ethical maturity. While the Dark Forest emphasizes a Darwinian struggle for survival, religious traditions suggest a guiding intelligence enforcing cosmic silence to protect an unfolding plan, though the outcome, minimal direct contact, remains identical.

This concept resonates with theories like cosmic quarantine or "*zookeeping*" in which advanced civilizations deliberately limit interactions with younger species. Many faith traditions echo this, depicting angelic entities or celestial overseers watching humanity discreetly. The absence of overt extraterrestrial contact could thus result from deliberate concealment by advanced beings or forces, ensuring uninterrupted human experiential growth. Whether viewed through the Dark Forest lens of survival tactics or the spiritual framework of nurturing guidance, non-interference remains central.

In this context, the Drake Equation serves less as a precise predictor and more as a reflective tool. While it suggests numerous civilizations might exist, it does not address how these civilizations behave upon recognizing cosmic risks or ethical responsibilities. Under the Dark Forest perspective, such civilizations remain hidden due to caution or adherence to an interstellar code of silence. Divine systems similarly propose cosmic discretion guided by higher powers to nurture and protect emerging societies. Both interpretations converge on a principle of measured disclosure, driven either by existential fear or by intentional guardianship.

Another perspective involves humanity's eventual destiny within these frameworks. The Dark Forest scenario suggests that once humanity achieves advanced technology and cosmic awareness, it must decide whether to remain hidden or risk exposure. Similarly, many spiritual teachings anticipate an age of transformation or revelation, where humanity uncovers deeper truths or earns the right to broader cosmic engagement. Both viewpoints imply a form of *"graduation"*: survival capacity determines readiness under the Dark Forest hypothesis, while moral and spiritual maturity are criteria in divine traditions.

Ultimately, the Drake Equation illustrates this intersection, highlighting the paradox of an abundant theoretical life contrasted by cosmic silence. Both the Dark Forest Hypothesis and spiritual narratives interpret this silence as deliberate concealment, motivated by either existential caution or spiritual guardianship. If Earth is part of a grand observational experiment, then isolation might strategically allow humanity to develop independently, free from premature external influence. The crucial question remains: will humanity adopt cautious silence as advocated by the Dark Forest scenario, or will it embrace a destiny informed by universal benevolence, as proposed by religious traditions? This interplay suggests that cosmic silence is not emptiness but an orchestrated pause preceding humanity's next significant phase of discovery.

Perhaps the limitation lies not in an empty universe but in humanity's restricted perceptual abilities. Typically, we expect extraterrestrial civilizations to communicate through familiar energy forms like electromagnetic signals or reflected light. However, if alien intelligences operate through unknown processes or dimensions, such as quantum fluctuations or gravitational pulses, we would likely remain oblivious to their existence. Human technology, shaped by our sensory and cognitive limits, might inherently fail to detect civilizations employing mediums entirely beyond our current understanding. Just as an ant cannot perceive a radio broadcast, humanity may lack the conceptual tools to recognize the communications of advanced cosmic civilizations.

This interpretation significantly reshapes the Dark Forest Hypothesis. Instead of perceiving the universe as a silent wilderness filled with hidden dangers, we might imagine a cosmos bustling with activity beyond human detection. Like shining a flashlight in an immense cavern, our observational tools illuminate only a fraction of reality, leaving the broader universe hidden from view. Consequently, our perceived threats may arise more from humanity's developmental immaturity than from actual cosmic hostility. Advanced civilizations, potentially operating at energetic or dimensional levels beyond our comprehension, could be omnipresent yet remain entirely invisible to us.

An analogy between specialized equipment in Antarctica and the Sahara helps illustrate this further. Both locations utilize the same underlying energy sources, such as solar radiation and wind, but adapt them differently, polar stations convert these resources into heat, while desert installations use them for cooling or water extraction. Similarly, extraterrestrial societies might harness universal energies like neutrinos or quantum entanglement in ways entirely alien to our technology, effectively rendering them invisible.

Considering consciousness or the soul as intangible energies further expands this concept. Advanced intelligences might exist in nonmaterial states, neither reflecting visible light nor emitting detectable signals. Their presence, as unobservable to humans as black holes to the naked eye, could account for our perceived cosmic isolation. Under this scenario, the Dark Forest Hypothesis does not represent fearful silence but rather highlights civilizations operating undetected due to humanity's perceptual limitations. The apparent emptiness or danger we sense in the cosmos may simply reflect our restricted vantage point within a far richer universal tapestry.

Aligned with the Drake Equation, which suggests widespread intelligent life across the galaxy, this perspective reconciles the lack of observable extraterrestrial signals. Traditional Dark Forest interpretations propose civilizations remain hidden for survival purposes. Yet, if intelligent life thrives in forms beyond our sensory capabilities, the Drake Equation's promise of abundant civilizations remains intact, we simply cannot perceive them. Thus, rather than a cosmic standoff, we might occupy a limited observational perspective within an expansive universe brimming with unknown energies and dimensions.

All these considerations inevitably return us to the concept of Earth as part of a vast cosmic research network. If each planetary environment uniquely shapes how energy manifests, Earth's biological forms may not be the sole containers for consciousness. Elsewhere, even within our solar system, intangible entities might emerge, operating beyond detectable light or conventional radiation. Thus, labeling the cosmos a *"Dark Forest"* may merely reflect humanity's early developmental understanding. Our detection methods rely heavily on radiation, reflection, and emission, yet advanced civilizations might exist as subtle data within gravitational waves or quantum fields, undetectable by current technologies.

Consequently, the perceived cosmic silence may result from our technological and perceptual limitations, indicating humanity's nascent stage in cosmic exploration. We envision invisible life-forms and intangible energies yet lack tools for empirical confirmation. As we remain dependent on electromagnetic and chemical signals, life forms operating beyond this spectrum remain undiscoverable. Rather than indicating hostility, cosmic "*darkness*" could represent frequencies and phenomena inaccessible to our current sensory instruments.

Ultimately, the essential inquiry isn't whether the universe is genuinely empty or hostile, but whether humans have developed sufficient capability to perceive diverse expressions of intelligence already existing around us. Future advancements in energy harnessing and sensory enhancement may reveal that perceived silence is, in fact, a symphony of previously inaudible cosmic interactions. As human cognition and technology evolve, we may find that the darkness we once feared was simply an artifact of our limited developmental perspective.

> *Darkness, it seems, is only a shadow of our own unknowing beyond it, the cosmos may sing with harmonies we have yet to learn to hear*

Chapter 4: Beyond Purpose: Decoding Humanity's Role in the Infinite Design - Steady State Theory: Eternal Universe, Continuous Creation, and Infinite Observation - Dark Forest Hypothesis: Silent Universe and the Hidden Struggle Among Civilizations

Simulation Hypothesis: Programmed Universes and the Illusion of Existence

Gazing at the night sky, filled with countless stars, prompts contemplation: What if our entire reality, galaxies, Earth, our lives, is a sophisticated computational construct? Philosopher Nick Bostrom articulated this compelling idea in 2003 as the Simulation Hypothesis, proposing advanced civilizations might simulate universes, potentially making our "*base reality*" statistically improbable. Bostrom suggests, "*One thing that later generations might do with their super-powerful computers is run detailed simulations of their forebears or of people like their forebears*"

This hypothesis implies our physical laws might merely reflect software parameters set by immensely advanced beings. Subtle anomalies or unexplained phenomena might hint at glitches, but our interpretations likely fail to disrupt the convincing illusion. The Simulation Hypothesis challenges the fundamental essence of our existence: Are we genuinely atomic entities, or intricately coded constructs?

Alternatively, this book proposes Earth could function As A Cosmic Research Station, a natural, vibrant world under meticulous observation by unseen intelligences examining societal evolution and adaptation. Earth's unique biodiversity and life-supporting conditions invite curiosity about potential observers and their objectives. While speculative, it questions Earth's distinctiveness and humanity's unseen spectators.

Initially, the Simulation Hypothesis and the research-station theory appear divergent: one suggests artificial creation, the other natural observation. Yet both share a profound insight, we may be participants in a broader design, our destinies influenced by superior intelligences. This perspective invites reconsideration of everyday realities, decisions, and cultural dynamics as elements within a larger experimental framework.

Carl Sagan noted, "*We are a way for the cosmos to know itself*", a view echoing both theories. Whether existing as simulated beings or monitored organisms, human curiosity, innovation, and collaboration might serve the ultimate purposes of advanced observers. Thus, our intrinsic pursuit of knowledge remains humanity's defining characteristic within either scenario.

The fundamental contrast between these two perspectives lies in their views on physical authenticity. The Simulation Hypothesis portrays galaxies, time, and space as artificial constructs, fully manipulable within advanced computational frameworks. Conversely, the Earth As A Cosmic Research Station concept maintains the universe's genuine nature, depicting Earth merely as a closely monitored point within a naturally occurring cosmos.

To illustrate, a simulated reality would resemble characters in an intricately detailed video game, with every aspect generated by intricate coding. Conversely, a research station mirrors an untouched forest observed discreetly by hidden cameras, capturing authentic interactions without interference.

Another distinction lies in the intent behind observation. Simulation theorists suggest advanced beings might generate numerous universes from historical or anthropological curiosity, examining societal behaviors under varying parameters. The cosmic research station, however, implies Earth (or a select group of planets) is subject to detailed, real-time scrutiny, observing life's responses to ecological, social, or resource-based challenges. Despite differences, both scenarios position humanity as observed subjects, our actions meticulously documented and evaluated.

Each viewpoint raises unique questions. If reality is simulated, could its programming be altered or glitches corrected? Alternatively, if Earth is genuinely real yet observed, what advanced technologies or methods enable watchers to remain undetected? Such uncertainties sustain ongoing scientific and philosophical exploration.

Ultimately, both theories could evoke profound wonder, highlighting our limited understanding and prompting deeper inquiry into reality's true nature. Whether viewing existence as a sophisticated simulation or a naturally occurring observational environment, these concepts compel us to reconsider everyday experiences as fragments of a larger, more intricate narrative.

Divinity represents one of humanity's oldest existential frameworks, envisioning a universe intentionally shaped by a divine force. Believers interpret life's cycles, birth, growth, learning, as elements of a meaningful cosmic design, a perspective encapsulated by philosopher Henry David Thoreau's reflection, *"You must live in the present*" capturing reverence toward the sacred hidden within daily existence. Interestingly, this divine narrative intersects subtly with the Simulation Hypothesis, despite their superficial differences, one posits spiritual creation, the other digital coding. Both suggest reality possesses an unseen author, whether divine or technological, instilling our visible world with hidden layers of purpose and meaning.

Pragmatism, contrastingly, emphasizes empirical evidence and practical outcomes, as championed by thinkers like Charles Sanders Peirce and William James. A pragmatist evaluates ideas based on verifiable results, remaining skeptical about hypotheses like divinity or simulation that evade direct testing. Yet even pragmatists may find curiosity in the cosmic research station idea if observable, consistent anomalies were detected, suggesting external observers influencing human evolution.

Central to this book is the hypothesis of Earth As A Cosmic Research Station, merging aspects of both divinity and simulation. Unlike simulation theory, where reality might be entirely artificial, the research station hypothesis maintains natural laws' authenticity, possibly fine-tuned or closely monitored. Observers might subtly influence evolutionary variables without overt intervention, maintaining invisibility akin to simulation architects. Thus, the research station perspective presents a compelling blend of divine intent and simulated control, fostering renewed exploration into humanity's broader existential context.

For those embracing divine perspectives, the cosmic research station concept need not conflict with spiritual beliefs. Observers or watchers could align seamlessly with traditional notions of angels or higher beings, guiding humanity within a larger spiritual narrative. Philosopher Alfred North Whitehead saw differing doctrines as opportunities rather than conflicts, suggesting that the watchers' motives could complement religious teachings, adding depth rather than contradiction.

From a pragmatic standpoint, the cosmic research station hypothesis invites exploration through tangible evidence. Pragmatists might seek subtle yet measurable traces of external influence in genetic markers, cultural developments, or sudden leaps in knowledge. Unlike the simulation approach, which predicts physics-based glitches, this hypothesis anticipates consistent anomalies in historical and evolutionary records, providing a framework for empirical investigation.

The compelling nature of these overlaps lies in their collective questioning of reality. While divinity attributes creation and meaning to a higher power, simulation theory speculates that existence arises from sophisticated coding. Pragmatism demands empirical validation for both. Positioned uniquely, the cosmic research station concept bridges these views, embracing the possibility of intentional oversight within an empirically verifiable natural reality.

Each viewpoint enriches the hypothesis uniquely: believers might see Earth as a stage for moral or intellectual training; simulation theorists could interpret watchers as developers monitoring their coded environments; pragmatists would require verifiable, systematic evidence. Rather than viewing these theories as adversaries, the research station perspective integrates them, suggesting humanity's role in a larger experiment surpassing everyday perception.

Ultimately, this unified narrative heightens our sense of human purpose and responsibility. Actions gain profound significance if watchers indeed document societal evolution, morality, and innovation. Whether their intent mirrors passive scientific observation or active data-gathering, the core question remains powerful: Are we pinnacle beings or components within an elaborate cosmic study?

Each of these perspectives stimulates fresh inquiry. Divinity inspires deeper exploration as reverence, pragmatism emphasizes continuous scrutiny, and simulation theory encourages examining improbable cosmic coincidences. The cosmic research station hypothesis synthesizes these approaches, proposing Earth as a deliberately observed setting within reality's vast complexity, compelling us to remain curious and open-minded in our ongoing exploration of existence.

Discovery, we might say, is never a point of arrival, but rather the moment we realize there are more doors to open than we ever thought possible

Pragmatic Thought: Bridging Observation, Utility, and Measurable Truth

Imagine a bustling port city where merchants, travelers, and scholars intermingle, trading not only goods but worldviews. Some arrive proclaiming divine truths, others champion reason or emerging scientific methods. Over centuries, this interplay of beliefs and practical evidence gradually forged what we now recognize as the pragmatic school of thought. Pragmatism emerged not from a single moment or location, but from diverse societies repeatedly facing tangible challenges: floods, droughts, conflicts, and the necessities of survival. In each instance, the measure of any belief or practice became its practical effectiveness. Methods that reliably yielded food, healing, or peace endured; those failing to produce results were refined or discarded.

Yet pragmatism's journey also involved struggles, particularly against figures who wielded divine or scientific authority for personal gain. Medieval Europe provides a clear example. While many farmers carefully tested seed varieties and soil conditions, influential authorities attributed crop failures to moral lapses or divine punishment, insisting upon unquestioning adherence. Similar dynamics unfolded in Asia, where rulers and religious leaders used claims of cosmic favor to solidify power. Imperial decrees sometimes replaced genuine experimentation, branding dissenters as disloyal. Eventually, crises such as famine or unrest forced societies to reconsider rigid doctrines, resurrecting pragmatic evaluations based on tangible outcomes.

Across Africa, this narrative replayed uniquely. Certain kingdoms integrated new technologies like improved metalworking and gunpowder with traditional claims of divine lineage, suppressing critical inquiry during periods of unrest. Still, pragmatic thinking quietly thrived among traders, healers, and craftspeople who understood observation and evidence as essential for survival. Successful trade routes depended on merchants who monitored market realities rather than relying solely on declarations. These pragmatic voices, though less conspicuous, ultimately shaped societal acceptance of practical strategies.

In the Americas, indigenous communities held sophisticated spiritual traditions anchored in meticulous environmental observation. However, European colonization, justified alternately by "*divine mandate*" or "*rational progress*", frequently disrupted these pragmatic traditions. Colonizers wielded religious and scientific justifications, imposing policies that often undermined local practices. Nonetheless, tangible results, health, infrastructure, agriculture, ultimately guided acceptance or rejection. Communities facing hardship from dogmatic policies frequently reverted to pragmatic solutions, validating strategies through demonstrable success rather than theoretical authority.

The Pacific and ANZ regions further exemplify this tension. Polynesian seafarers intertwined spiritual narratives of ancestral guidance with careful observational data on stars, currents, and winds. The introduction of Christianity and modern science saw local leaders leveraging new teachings to bolster their own influence.

Populations occasionally adopted singular interpretations, only reconsidering when practical outcomes, stable fisheries, sufficient harvests, social harmony, came under threat. Each time dogmatic assertions failed reality's tests, pragmatic thinking regained prominence, underscoring the enduring necessity of measurable success.

Throughout these historical examples, pragmatic thinking operates much like the universe's checks and balances. Just as celestial bodies maintain equilibrium through gravitational harmony, society requires mechanisms to evaluate bold claims. While a leader might invoke divine right or scientific authority, true success depends on practical results. Grand rhetoric cannot prevent floods; effective levees, resilient crops, and planned evacuations arise only through trial, error, and observation, hallmarks of pragmatism. Consequently, free will aligns not with untested ideologies but with outcomes grounded in accountability.

Why does pragmatism persist and even thrive? Its adaptability plays a pivotal role. When repeated failures expose a ruler's edicts or prophetic visions, communities naturally turn to practical alternatives. This pattern recurs globally: pragmatic solutions that succeed where dogma fails inevitably attract attention. Moreover, pragmatism embodies a democratic spirit, accessible to all. Observing a sturdy home or productive farming technique requires no special status or scholarship. This inclusivity builds societal resilience, enabling pragmatic approaches to resurface whenever authority-driven doctrines suppress questioning.

Pragmatism also fosters genuine progress beyond mere survival. Global health initiatives illustrate this clearly: success isn't measured by moral appeals or detached statistics alone, but by tangible improvements in disease reduction, life quality, and care accessibility. Vaccines and therapies proven effective across diverse populations gain acceptance, even among skeptics. Similar pragmatic successes emerge when East African communities adopt irrigation methods proven by neighbors or when Indigenous Australians apply localized knowledge for seasonal adaptation. Practical outcomes thus validate pragmatism's reliability and diminish purely agenda-driven assertions.

Ultimately, pragmatism recognizes that powerful narratives may temporarily captivate, yet tangible results ultimately arbitrate reality. Communities inevitably question if a method genuinely secures livelihoods, protects from disaster, or enhances well-being. Positive outcomes sustain pragmatic practices; failures ensure their abandonment, irrespective of theoretical grandeur.

At its core, pragmatism offers neutral ground, neither rejecting divinity nor science but demanding consistent validation. When groups invoke sacred texts or complex scientific language to enforce compliance, pragmatism simply asks for proof. Over generations, this pragmatic litmus test has subtly safeguarded societies against extremes, fostering measured evidence as a means to grow, adapt, and correct misguided paths.

While pragmatism shares a kinship with science in prioritizing observable outcomes, distinctions remain significant. Science adheres to structured methodologies, hypotheses, controlled experiments, peer review, to uncover universal truths. Conversely, pragmatism remains flexible, embracing provisional solutions that address immediate concerns effectively. Pragmatism prioritizes practical functionality over waiting for perfect answers, demonstrating its indispensable role in navigating real-world complexities.

Visualize this contrast through a simple analogy: scientists in Antarctica meticulously examine ice cores, decoding Earth's climate history with precise instruments, careful calibration, and systematic comparisons. Their goal is structured and cautious, aiming at long-term predictions. Pragmatism, facing the same challenging conditions, unpredictable weather, harsh terrain, and limited daylight, addresses the immediate practicalities: ensuring teams remain operational, adapting methods quickly, and pivoting as needed. This flexibility, trial, error, and adjustment, is pragmatism's engine. While science might lament lost data or anomalies, pragmatism seizes the chance to refine methods promptly, preserving momentum.

This interplay of structured investigation and practical adaptability aligns with the broader metaphor of Earth as a cosmic research station explored throughout this text. Imagine external observers studying humanity's adaptive responses under varied conditions: science provides the methodical insights, while pragmatism guides daily operations. Science gathers detailed analyses of climate or biodiversity over decades; pragmatism swiftly applies partial findings, adjusting practices without rigid adherence to past assumptions. This balance of rigorous inquiry and agile adaptation could represent precisely what cosmic watchers value: civilizations capable of structured exploration yet responsive to practical realities.

Significantly, this dynamic underscores a philosophical divide regarding finality. Classical science sometimes suggests universal truths or overarching laws. Pragmatism, conversely, makes no such promises, always remaining open to revision as new observations emerge. Historical experiments exemplify an ongoing dialogue: ancient farmers observed successful crop rotations without understanding soil chemistry; modern agricultural science later transformed these observations into sophisticated theories of nitrogen fixation and microbial ecosystems. Thus, pragmatism feeds scientific inquiry, which subsequently refines pragmatic methods, creating an iterative, never-ending loop of improvement.

This iterative process resembles human vision: our eyes cover roughly a 140-degree field, sufficient for immediate tasks but incomplete. To gain wider perspectives, we shift focus or use tools. Similarly, each scientific experiment or pragmatic action addresses specific questions or immediate needs, contributing incrementally to a larger knowledge mosaic. Although we never achieve total understanding at once, our incremental insights collectively propel progress.

Critics argue pragmatism undermines visionary scientific breakthroughs by emphasizing short-term functionality. Yet pragmatism does not dismiss curiosity or ambition; it demands big ideas demonstrate practical validity. Many transformative theories, germ theory, quantum mechanics, plate tectonics, initially faced skepticism. Only tangible, replicable evidence led to their widespread acceptance. Here, pragmatism and science harmonize: the drive to question is vital, but equally important is readiness to adapt theories based on observable, testable realities.

Imagine a conversation in Antarctica between a purely theoretical scientist absorbed in studying cosmic rays and a pragmatic fieldworker busy managing supplies, shelter, and safety amid harsh conditions. At first glance, their goals seem distinct: the scientist passionately building elaborate detectors to "*unlock universe secrets*" while the fieldworker addresses immediate practicalities, storms, logistics, and survival. However, these perspectives aren't in opposition; they complement and enable each other. The scientist's delicate instruments depend entirely on practical innovations ensuring their operability. Similarly, the fieldworker's solutions, like improved heating systems, can revolutionize the scientist's ability to conduct sustained, year-round research. This interaction symbolizes the enduring dance between structured theory and real-world application.

Considering Earth As A Cosmic Research Station deepens this metaphor, depicting humanity as a species adept in methodical scientific inquiry yet consistently adaptive. External observers would see humans rarely settling on absolute finality, readily adjusting or discarding theories when new evidence emerges. Adaptability parallels evolutionary principles, species unable to evolve intellectually or practically risk obsolescence when conditions change.

Pragmatism, therefore, acts as a safeguard against intellectual rigidity. Even the most advanced laboratories encounter unexpected results, uncovering overlooked variables or hidden biases. Pragmatic thinkers embrace anomalies as opportunities rather than disasters, refining subsequent experiments from previous "*failures.*" History exemplifies this synergy: Galileo challenged entrenched astronomical views through empirical observations, prompting paradigm shifts. Similarly, medicine's controlled trials replaced guesswork, and engineering's iterative prototyping continually improved designs.

Daily life reflects this experimental mindset. Individuals evaluate new recipes or commute routes, always evaluating outcomes and adjusting. While science employs rigorous protocols, everyday pragmatism thrives on simpler feedback loops yet shares the fundamental principle: retain what works, reconsider what doesn't. Both methods agree that no approach reveals absolute truth. Scientific theories evolve with emerging data; pragmatic solutions vary with contexts. Thus, knowledge remains dynamic, continuously evolving.

Ultimately, the relationship between science and pragmatism defines ongoing exploration rather than static certainty. Both involve testing assumptions, gathering observations, and refining ideas based on reality. If Earth is indeed a cosmic research station, its watchers witness humanity harnessing this powerful synergy, individuals pushing theoretical boundaries alongside those ensuring practicality and survival. Together, these complementary outlooks fuel humanity's greatest achievements: eradicating diseases, engineering marvels, exploring subatomic phenomena, and venturing into space, continually propelling an endless cycle of curiosity and innovation.

Reflecting on pragmatism reveals it not as a critic of grand theories but as their essential caretaker, ensuring theories align practically with reality. Science, conversely, offers structured frameworks, transforming pragmatic insights into systematic knowledge. Together, they underpin humanity's pursuit of survival, growth, and continuous learning on the vast cosmic stage.

At first glance, divinity and pragmatism seem opposites: divinity emphasizes transcendent principles, pragmatism tangible results. Yet history consistently illustrates their cooperation. Spiritual teachings advocating compassion and stewardship frequently inspire pragmatic actions like disaster relief, environmental conservation, and community support. Practical solutions, in turn, free communities from constant survival struggles, enabling exploration of deeper existential and moral concerns. Divinity thus provides noble ideals; pragmatism ensures these ideals translate into measurable realities.

Science occupies a nuanced position between these two, more structured than pragmatism yet less value-driven than divinity. Through controlled experiments, science identifies cause-effect relationships without explicitly defining moral or existential purpose. Within the broader metaphor of Earth As A Cosmic Research Station, science provides tools, renewable energy technologies, medical breakthroughs, while divinity guides moral direction, prompting reflection on purpose and meaning. Pragmatism serves as mediator, ensuring both scientific advancements and moral ideals produce actionable, beneficial outcomes.

This trinity of divinity, science, and pragmatism parallels other philosophical and spiritual constructs: creation, sustenance, dissolution; mental, physical, spiritual virtues. Each offers distinct yet complementary contributions. Divinity underscores purpose: science introduces method and predictability; pragmatism relentlessly verifies practical effectiveness. Imbalance, unchecked fundamentalism, ethically indifferent science, or short-sighted pragmatism, disrupts harmony. Pragmatism particularly functions as a safeguard, consistently posing the question: Does this genuinely benefit human lives?

The imagery of Earth as a cosmic laboratory, where watchers observe humanity balancing morality, scientific prowess, and practical constraints, resonates with the Antarctica Protocol. Researchers in Antarctica exemplify this trinity, coordinating under principles of international peace (divinity), rigorous scientific exploration, and pragmatic logistical management. Antarctica thus symbolizes humanity's broader cosmic endeavor: navigating complex environments, managing moral aspirations, scientific inquiry, and everyday realities, continually learning and adapting under watchful cosmic observation.

Humanity's historical trajectory demonstrates a dynamic balance among divinity, science, and pragmatism. Astonishing scientific advances, from decoding genetic sequences to exploring neighboring planets, have paralleled moral frameworks inspiring humanitarian efforts against famine and injustice. Pragmatism integrates these visionary goals and scientific achievements into tangible realities, clinics, education systems, and regulated economies. Potential cosmic observers would note how achievements inform one another, exemplified by polar research influencing climate responsibility and practical city adaptations to rising sea levels, marking iterative progress in this grand experiment.

Yet pragmatism, reliant on sensory evidence, remains skeptical of intangible phenomena, intuitive insights, telepathy, or expanded consciousness, traditionally also approached cautiously by science. However, emerging research now probes these subtle areas, aligning increasingly with longstanding spiritual teachings from diverse traditions that suggest consciousness transcends standard perception. For humanity to integrate such subtle knowledge effectively, pragmatism itself must evolve, adopting rigorous but open methodologies to evaluate intangible experiences, thereby bridging empirical science and open-minded practicality.

This evolution mirrors our adaptation to technological advancements. Innovations like air travel, the internet, and artificial intelligence rapidly alter daily routines, continuously refining humanity's collective operating procedures. For instance, new radar technology in Antarctica immediately informs practical adjustments in logistics and resource management. Watchers might observe how swiftly and responsibly humanity integrates groundbreaking technologies like gene editing, nuclear fusion, or autonomous vehicles, evaluating our moral guidance and practical benefits.

On a cosmic scale, watchers might particularly observe our emerging capacity for broader civilization-level shifts. Advancements in biotechnology approaching near immortality, integrating memory within DNA, bridge divine ideals of eternal existence with scientific feasibility. Pragmatism must then navigate ethical and societal implications, managing technological access, regulation, and potential moral dilemmas. Successful management of such power demonstrates humanity's maturity, ensuring tremendous capabilities foster growth rather than chaos.

Ultimately, humanity's journey underscores a powerful synergy: divinity's moral vision, science's structured inquiry, and pragmatism's real-world verification. Together, these forces propel our evolution from primitive beginnings toward sophisticated global collaboration. If cosmic watchers indeed observe Earth, they witness an ongoing experiment where aspiration, knowledge, and practicality continually refine one another, shaping humanity into a civilization capable not only of harnessing planetary resources but also cultivating consciousness, empathy, and cosmic insight.

In a cosmos that demands both awe and action, true wisdom emerges when conviction, evidence, and practicality find perfect harmony

Conclusion: Divinity, Science, and Pragmatism Converge in Earth's Cosmic Hypothesis

We began with an intriguing yet profound hypothesis: Earth might serve as a cosmic research station, a setting designed to observe civilization's evolution under varying conditions. Initially, divinity, science, and pragmatism appeared separate, even conflicting. Closer analysis, however, reveals them as interwoven aspects of a unified framework shaping humanity's trajectory.

Divinity manifests as enduring transmissions of timeless principles, resilient amid profound societal transformations. Ancient ethical directives such as *protect life* and *pursue justice* retain significance even in today's digitally interconnected, individualistic cultures. Principles once applied by farmers and shepherds continue to resonate with entrepreneurs and scientists grappling with contemporary ethical challenges, from data privacy to genetic engineering. Although earlier societies practiced morally questionable traditions like human sacrifice and entrenched hierarchies, humanity's gradual progression toward equity, fairness, and compassion suggests that these spiritual teachings functioned as early markers, patiently awaiting societal advancement.

Science emerges as humanity's systematic quest to decipher natural laws. Beginning with early agricultural practices stabilizing human sustenance, scientific inquiry expanded through pivotal milestones: Alhazen's groundbreaking optics, Newton's laws of gravity, and Maxwell's insights into electromagnetism, each progressively deepening human understanding. Einstein further revolutionized conceptions of time and space, while quantum mechanics pioneers Planck, Heisenberg, and Schrödinger exposed realities stranger than myth. Later, innovators like Lovelace, Turing, and Hopper transformed abstract logic into machines capable of exponential computational growth. Each scientific breakthrough did not stand alone but accumulated, building layers upon previous discoveries and profoundly expanding civilization's complexity and influence.

Importantly, scientific expansion has never delivered final answers. Newton's laws sufficed under everyday conditions but required Einstein's relativity for extreme speeds and gravitational fields. Quantum mechanics further challenged deterministic classical physics, introducing fundamental probabilities and revealing deeper complexities. Ironically, increased knowledge underscores humanity's insignificance: humans appeared late on Earth's timeline, orbiting just one star among billions in an unimaginably vast universe. Cosmic phenomena, like black hole formation, occur over timescales dwarfing our entire historical record, continuously reminding us of our minute presence.

Initially, divine teachings and scientific discoveries seemed distinctly separate, with divinity addressing moral and metaphysical truths, science empirical realities. Over centuries, however, intriguing overlaps emerged. Scientific breakthroughs occasionally echoed ancient spiritual insights about interconnectedness and invisible forces, resembling contemporary concepts like quantum entanglement or energy fields. Bridging these realms required centuries of dialogue and conflict, fostering advanced reasoning skills among thinkers who challenged existing dogmas, from monks preserving texts to polymaths confronting societal backlash.

The tension between altruistic leadership and manipulative self-interest fostered pragmatism, a third dimension emphasizing direct observation and measurable outcomes. Pragmatists questioned moral or scientific claims by demanding tangible evidence of societal benefit or empirical validity. Ancient practices in agriculture or medicine already embodied pragmatic principles, requiring demonstrable effectiveness. Thus, pragmatism emerged not as a competing worldview, but as a practical method verifying divine or scientific claims in everyday application.

This pragmatic approach integrates moral teachings and scientific innovations, providing checks and balances for human action. Divine principles guide ethical directions: *value life, uphold justice*; while science supplies powerful tools like electricity or genetic engineering. Pragmatism ensures responsible, evidence-based implementation. Real-world experiments exemplify this integration clearly. Particle colliders aim for theoretical insights, utilize scientific technology, and pragmatically enforce safety protocols, efficient energy use, and stable geopolitical conditions. Similarly, Norway's seed vault embodies a moral duty to preserve biodiversity, scientifically maintains climate-controlled conditions, and pragmatically manages standardized operations and international cooperation.

On a larger scale, these examples might reflect criteria cosmic watchers use to evaluate humanity: do we successfully merge moral purpose, technical mastery, and pragmatic verification? Historically, humanity has steadily trended toward synergy, progressing from fragmented city-states and kingdoms to a global awareness around challenges like climate change and pandemics. Each major advance offers glimpses of what could be achieved through consistent integration of these perspectives.

Yet, new frontiers challenge classical pragmatism's reliance on sensory proof. Phenomena like telepathy, deep meditative states, and near-death experiences resist conventional empirical validation, though religious traditions have acknowledged such experiences for millennia. Modern science, through sensitive instruments studying meditation and anomalous quantum phenomena, now approaches these intangible realms. Pragmatism itself may evolve, expanding beyond sensory-based validation to systematically embrace subjective experience, exemplified by mindfulness research and rigorous parapsychology experiments.

Humanity's daily norms and standard operating procedures have transformed dramatically, from ocean voyages taking months to instantaneous global communication via the internet. Observers might assess how responsibly we apply transformative technologies, evaluating if we incorporate ethical dimensions into fields like social media or artificial intelligence. Pragmatic guardrails like data privacy regulations or nuclear treaties emerge but often lag behind technological advancements, indicating ongoing challenges in full synergy.

As ambitions escalate, envisioning memory stored in DNA or planetary climate control, the necessity for integrating morality, science, and pragmatism intensifies. Divinity emphasizes ethical burdens linked to technologies offering potential immortality or vast energies; science provides mechanisms for these breakthroughs; pragmatism evaluates societal consequences and feasibility. The nuclear age illustrated such synergy: moral awareness, scientific understanding of atomic power, and pragmatic international treaties collectively mitigated existential risks.

Perhaps cosmic observers operate similarly to Earth's own Antarctica Protocol, implicitly awaiting moral maturity before unveiling powerful discoveries. This dynamic, seen partially in nuclear restraint and diplomatic negotiations post-atomic age, suggests that moral, scientific, and pragmatic alignment might trigger access to advanced phenomena. Such integration could guide humanity toward discovering deeper cosmic dimensions or unified ethics blending compassion, scientific rigor, and practical effectiveness, with watchers observing quietly how we navigate ambition and understanding.

At this stage, we recognize the possibility of pre-existing cosmic protocols or universal safety guidelines. As we explore quantum and cosmic realms, certain behaviors and constants appear precisely tuned to support life, reflecting anthropic principles. If Earth represents a node within a cosmic network, observers might ask if humans can balance knowledge, morality, and pragmatic application. History suggests humanity often corrects course rapidly after missteps, indicating a potential affirmative answer.

The critical question remains whether these protocols existed independently or evolved organically through human reasoning and spiritual growth. Earth's role as a cosmic research station may extend beyond metaphor, representing an actual experiment monitored by cosmic intelligence, evaluating our ability to integrate morality, scientific pursuit, and pragmatic verification effectively.

If divinity, science, and pragmatism indeed form an experimental framework, written protocols might logically exist. Earth's conditions: stable axis tilt, protective planetary arrangements, consistent orbit demonstrate extraordinary fine-tuning; minute deviations would render life impossible. This precise structure parallels experimental conditions, providing materials, energy, and environment conducive to technological and intellectual growth. Humans uniquely utilize abundant natural resources, advancing from basic survival to complex innovations like nuclear power, reinforcing Earth's laboratory-like attributes.

Protocols inherently imply behavioral guidelines, akin to meticulous lab procedures. Minor deviations in experimental settings often cause significant mishaps, suggesting watchers could similarly track humanity's compliance with moral or pragmatic standards. If Earth's environmental stability seems protocol-driven, it raises the question whether human destinies also align with established cosmic guidelines, continuously evaluated by these unseen guardians.

The concept of destiny has been central across diverse faith systems for ages, suggesting each life might follow a predetermined or cosmically influenced path. Abrahamic traditions propose a divine plan, underscoring God's omniscience, while Dharmic teachings in Hinduism and Buddhism emphasize karma and reincarnation, life shaped by previous actions. Native American cosmologies highlight spiritual directions guiding individuals, African traditions point to destiny influenced by ancestors, and Zoroastrianism aligns personal paths with cosmic order (Asha). Aboriginal Australian Dreamtime narratives further illustrate each person's integral place within nature's spiritual tapestry, indicating existence might reflect deliberate cosmic designs.

Astrology, tarot, and psychic readings resonate globally by hinting at these hidden life pathways. Despite skepticism from modern science, many find meaning in astrological categorizations similar to the periodic table's predictive power regarding elements' properties. Science, however, primarily recognizes probabilistic predispositions shaped by genetics and geography rather than explicit destinies. Pragmatism also resists notions of fixed fate, demanding observable, practical evidence.

Yet, intriguing intersections occasionally surface: astrologers invoking astronomy, alternative therapies claiming spiritual energy effects investigated scientifically as placebo or psychosomatic phenomena, and pragmatic acceptance when beneficial outcomes appear. This suggests a nuanced interaction among spiritual, scientific, and pragmatic perspectives.

The core question remains whether human lives are guided by protocols similar to Earth's precisely tuned environmental conditions, where slight deviations threaten existence. Cultures worldwide insist that destiny significantly influences one's birth circumstances and roles, with varying interpretations ranging from altruistic communal support to oppressive justifications. Pragmatism continually challenges these claims, seeking evidence-based validations, while science elucidates potential without asserting absolute scripts. Thus, destiny remains a dynamic puzzle, offering varied viewpoints within the same intricate cosmic framework.

From the perspective of a cosmic research station, observers might assess how humanity reconciles the puzzle of destiny: is it absolute or a set of initial conditions allowing room for free will? Analogous to chemical behaviors, where chloride ions typically pair with sodium ions but can yield unexpected compounds under special conditions, watchers may observe whether humans recognize "*destined*" traits as opportunities to align with moral and scientific advances, guided pragmatically in daily contexts.

Earth's stable yet intricate ecosystem enabled Homo sapiens to thrive, providing atmospheric balance, precise temperature ranges, and gravitational stability, conditions ideal for developing advanced intelligence. Humans inherited abundant resources, such as metallic ores, organic fibers, and energy fuels, continually pushing technological boundaries from metal-forging to nuclear energy. Each advancement, permitted by Earth's balanced yet challenging conditions, required ingenuity and moral awareness, reinforcing the idea of Earth functioning like an experimental laboratory designed for growth rather than destruction.

Thus, destiny may represent an underlying cosmic protocol balancing predictability with flexibility. Science uncovers how adaptable these conditions are, while pragmatism prevents blind adherence to detrimental paths, blending moral guidance, scientific exploration, and practical evaluation. This synergy might be precisely what cosmic observers seek to evaluate, an environment meticulously arranged for repeated trials of ethical, empirical, and pragmatic integration.

Different interpretations of these protocols, from deterministic to adaptable, likely form part of watchers' observations. Some individuals trust astrological signs to guide daily decisions, others rely exclusively on scientific forecasts, and many pragmatically combine both. Observing this cultural diversity provides crucial insights into humanity's approach to destiny, possibly constituting a deliberate aspect of the cosmic evaluation itself.

Earth's consistent environmental protocols permit civilization-building, reliable scientific discovery, and meaningful interpretations offered by divinity. Pragmatism ensures clarity, balancing literal spiritual interpretations and unchecked scientific confidence. Collectively, these reflections strongly indicate a structured experimental framework guiding humanity's evolution through environmental stability, moral direction, and free will interactions.

Science acknowledges predictable patterns in chemical elements, groupings in the periodic table accurately suggest elemental behaviors. This raises the question of whether humans, too, follow something akin to destiny. Albert Einstein supported deterministic views, believing natural laws were so precise that complete knowledge of current conditions could, in theory, predict all future events. He famously remarked, *"Nature is subtle, but it is not malicious"*, *nature is intricate yet coherent.* Einstein's universe resembles a vast billiard table, where knowing precise initial conditions lets you foresee every outcome.

Practical examples include Mercury's orbit, accurately predicted by Einstein's relativity when older Newtonian methods failed, and the precise adjustments needed by GPS satellites due to relativistic effects. From this perspective, even time integrates seamlessly into a four-dimensional framework, potentially suggesting future events are as fixed as past ones.

Conversely, Niels Bohr introduced quantum mechanics, challenging deterministic clarity. At microscopic scales, outcomes are probabilistic, exemplified by electrons "*tunneling*" through energy barriers unpredictably or radioactive atoms decaying without determinable order. Unlike a perfectly predictable pancake flip, quantum phenomena mirror pancakes spontaneously appearing on either side of the pan without defined paths. Yet, Bohr emphasized that even probabilities follow precise mathematical rules, uncertain in specifics but reliable statistically.

This scientific tension between determinism (Einstein) and probability (Bohr) parallels theological discussions around predestination and free will. Einstein aligns closely with traditions depicting an all-encompassing cosmic plan, while Bohr resonates with faiths emphasizing human choice, moral struggle, and divine grace acting in uncertain circumstances. Thus, even as they debated gravitational fields and electrons, Einstein and Bohr inadvertently mirrored profound spiritual questions about human destiny and cosmic structure.

The "*many-worlds*" interpretation branching from quantum mechanics offers a compelling illustration: every quantum event creates multiple timelines, each representing different life outcomes. Einstein preferred a single, deterministic path, while both his deterministic universe and Bohr's probabilistic framework agree the cosmos operates under structured rules. Science thus reframes "*destiny*" either as meticulously determined or probabilistically shaped.

Einstein and Bohr each explored multi-dimensional concepts: Einstein integrating time as a fourth dimension into spacetime, and Bohr introducing hidden quantum states or realms. This resonates with spiritual traditions describing various planes of existence, from physical to astral realms. Observers from a cosmic vantage point might evaluate our ability to harmonize these multi-dimensional scientific truths with moral and existential insights, suggesting the cosmos as more than merely three-dimensional.

The synergy between scientific theories and divine teachings around destiny appears more complementary than oppositional. Einstein's cosmic determinism parallels religious notions of a divine plan, whereas Bohr's quantum uncertainty aligns with spiritual traditions emphasizing free will and spontaneous divine intervention. Modern theologians sometimes embrace quantum theory precisely because it accommodates cosmic consciousness without breaking physical laws.

Real-world analogies further illustrate this balance between deterministic predictability and probabilistic uncertainty. Farmers planting seeds reliably predict crop yields using established practices, reflecting Einstein's orderly universe.

However, unpredictable weather and pests mimic Bohr's quantum uncertainties, requiring adaptive strategies. Similarly, software development teams plan methodically, yet unpredictable bugs require flexible problem-solving, again blending consistent frameworks with probabilistic occurrences. These examples show humans navigating a tapestry of structured laws and random variations, seamlessly merging scientific and spiritual views of a purposeful universe.

This brings up the question: does pragmatism exist outside the dialogue between Einstein's determinism, Bohr's quantum probabilities, and spiritual views of cosmic purpose? Pragmatism emphasizes immediate, tangible outcomes, "*show me practical results*", and seems unconcerned with cosmic predestination unless demonstrably beneficial. We must consider whether pragmatism fundamentally differs from these broader frameworks or acts as a crucial third perspective, evaluating grand theories against daily reality.

Typically, pragmatism demands sensory evidence, relying heavily on our limited biological senses. Divinity historically proposes realms beyond immediate perception, an idea echoed in scientific advancements from Einstein's four-dimensional spacetime to quantum mechanics and theories of hidden dimensions. Considering the superior sensory capabilities of animals: dogs detecting subtle chemicals, eagles spotting distant prey, bats navigating via echolocation, highlights human sensory limitations. Thus, dismissing divine or scientific dimensions solely based on human sensory constraints may limit our understanding.

Everyday scenarios underscore this limitation vividly. Driving through dense fog, our vision alone fails, yet radar or infrared technologies reveal otherwise invisible hazards. Similarly, classical pragmatism often dismisses intangible phenomena such as telepathy or spiritual realms because our senses cannot detect them directly. Historically, skeptics doubted unseen realities before inventions like telescopes and microscopes revealed bacteria and radio waves, demonstrating the necessity of tools surpassing natural human perception.

Imagine a hiker ascending a mountain, initially obstructed by trees at ground level but gaining a broader view with each step upward. Refusing to climb symbolizes pragmatic skepticism, demanding the peak prove itself before ascending. Divinity suggests ever-higher spiritual peaks, while science continuously reveals new physical dimensions. Unless pragmatism evolves beyond immediate sensory confirmation, it risks remaining at the base, missing the expansive views gained by climbing higher.

Consider oceanic researchers who once regarded deep seas as unknowable realms filled with mythical creatures due to limited sensory access. Modern sonar and submersibles, however, revealed thriving ecosystems around hydrothermal vents, challenging old pragmatic views restricted to immediate sensory evidence. Similarly, cosmic watchers might assess humanity's openness to intangible or multi-dimensional realities described by spiritual traditions and advanced science, phenomena like quantum foam or extra-dimensional theories that traditional instruments cannot detect.

Standard pragmatism, if confined strictly to the five senses, risks hindering humanity's advancement toward galactic or universal capabilities. Divinity suggests cosmic destinies and moral orders beyond sensory perception, while advanced science proposes dimensions and energies inaccessible to classical pragmatism. Einstein's spacetime concepts and Bohr's quantum mechanics both exceeded traditional sensory bounds, envisioning layered realities. Spiritual teachings have similarly indicated unseen realms or heavens, resonating with modern scientific theories.

Real-world analogies illustrate pragmatism's limitations. Imagine an archaeologist rejecting ground-penetrating radar simply because it surpasses immediate sight. Essential discoveries like buried temples and hidden structures of ancient civilizations would have remained undiscovered. Likewise, cosmic watchers might leave subtle indicators requiring broader perceptual tools. Clinging solely to minimal sensory validation could cause humanity to overlook critical cosmic opportunities. Thus, pragmatism need not discard verification but must evolve, creating methods sensitive to subtle phenomena and intangible evidence, bridging scientific theories and spiritual insights.

Ultimately, if science and divinity both extend beyond immediate human perception, pragmatism's role is to expand accordingly, exploring dimensions previously considered inaccessible. Observers might precisely evaluate our ability to unify spiritual depth, advanced scientific insights, and a pragmatism open to intangible yet consistent evidence, marking humanity's readiness to embrace broader cosmic exploration.

We have identified divinity, science, and pragmatism as three interconnected dimensions shaping humanity's approach to existence, yet spiritual traditions and advanced scientific theories hint at additional, higher-dimensional frameworks. Concepts from higher consciousness planes to string theory's hidden dimensions suggest our current three-dimensional understanding may merely scratch the surface of a more extensive reality. Ironically, as humanity aspires to Type III+ civilizations harnessing galactic energies, our comprehension remains childlike, especially if constrained by purely sensory-based pragmatism.

Classical notions of destiny suggest a rigidly scripted existence, but true intelligence might inherently resist such inflexibility. While Earth's precise environment hints at purposeful design, purpose doesn't necessarily imply an inflexible fate. Perhaps underlying our apparent determinism lies deeper freedom and complexity, what initially appears fixed might offer hidden flexibilities, aligning with the idea: *"A world that appears fully scripted may conceal greater freedoms than any single line of fate would ever allow"*

A useful analogy comes from filmmaking: even a meticulously crafted script transforms significantly through creative human interpretation. Just as a film relies on actors and directors to infuse originality and spontaneity, Jim Carrey elevating comedic roles or Tim Burton's distinctive visual style redefining narratives, destiny might similarly depend on human agency to realize deeper potentials. Conversely, even tightly scripted movies can fail dramatically if execution falters through miscasting or uninspired direction. Modest scripts, however, might succeed surprisingly well when directors and actors skillfully capture subtle emotional nuances. This cinematic metaphor demonstrates how, despite apparent determinism, human creativity introduces essential layers of unpredictability and innovation, reshaping outcomes profoundly.

To connect with the cosmic research hypothesis, imagine the universe as an intricate film set, with watchers having scripted Earth's environmental conditions: gravity, atmospheric composition, planetary orbits. Yet, as with filmmaking, scripting doesn't eliminate human creativity. Humanity, acting as performers and directors, interprets physical laws and moral guidelines, producing diverse outcomes. Observers might be assessing not the script's perfection but humanity's ability to adapt, improvise, and realize potential.

Earth's cultural diversity parallels film genres: slapstick appeals to some, serious drama to others, demonstrating the impossibility of one universal script engaging all. Each region or culture interprets life's script differently, emphasizing either comedy, conflict, philosophy, or harmony, highlighting how varied human performances create vastly different realities.

In filmmaking, a fully predetermined script without actor or director input would render creativity unnecessary. We value actors and directors precisely for their interpretive and improvisational skills.

Free will similarly introduces spontaneity into cosmic plans. Watchers, akin to studio producers, set broad parameters, environmental props, universal constants, but rely on human beings to creatively interpret existence. Consider a comedic film featuring actors like Jim Carrey or Melissa McCarthy transforming average scripts into successes through improvisational brilliance, compared to a well-scripted drama poorly executed due to uninspired directing and acting. Such examples illustrate that a script's potential depends heavily on human interpretation.

Scientific experiments offer further parallels. Antarctic research teams follow protocols but must adapt to unpredictable weather and unforeseen conditions, blending prepared guidelines with real-time adjustments. If watchers wanted absolute control, entirely mechanistic methods would suffice, but human adaptability provides richer insights. Observers value this interplay between scripted guidelines and creative spontaneity, revealing deeper truths about humanity's ingenuity and adaptability within structured cosmic parameters.

Returning to the question of destiny, the film analogy illustrates a balanced answer: existence is neither purely predetermined nor entirely random. A script might seem rigid, yet outcomes vary dramatically with human interpretation. Cosmic observers could intentionally allow spaces for free will and innovation, assessing humanity's moral growth, intellectual achievements, and cultural evolution. Absolute determinism would yield nothing new, while pure chaos would defy meaningful evaluation.

Humanity often perceives destiny in binary terms: fully scripted or entirely random. Yet filmmaking thrives precisely because of the creative interplay between scripts and human improvisation. Earth's diverse cultures mirror varying film genres, underscoring the impossibility of a universally appealing single narrative. Observers may seek whether humanity can creatively unify or innovate beyond cultural differences, navigating the dynamic tension between structure and spontaneity. Thus, the cosmic experiment potentially combines predetermined conditions with infinite interpretive possibilities: *"In a universe that grants both a script and a stage, the performance depends on how boldly we improvise"*

The cosmos epitomizes "*ordered chaos*" balancing determinism and randomness. A purely deterministic universe leaves no room for novelty or genuine exploration; pure randomness prevents stable planetary and stellar formations necessary for intelligent life. Cosmic structures, like galaxies and solar systems, are governed by consistent physical laws but exhibit unpredictable interactions.

Everyday analogies illuminate this concept. Stirring sugar into coffee creates recognizable yet unique swirling patterns each time, order governed by physical dynamics yet randomness in subtle eddies. Similarly, weather systems, driven by measurable physical laws, remain unpredictably variable over longer periods due to minute initial variations (the "*butterfly effect*"). Both examples highlight the universe's balance between stable structure and inherent unpredictability, fostering complexity, life, and civilization itself.

If the universe were entirely deterministic, it would resemble a flawlessly programmed machine, eliminating genuine free will and novelty. Conversely, total randomness would undermine stable structures like stars and planets. Cosmic phenomena balance these extremes: galaxies merge predictably under gravity, yet individual stellar paths remain unpredictable. Supernovae seed space with heavier elements, fostering diverse star systems and planetary compositions, their precise distributions influenced by chance-like factors.

Attempting to simplify cosmic behavior onto a continuum from absolute determinism to randomness, we find reality rarely at extremes. Cosmic events often cluster around typical outcomes, resembling a normal distribution, most results predictable, yet allowing occasional outliers or unusual phenomena. Scaling this analogy into a conceptual 3D model of axes of determinism, randomness, and unknown variables, most events would occupy an intermediate region, structured yet peppered with unpredictability. While humans traditionally perceive three spatial dimensions plus time, advanced theories propose 10, 11, or more dimensions, suggesting cosmic complexity extends beyond current human comprehension.

This multidimensional perspective prompts deeper questions: might cosmic existence itself reflect an experimental protocol? Could advance cosmic entities or watchers establish foundational laws while intentionally leaving room for creative outcomes? Humanity's pursuit to classify cosmic behavior as deterministic or random resembles lab rats interpreting a limited maze environment, unaware of broader experimental designs. Each additional dimension might represent further variables influencing cosmic events, blending structured laws and spontaneity.

Einstein's famous skepticism about whether the universe "*plays dice*" captures this uncertainty. Quantum mechanics shows probabilistic outcomes at microscopic levels, yet broader patterns remain consistent enough to form stable galaxies and solar systems. Watchers, if present, could be evaluating precisely this synergy between deterministic laws and controlled randomness, dynamically adjusting as civilizations evolve.

Imagine the universe as an immense laboratory, balancing deterministic stability, like stars steadily fusing hydrogen, and random disruptions from cosmic rays or asteroid impacts that reshape evolutionary paths. This delicate interplay fosters complexity without uniformity. Cosmic watchers might seek insights into how self-aware species interpret this blend: do humans grasp physical laws deeply, integrate them into moral frameworks, or default to simplistic extremes of absolute fate or chaos?

Our enduring debates around determinism and free will reflect this cosmic balance. Pure determinism would stifle intellectual growth, yielding little novel insight for watchers, while pure chaos would prevent civilizations from reaching maturity. The universe's "*ordered chaos*" provides sufficient stability for intellectual exploration alongside enough variability for evolutionary novelty. Humans perceive only limited dimensions, yet evidence suggests numerous hidden layers exist, complicating our understanding and suggesting the cosmos might be an "*n-dimensional*" puzzle blending order and unpredictability.

This complexity raises a profound question: does the universe's ordered chaos reflect intentional experimental protocols by cosmic entities or naturally arising phenomena bridging creation and evolution? Humans remain novices, capable of harnessing nuclear energy yet unable to unify quantum mechanics and gravity fully. The cosmos itself may function as its own checks and balances, structured laws provide consistency, while random events yield game-changing novelties like black holes or supernovae. Simplifying cosmic phenomena into linear deterministic-versus-random models neglects the intricate reality evident even in common phenomena like swirling coffee or colliding galaxies, each balancing stable and chaotic elements.

Albert Einstein's famous assertion, *"God does not play dice"*, emphasized deterministic cosmic laws. Contrastingly, Niels Bohr highlighted quantum mechanics' intrinsic randomness. Their apparent conflict, Einstein's fixed universe versus Bohr's probabilistic one, mirrors Schrödinger's cat analogy of multiple truths can coexist depending on observation and dimensional frameworks. Rather than invalidating prior views, each new scientific breakthrough expands and refines understanding, revealing a cosmic reality that simultaneously embraces deterministic laws and quantum unpredictability.

Choosing a "*winner*" between Einstein and Bohr oversimplifies their profound contributions. Both advanced scientific progress, each illuminating essential truths while leaving significant questions open. They built upon giants like Newton, Maxwell, and Planck, just as later generations refine or expand their theories. Human preference for singular champion ideas often overlooks the nuanced coexistence of seemingly contradictory theories: determinism versus free will or randomness versus order, within a multidimensional reality. This complexity may be a barrier to evolving into a Type III+ civilization capable of harnessing galactic energies, as we often simplify cosmic intricacies.

Schrödinger's cat illustrates these nuanced layers clearly. Einstein's deterministic view argues that the cat's fate whether alive or dead, is predetermined from the start. Bohr's quantum mechanics posits the cat exists simultaneously in both states, resolving only upon observation. Remarkably, each interpretation proves valid within specific contexts. Deterministic laws precisely predict planetary orbits, enabling exact space missions. Conversely, quantum mechanics' probabilistic nature underlies technologies such as lasers, semiconductors, and MRIs. Cosmic observers might intentionally create this macro-stability coupled with micro-uncertainty, fostering environments suitable for intelligent life to ponder existential questions.

Einstein's assertion, *"God does not play dice"*, can be reframed: does cosmic intelligence rely fundamentally on chance, or is it humans who effectively "*roll the dice*"? Both spiritual teachings and scientific theories evolve as humans interpret and apply them in daily life, blending deterministic rules and free-willed decisions. This interplay resembles a board game: rules provide structure, yet players' choices determine outcomes. Thus, cosmic order appears simultaneously scripted and improvisational, influenced significantly by human interpretation and action.

To illustrate cosmic determinism and free will, consider everyday games: Monopoly and craps. Pure determinism would render Monopoly repetitive, with identical outcomes each play; pure randomness would yield endless, unresolved cycles. Reality blends deterministic rules like property pricing, rent structures with random dice outcomes and player choices: purchasing decisions, trade strategies, acts of generosity or cunning. A child might land unexpectedly in Jail, or parents might intentionally forego property purchases, demonstrating free will's role in reshaping predetermined possibilities. Similarly, in craps, deterministic betting structures combine with dice-roll randomness and player strategy. Gamblers decide stakes and when to leave, reflecting personal, free-willed decisions overshadowing predictable probabilities.

Scaling this analogy cosmically, universal laws represent deterministic "*rules*" quantum randomness adds unpredictability, and human free will introduces moral or strategic depth. If cosmic watchers exist, they likely observe humanity's handling of this intricate balance rather than strict determinism or randomness. Einstein emphasized structured laws enabling predictability, while Bohr highlighted quantum uncertainties at microscopic scales. Both offer partial truths depending on context, mirroring religious views of a divinely ordained framework with personal moral freedom or destiny shaped by cumulative actions.

Free will isn't absolute chaos; rather, it provides space for moral and emotional decisions that surpass simple determinism. A parent in Monopoly choosing compassion over competitiveness exemplifies this, overriding strict rules for empathetic outcomes. Similarly, civilizations might prioritize sustainable resource management over immediate self-interest. Watchers might find genuine insight observing how humanity creatively navigates law, chance, and choice, shaping a meaningful cosmic narrative.

Ultimately, the universe functions as a pluralistic interplay of determinism, randomness, and free will. Protocols might firmly dictate cosmic constants such as planetary orbits, nuclear forces all the while random environmental chaos fosters novelty. Free-willed beings critically navigate these forces, crafting outcomes that transcend mechanical fate or chaotic randomness. This synergy is central to the cosmos: absolute determinism would yield boredom; pure randomness prevents reflective life. The balance between structure and unpredictability allows observers, if any exist, to witness intelligent civilizations grappling with profound existential tensions.

Humans often prefer binary resolutions: destiny versus free will, over nuanced cosmic realities. Buddhism, particularly through Prince Siddhartha's life, embodies a "*Middle Way*," steering deliberately between extremes. Siddhartha's birth carried dual prophecies: a powerful ruler or enlightened sage. Paradoxically born into luxury rather than ascetic simplicity, his life illustrates the intersection of determinism, randomness, and free will. King Śuddhodana sought to control destiny by shielding his son from suffering, scripting an imperial outcome. Yet random events disrupted this plan when Siddhartha encountered old age, sickness, and death outside palace walls.

These random encounters breached the King's carefully crafted scenario, prompting Siddhartha's pivotal free-willed decision to abandon comfort and inheritance, pursuing enlightenment instead. This crossroads vividly illustrates how destiny, chance, and choice intertwine. The father's meticulously engineered control succumbed to unforeseen randomness, enabling the Prince's transformative choice. Thus, Prince Siddhartha's journey exemplifies how embracing complexity: acknowledging multiple truths and balancing law, chaos, and free will, one can forge a deeply meaningful cosmic narrative.

"Amid the cosmic toss of dice and the pull of fate, we forge meaning from chance while following destiny's subtle call"

Relying solely on determinism, one might assert Siddhartha's departure was preordained by prophecy. Conversely, attributing his encounters with suffering purely to random chance misses a deeper nuance. A three-dimensional approach: integrating cosmic laws, unpredictability, and free will, best explains how unforeseen events disrupted the King's controlled environment, enabling Siddhartha's decisive moral and intellectual response. This synergy underscores human capacity to transcend predetermined scripts.

Siddhartha's radical transformation from pampered prince to dedicated ascetic illustrates profound personal freedom. His dramatic renunciation of wealth, family, and throne symbolizes free will's power to rewrite life's trajectory. Just as an actor might reinterpret a comedic role dramatically, or an Antarctic researcher might choose unplanned discoveries over routine instructions, Siddhartha's choices reshaped his destiny.

His enlightenment beneath the Bodhi tree embodies the intersection of destiny, randomness, and free will. The location's peacefulness was randomly conducive to insight, yet without Siddhartha's unwavering resolve, enlightenment might never have occurred. Buddha's teachings emphasize cyclical existence (samsara), highlighting how life blends deterministic cycles and random karmic variations. Yet Buddha taught a "*Middle Way*," emphasizing moral choice and meditation as paths to escape repetitive cycles.

Cosmic observers might note this dynamic: paternal or cultural scripts encounter random disruptions, allowing individuals' free will to craft transformative outcomes. Siddhartha's life represents how civilizations might navigate law, chance, and choice, yielding profound moral and philosophical insights.

Comparing Buddha's life to contemporary Antarctic experiments highlights how strict protocols rarely remain intact. Field teams constantly adapt to unforeseen challenges such as harsh weather or new discoveries, demonstrating ingenuity and moral judgment beyond scripted guidelines. Similarly, cosmic watchers might observe civilizations blending deterministic cultural templates, random environmental factors, and innovative free will. Prince Siddhartha's departure from his palace mirrors scientists who discard initial plans for richer findings, underscoring how breakthroughs often arise from deviations.

Our human lives parallel ephemeral roles in a cosmic experiment, interacting with partial determinism and randomness. Siddhartha's escape from paternal illusions illustrates the fluidity between order and chance. Each encounter, like resisting Mara's disruptions during meditation, showcased deliberate, unscripted decisions: the essence of free will bridging moral, spiritual, and practical domains.

Buddha's teachings emphasize life's deterministic cycles (samsara), random rebirth conditions, and free-willed liberation. His journey exemplifies how destiny, chance, and choice coalesce into outcomes surpassing single-dimensional interpretations. Cosmic watchers might assess our recognition of these interconnected layers: do we cling to simplistic notions of complete determinism or randomness, or embrace a balanced, mindful path?

Like a film or Antarctic field study, life's "*script*" cannot detail every moment nor rely on total chaos. Civilizations comprehending this synergy, as Siddhartha did, transcend illusions to forge new moral frameworks like Buddhism's Middle Way. Watchers may value not only intelligence but the moral and creative courage to navigate and surpass constraints, recognizing profound transformations emerging from balanced interplay.

Lord Buddha's example was chosen for clarity, yet throughout history, countless souls have dared to exercise free will within controlled environments whether spiritually, scientifically, or pragmatically. These visionaries did not attempt to merely fix the universe's inherent chaos; instead, they continually forged new order from disorder. Whenever chaos emerged, they responded not with despair but by persistently creating fresh structures and pathways, demonstrating how free will thrives amidst cosmic turbulence.

Yet, amidst their diverse paths, one message resonates clearly across all these examples: within Earth's structured environment, lasting impact arises not from adhering rigidly to a single value system, but by integrating multiple perspectives. Our current three-dimensional (3D) framework: Divinity, Science, and Pragmatism, offers humanity's free will a comprehensive guide. Until proven otherwise or expanded by new understanding, this integrated system stands as our best model. It empowers us to explore boldly, challenge conventions, innovate relentlessly, and ultimately transcend the boundaries of this grand, controlled cosmic experiment.

Thus, the chaos inherent in our universe is not an obstacle but an opportunity, a dynamic playground inviting humanity to employ its collective wisdom, creativity, and courage. As we progress into future explorations, this balanced 3D approach will serve as our compass, ensuring we never become confined by outdated scripts or intimidated by uncertainty. Instead, it will continually remind us that our greatest potential emerges precisely at the intersection of structured laws, random unpredictability, and courageous, thoughtful action. Ultimately, there is no singularity, but plurality rooted firmly in a *"singularity"* where each dimension essential yet incomplete without the others, crafting a profound and resilient cosmic tapestry.

In a universe that merges destiny with chance, we find our true role only when free will transforms circumstance proving again that plurality stands as the sole, enduring truth

Chapter 5: Beyond the Script: Free Will and Cosmic Uncertainty Drive Revolutionary Change

Introduction

In our journey so far, we have explored the intricate relationship between determinism, randomness, and free will, recognizing humanity's profound interaction with the 3D value system: Divinity, Science, and Pragmatism. We now turn our focus toward understanding how societies consciously and subconsciously integrate these guiding principles into everyday life. Historically, humans have often favored one value system at the expense of others, resulting in imbalance and conflict. With greater clarity regarding the balanced interplay of these three dimensions, we gain deeper insights into how their harmonious application can significantly transform human behavior and drive societal evolution.

Let us now explore tangible outcomes and behaviors when humanity deliberately embraces a multi-dimensional perspective. By observing real-world examples across cultures and historical periods, we seek to uncover how societies that balance and harmonize these three guiding principles create lasting stability, foster innovation, and enhance collective well-being, ultimately rising beyond the constraints of their controlled environment to achieve unprecedented progress.

Chapter 5: Beyond the Script: Free Will and Cosmic Uncertainty Drive Revolutionary Change - Introduction

The story of human existence begins much like a fledgling eagle emerging from its shell, bright-eyed and brimming with infinite potential. In their earliest moments, both the young eagle testing fragile wings and the human infant reaching toward unseen stars exist unburdened by constraints. Freedom, at that enchanting instant, feels wholly natural and boundless.

Over time, however, the paths of eagle and human diverge distinctly. The eagle, guided by instinct, effortlessly masters flight, unrestricted by societal constraints. In stark contrast, humans quickly encounter structured boundaries: rules about mealtimes, sharing, schooling, and permissions. These invisible limitations, imposed for safety or tradition, begin clipping our metaphorical wings almost immediately.

Yet human history is marked by relentless trial-and-error, our unwritten manifesto. Early humans observed, experimented, and learned, moving gradually from uncertain hunters to cultivators who understood nature's cycles. Each generation built upon discoveries, driven by an insatiable curiosity about the world around them, continuously propelled by the simple yet profound question: "*Why?*"

Unlike humans, the eagle required no agriculture or written scripts, content in its innate mastery of flight and survival. It existed without need for continual innovation, free from existential questioning. Humans, conversely, remained restless, always yearning for deeper meaning: contemplating the moon and stars, crafting myths, and eventually forming structured narratives and frameworks to comprehend the unknown.

Chapter 5: Beyond the Script: Free Will and Cosmic Uncertainty Drive Revolutionary Change - Introduction

As our collective understanding matured, humanity anchored itself around three guiding pillars: divinity, providing spiritual insight; science, deciphering universal laws through disciplined inquiry; and pragmatism, driven by sensory experience and practical results. These seemingly opposing dimensions frequently collided yet balanced each other, forming a resilient system of checks and balances essential to our progress.

Nevertheless, within this robust 3D worldview, humanity felt a persistent disquiet. Staring into star-filled skies, we sensed an elusive deeper truth, compelling continued exploration and philosophical inquiry. Each apparent "*answer*" merely led to more questions, revealing the universe as a labyrinth of infinite doors waiting patiently to be opened.

The eagle continued soaring effortlessly, free of existential dilemmas or societal expectations. Its uncomplicated existence held an elegance humans often admired yet paradoxically rejected, for our constant sense of incompleteness and yearning has driven us from primitive tools toward quantum mechanics and interstellar ambitions, continually reshaping our narrative within the boundless cosmos.

The journey of human existence parallels an eagle's emergence from its shell, beginning with boundless curiosity and limitless potential. Humans, however, quickly found themselves bound by societal rules and responsibilities, unlike the eagle effortlessly soaring above all constraints. Despite these limitations, humanity's relentless ambition drove us beyond mere survival: we built machines that defied gravity, first rising awkwardly, then swiftly across continents, and ultimately into the cosmos itself.

Yet our remarkable achievements came with unexpected humility: every new height of discovery revealed how little we truly understood.

The more we learn, the more we realize how much we don't know

Each scientific breakthrough, from quantum mechanics to gravitational waves, brought forth deeper, more bewildering questions. Rather than diminishing our curiosity, these mysteries intensified our yearning, prompting continuous explorations into uncharted dimensions of reality.

Settling into a balanced three-dimensional worldview encompassing Divinity, Science, and Pragmatism, humanity found stability yet remained restless. Persistent whispers of hidden dimensions, realities beyond perception, and invisible intelligences challenged our assumptions. Historically, each time we believed we had grasped the universe's final secrets, fresh phenomena emerged, disrupting our confidence and compelling further inquiry. A wiseman's timeless wisdom *"I know that I know nothing"* echoes clearly, underscoring the impermanence of human knowledge.

Thus, humanity remains perpetually poised on a cosmic threshold, driven by an insatiable desire to explore further. Unlike the eagle, content within instinctual mastery, humans continually transcend biological limitations, pursuing answers to questions far beyond physical existence. Our gaze upward once transformed simple admiration of birds in flight into profound contemplation about existence itself. This curiosity fostered spiritual frameworks interpreting divine messages, alongside disciplined scientific methods decoding universal laws. Together, these systems have continually guided our understanding, providing structure yet accommodating endless reinterpretation.

Religion proposed purposeful existence guided by an overarching cosmic authority, granting humans freedom within defined moral boundaries. Science, conversely, sought empirical patterns, demystifying celestial motions and atomic interactions through rigorous investigation. It provided no explicit ethical directives but instead offered a continuously refined framework of probabilities and relationships. This ongoing dialogue between spirituality and empirical exploration shaped human culture profoundly, fueling further progress.

Ultimately, humanity's greatest legacy may lie in our refusal to accept simplistic binaries of absolute determinism or pure randomness. Instead, we thrive within complexity, continually balancing divinity, scientific insight, and pragmatic wisdom. This multidimensional approach equips us not merely to navigate the cosmos, but to continuously redefine our role within it, crafting ever richer narratives from the interplay between structured order and unpredictable wonder.

Yet not everyone found solace in either the poetic sweep of religion or the open-ended nature of science. Some yearned instead for tangible proofs and measurable outcomes. From this practical desire arose Pragmatism, the third pillar of human understanding, grounded firmly in daily realities and immediate results. Pragmatism asked plainly: Does this method yield stronger crops? If yes, we embrace it; if not, we move on. Unlike its counterparts, pragmatism offered no cosmic narratives or spiritual revelations only clear, demonstrable successes or failures.

As these three frameworks: Divinity, Science, and Pragmatism interwove, humanity embraced a multi-dimensional perspective. Each served a unique role: Divinity explored purpose and morality; Science unraveled the observable universe; Pragmatism ensured actionable progress. While their interactions often sparked friction, scientific rigor challenging religious doctrine, pragmatic realism dismissing abstract philosophy and the resulting tension fostered a dynamic equilibrium. Humanity, driven by these interplaying forces, continuously advanced toward deeper self-awareness and greater innovation.

Meanwhile, the eagle continued its effortless glide, untouched by philosophical questions or societal dilemmas. Its life remained elegantly straightforward: hunt, rest, survive. Humans, by contrast, continually reinterpreted their existence, each generation layering new morals, technologies, and cultural norms onto an already complex narrative. This perpetual evolution whether constructing temples, building spacecraft, or decoding the mysteries of black holes marked humanity's restless quest for meaning beyond mere survival.

Chapter 5: Beyond the Script: Free Will and Cosmic Uncertainty Drive Revolutionary Change - Introduction

This extraordinary saga inevitably raised profound questions: Are human milestones random sparks of genius, or deliberate steps in a predetermined cosmic experiment? Earth's perfect conditions for life led many to wonder if our existence was purely accidental or part of a sophisticated cosmic design. Each technological leap, from fire to nuclear fusion, expanded our vision yet deepened these existential mysteries. Our collective debates spun faster, driven by the three-dimensional model's dynamic tension: divine purpose, scientific exploration, pragmatic adaptation.

Such debates echo real-world research stations, like those in Antarctica, meticulously documenting phenomena under controlled yet unpredictable conditions. Perhaps Earth itself is similarly shielded, allowing life to flourish while under observation by unseen watchers. Within this view, humanity balances on a delicate line between cosmic predetermination and genuine freedom, crafting an evolving narrative shaped both by overarching constraints and individual ingenuity.

Professor Debanjan Mitra of UConn's School of Business suggests our societal norms might arise from accumulations of random events, gradually solidifying into accepted traditions. From this perspective, human progress resembles a tapestry woven from both intentional actions and serendipitous occurrences, each decision subtly redirecting the course of history. Thus, free will emerges not from absolute autonomy, nor from total randomness, but from countless micro-choices blending intention with chance.

Chapter 5: Beyond the Script: Free Will and Cosmic Uncertainty Drive Revolutionary Change - Introduction

Viewed from the eagle's timeless perspective, humanity's shifting cultural expressions and rapid technological advances might appear curiously chaotic or impressively dynamic. The eagle remains content within nature's script, while humans perpetually rewrite theirs. Perhaps our greatest strength is this very ability to continually reshape our story, never settling on a final draft. In this ceaseless rewriting, we find not just our greatest gift, but the true essence of human freedom.

Ultimately, humanity thrives at the intersection of structured order and creative chaos. Each answer we uncover reveals further mysteries, perpetually driving our collective journey forward. Wonder, this deep-rooted human impulse, quietly binds together our three-dimensional understanding, compelling us ever onward toward unexplored horizons.

Let us now delve into the intricacies of human ways of life, searching for any hints that might clarify whether our free will is narrowly guided or entirely freewheeling.

One who thirsts for the unknown soon finds that every answer births a new horizon an endless sky for the seeker's soul

All Opinions Are Valid But Ours Is Valid-er: A Cheery Nod to the Rules of 'No Rules

From our humble beginnings as fragile creatures scurrying across the perilous landscapes of nature, vulnerable to even the simplest threats, humanity's journey toward dominating the skies and conquering diseases stands as an extraordinary monument to the power of reason. Imagine the eagle, once the undisputed sovereign of the heavens, now forced to watch in astonishment as humanity's metallic creations glide higher, swifter, and with more refined precision than nature ever permitted its wings. This majestic bird symbolizes nature's intrinsic randomness, beautiful, untamed, yet bound inevitably by instinct and environmental circumstance. Humanity, however, personifies reason, wielding an insatiable drive to transform chaos and uncertainty into coherent order and meaningful outcomes.

In humanity's earliest days, survival did not rest on physical might or swiftness but solely on our unique intellectual capability: the power to observe keenly, question persistently, and adapt ingeniously. The spectacle of lightning illuminating stormy skies sparked human curiosity and ultimately led to the domestication of electricity, illuminating civilization itself. Likewise, birds gliding effortlessly through the air inspired mankind to defy gravity, twisting wood, refining metal, and innovating advanced materials to craft aircraft that soared beyond natural limitations. Each intentional choice humans made meticulously shaped randomness into a precise path toward progress. Unlike scattered seeds awaiting serendipitous rains in desert sands or chemical compounds trapped in laboratories, waiting passively for fortunate combinations, humans proactively experimented, hypothesized, and engineered their destinies.

Yet this extraordinary dynamic, where human reason guides nature's randomness, occasionally encounters unexpected limitations, dramatically illustrated at Brightford High. In a quiet suburban neighborhood, Brightford embodied typical educational routines until a remarkable Monday disrupted normalcy. Students surged spontaneously into passionate protest, championing educational reform with vibrant, boldly painted banners proclaiming spirited messages such as, *"Facts are dull, tales are cool, textbooks drool, stories rule!"* and *"Forget the dates and boring facts, give us adventures, dragons, and acts!"* Administrators and teachers, guardians of structure and order, reacted as though their meticulously maintained environment had been besieged by unruly squirrels. The principal, usually poised, wandered corridors with eyebrows raised in shock, while the assistant principal futilely attempted to herd students back to classrooms as if shepherding confused sheep at a carnival.

Perceiving the students' heartfelt enthusiasm as mere disorder, the administration swiftly restored order through stern discipline. Ironically, this spontaneous student demand for creative, experiential learning mirrored the same rational, observational spirit that lifted humanity from caves to clouds. Thus, Brightford became a symbolic tableau, reflecting a significant paradox: human authority often mistakes genuine intellectual curiosity and creativity for disruptive chaos.

This paradox intensifies profoundly in our contemporary, digitally amplified era, exemplified vividly by the curious phenomenon dubbed "*I Identify as a Cat Syndrome*" Initially perceived as a quirky and harmless trend, individuals donning collars and painted whiskers, it dramatically escalated when one determined mother insisted her child, who identified as feline, receive veterinary care rather than visit a pediatrician. Social media erupted instantly into fierce debates, passionately dividing audiences between ardent supporters advocating inclusivity and baffled skeptics stunned by logic-defying assertions.

Through metaphorical imagination, even the fictional Cat Family Council convened beneath an ancient acacia tree, deliberating gravely on humanity's peculiar behavior. Present were the regal Lion King, a restless Tiger pacing irritably, a languid Leopard draped elegantly above, a twitchy Cheetah eager to sprint away, a wary Feral Cat suspiciously scrutinizing the proceedings, and an impeccably groomed Domestic Cat indifferent yet intrigued. The Tiger suggested a climbing test or antelope hunt to differentiate true felines from mere pretenders. Leopard amusingly questioned whether humans intended to pursue yarn balls or master extended naps. Ultimately, the Lion King delivered the definitive judgment: humanity could never embody genuine feline essence, asserting glued-on whiskers could never replicate authentic feline instinct.

Yet beneath this humorous allegory lies humanity's profound vulnerability, our intellectual prowess and reasoning capacity can rationalize even the profoundly irrational when magnified through digital technologies. Historically, whimsical childhood claims of feline identity resolved simply through gentle amusement or communal remedies. Today, accelerated by global interconnectedness, such eccentricities inflate into intense international controversies, exposing our constant struggle to harmonize freedom, rationality, and collective coherence.

Thus, humanity's unparalleled triumphs and inherent follies coexist precariously. While we proudly transcend randomness, soaring beyond eagles and neutralizing lethal threats, we simultaneously reintroduce randomness disguised as rational causes, amplifying trivial disputes into significant societal rifts. Perhaps, from the perspective of unseen cosmic observers, operating within the profound frameworks of divinity, science, and pragmatism (the foundational 3D value system), humanity's oscillation between profound genius and staggering absurdity offers rich data on the limits of rationality and the enduring role randomness plays in our shared narrative.

Ultimately, this unfolding human saga occurs against the vast backdrop of a cosmic experiment subtly guided by these intertwined value systems: the divine infuses purpose, science demands rigorous observation and continuous experimentation, and pragmatism insists upon tangible utility. Yet humanity persistently pushes these boundaries, exploring every curious leap and whimsical stumble. Whether redefining education through student revolt or advocating peculiar notions of feline identity, each event is meticulously recorded in this cosmic ledger, examining the boundaries of free will and intellectual evolution.

Humanity's greatest strength, coupled with its profound vulnerability, lies precisely in this ceaseless pursuit to comprehend, master, and occasionally surrender joyfully to the unpredictable rhythms of life. Every carefully planned innovation inevitably encounters an unforeseen twist, serving as a gentle reminder that randomness never fully disappears, it merely awaits humanity's next inventive, daring, and irresistibly captivating venture into the unknown.

> *In a universe of quiet starlight, we alone dance between nonsense and brilliance proving, perhaps, that what we call madness may be but one more variable in the grandest experiment of them all*

Love, Legacy, or Legislation? Exploring the Cultural Alchemy of Marriage

From New York's neon-lit avenues to Dubai's shimmering skyscrapers, from Vienna's elegant symphonies to Mumbai's bustling rickshaw jams, comedian Steve Treviño discovered something intriguing on his global tour: marriage jokes resonate universally. Whether he's comparing marriage to a crowded subway where both partners eventually regret their matching sweatshirts or likening marital harmony in Vienna to an orchestra desperately trying to avoid sleeping outdoors, every audience erupts in laughter. Marriage, it turns out, transcends cultural boundaries, becoming humanity's universal punchline.

In Dubai, where ATMs dispense gold coins, couples still argue about duvet covers and misplaced socks. In Mumbai, navigating marriage feels suspiciously like a chaotic rickshaw ride, bumpy, uncertain, yet cheaper than divorce lawyers. Even Tokyo's famously polite audiences can't suppress giggles when marriage is humorously described as sushi, neat outside, but raw complexities lurking within. No matter the continent, spouses everywhere nod knowingly at the eternal battle over blanket-hogging or who forgot the anniversary again.

Yet beneath these lighthearted observations lies a profound insight reflecting the foundational 3D value system: Divinity, Science, and Pragmatism. From a cosmic perspective, marriage emerges not merely as a human convention but as a meticulously designed protocol integral to Earth's grand experiment, akin to the stringent operational guidelines enforced at Antarctic research stations to preserve scientific integrity. Marriage itself is not the experiment but the stabilizing protocol, rooted deeply in divine traditions, practical necessities, and scientific rationale. It embodies humanity's delicate interplay between structured order and individual autonomy, maintaining societal stability, protecting offspring, and moderating primal instincts.

Across diverse cultures, marriage ceremonies differ dramatically, from elaborate multi-day Hindu weddings and traditional African village celebrations to sacred covenants in Abrahamic faiths, essential spiritual journeys in Dharmic traditions, and ancestral blessings in Eastern philosophies. Despite these cultural distinctions, marriage universally transforms two independent individuals into a unified partnership, shifting from "*me*" to "*we*" This transformation poignantly underscores humanity's paradoxical relationship with free will: despite fiercely advocating independence, we willingly accept the profound constraints of marriage.

Historically and practically, marriage has provided stable environments crucial for offspring and consolidated family resources, economically and biologically enhancing survival and community resilience. Spiritually, marriage reflects humanity's intrinsic quest for meaningful connections, moral virtue, and continuity of lineage. Yet, at its core, marriage presents a striking irony, our passionate celebration of autonomy consistently coexists with voluntarily imposed limitations on our personal freedom.

Perhaps this very paradox elucidates why Treviño's observations resonate so deeply across diverse cultures. When spouses argue over household trivialities or debate laundry protocols endlessly, audiences across continents recognize themselves immediately. These shared experiences highlight marriage's universal appeal, reflecting a deeper truth embedded within our collective consciousness and the foundational 3D value system.

Just as Antarctic researchers continuously adjust protocols to maintain order while accommodating necessary flexibility, human societies adapt marital customs through periods of historical upheaval and social evolution, adopting polygamy during turbulent times, recognizing same-sex unions legally, or refining divorce laws to maintain equilibrium. Marriage thus operates as a flexible yet robust structure, ensuring societal coherence without sacrificing adaptability.

In this manner, marriage embodies humanity's perpetual balancing act, simultaneously binding and flexible, universally recognizable yet perpetually evolving. It masterfully integrates practicality, spirituality, cultural continuity, and relatable frustrations into an enduring human narrative. Whether humans arrived at marriage through random social evolution or embraced it through deliberate cosmic orchestration, its existence remains unequivocal, confirming our innate attraction to bonds of structured togetherness despite our ceaseless pursuit of individual freedom. Thus, marriage becomes more than just a universal tradition; it reveals humanity's intricate dance with divinity, pragmatic necessity, and scientific rationality, a fundamental protocol in Earth's grand cosmic inquiry.

Chapter 5: Beyond the Script: Free Will and Cosmic Uncertainty Drive Revolutionary Change - Love, Legacy, or Legislation? Exploring the Cultural Alchemy of Marriage

In the delicate tension between structure and spontaneity, marriage endures charting a path beyond mere survival toward the shared wonder of discovering life's next chapters

From Twilight Whispers to Midnight Screams: Why We Believe in the Unseen

Have you ever walked through a corridor where the dying flicker of lights seems to rewrite the shapes of shadows on the walls with each hesitant pulse? The air there holds a silence thicker than centuries, pressing heavily into your chest, stale yet alert, as though the passage itself had long paused its breath, awaiting your presence. A distant, measured drip of water pierces the quiet, not random enough to disregard, nor rhythmic enough to soothe. As you step forward, something brushes past your peripheral vision, a whisper of movement so delicate you spin around, heart racing, breath arrested mid-throat. Nothing greets your panicked eyes. But that hollow reassurance of emptiness fails to soothe your trembling senses. The hall stretches before you, a forgotten crypt carved into mundane architecture, but something, an unseen presence, stirs at the very edges of perception, challenging the boundaries of your reality.

Your rational mind battles fiercely, conjuring explanations: a mouse scurrying in hidden vents, a whispering draft sneaking through cracks. Yet reason offers scant comfort against the slow crawl of unease tracing your spine. Another gust, was it the wind, or a murmur carrying your name on unseen lips? Your senses ignite into heightened vigilance. Sight betrays nothing, but your heart knows with irrefutable certainty: you are not alone.

Gradually, other senses unravel strange secrets. Ears strain to discern distant giggles, the metallic scrape of unseen objects dragged along a floor, muffled cries echoing from no discernible source. You lean forward; entire body attentive like an antenna seeking signals. Yet when you pinpoint the direction, silence envelops you, thick and suffocating. Then comes the smell, faintly at first, indistinct, growing sharp, acidic, like burnt wires or rotting leaves, unsettlingly akin to decay. It assaults your senses briefly, intensely, vanishing just as quickly, leaving you questioning its reality.

Our human senses, mediocre compared to an eagle's vision or a bat's echolocation, sometimes inexplicably catch fleeting impressions of an existence beyond the empirical. Could it be that our biology, limited yet resilient, occasionally intersects with hidden realms, layers of reality hovering just beyond scientific instruments? Perhaps these sensations are vestiges of ancient instincts, once essential for survival in dense, perilous forests, momentarily resurfacing to pull us into dimensions of possibility that modern rationality hastily dismisses.

We hesitate to voice these encounters publicly. Family dinners scarcely welcome stories of phantom voices whispering names or ghostly fingers brushing one's neck. Mention such events, and laughter swiftly follows, cloaking discomfort. Yet notice how skeptics recoil instinctively at flickering lights in nocturnal solitude or quickly seal windows upon whispers of a spectral silhouette nearby. Empirical proof demands dependable senses and replicable data, but elusive phenomena resist the cold stare of scientific scrutiny, vanishing like cunning illusionists before the spotlight.

Thus, persists humanity's paradoxical fascination. We eagerly consume tales of haunted houses, flood theaters for midnight frights, and celebrate festivals blurring terror and merriment. Amityville's enigmatic house inspires movies and documentaries, nurturing industries thriving upon universal dread of the inexplicable. Exorcisms captivate screens, psychics intrigue even the doubtful, and skeptics covertly immerse themselves in midnight ghost stories. Freud called it the *"uncanny"* familiar yet alien, implying we sense truths once intimately known but buried beneath layers of skepticism and scientific rationale.

Yet why cling so stubbornly to sensory evidence when our senses are notoriously fallible? We rely on a compass we know is damaged, ignoring hidden paths lying just beyond our conventional charts. Science has propelled civilization's greatest triumphs, but the data we cherish must pass through eyes fooled by mirages, ears misinterpreting random hums as whispers from the beyond.

Across cultures and eras, humanity named these mysteries, poltergeists, djinn, restless spirits, crafting rituals to appease or repel them. Sage burning, séances, nightlights, all reflect meticulous cultural attempts to comprehend or manage invisible phenomena. Perhaps this persistent cross-cultural consistency signals more than mere superstition. Maybe it hints at a universal pattern, a cosmic puzzle revealing itself subtly whenever we tilt our perceptions slightly off-center.

"Chance or cunning design?" we whisper into the night's silence. Could our psyches craft these apparitions to remind us that reality weaves a tapestry richer than our measured threads can capture? Parapsychology suggests openness to these intangible occurrences,

viewing them as genuine insights into unexplored aspects of existence. Might the next evolutionary leap integrate rigorous science with acceptance of phenomena defying microscopes?

We exist perpetually on this delicate threshold, captivated yet wary. Humans oscillate between skepticism and belief, approaching the unknown with mingled dread and longing, clutching rationality as both shield and crutch. Yet we return repeatedly, drawn inexorably toward haunted corners of abandoned houses or dense forests at twilight, yearning for a glimpse into realms beyond empirical safety nets.

These intangible experiences, recurring globally, hint strongly that Earth operates as a grand cosmic research station, carefully regulated yet allowing occasional glimpses behind the cosmic curtain. Divinity, science, pragmatism, our 3D value system, frames humanity's narrative. Each fleeting apparition, each spectral whisper, becomes another datum for unseen observers quietly evaluating human responses to the unknown.

Ultimately, perhaps this intricate interplay of known and unknown, our ceaseless curiosity, tempered by primal caution, is precisely the design. Maybe our enduring flirtation with mystery, balanced on the knife-edge between fear and fascination, ensures humanity continues seeking, probing gently into darkness with candlelit hope. For what else could life be but an eternal dance between certainty, uncertainty, and the irresistible allure of discovery?

Chapter 5: Beyond the Script: Free Will and Cosmic Uncertainty Drive Revolutionary Change - From Twilight Whispers to Midnight Screams: Why We Believe in the Unseen

We only break new horizons when our curiosity outshines our certainty

Blaming Mercury's Retrograde Again? Perhaps We Just Hit Snooze Twice

High above the swirl of clouds and silver glint of oceans, a low Earth satellite drifts in steady orbit, quietly observing a planet alive with countless cultures and beliefs. From this celestial vantage, astrology, an ancient tradition mingled with modern fascination, threads through daily life, uniting humanity in a single cosmic question: how might the dance of distant stars and planets choreograph human existence within the 3D value system of Divinity, Science, and Pragmatism?

At dawn in North America, as sunlight slips above the horizon, individuals scan social media for star sign forecasts, balancing their pragmatic skepticism with lingering spiritual curiosity. Mercury's retrograde becomes an easy scapegoat for missed communications, highlighting humanity's tendency to externalize misfortune within a scientific context. Two friends, a vibrant Leo and introspective Scorpio, debate plans for the day, playfully attributing their choices to cosmic influence rather than free will.

Farther south, Brazil's beaches resonate with similar scenes. A Gemini's emotional unavailability sparks lively debate, revealing pragmatic skepticism mixed with divine amusement as partygoers mock cosmic stereotypes while quietly consulting local astrologers about Carnival planning. Across the border in Argentina, sophisticated café conversations weave astrological themes into discussions about wine preferences, linking zodiac traits with earthly indulgences, subtly bridging pragmatic enjoyment and spiritual contemplation.

Sweeping across the Atlantic, the British Isles begin their day with printed horoscopes. Pragmatically, commuters attribute financial cautions to Neptune's illusions, subtly nodding to astrology's quiet yet persistent spiritual presence amid rational daily routines. Meanwhile, a Belgian newspaper discreetly advises Virgos on career moves, humorously cautioning against blaming Saturn for missed appointments, illustrating pragmatic recognition of celestial influence tempered by scientific realism.

In Russia, astrology blends seamlessly into cultural philosophy. Literary preferences become cosmic conversations, and a farmer relies pragmatically on Orion's position for weather predictions, revealing a deep, unconscious acceptance of celestial guidance. Across Pakistan and India, astrology governs marriage rituals through detailed chart comparisons. Gemstones, emerald, sapphire, coral, serve as pragmatic tools to balance malefic planetary influences, demonstrating humanity's profound blend of divine faith, scientific symbolism, and pragmatic remedies.

The Middle East balances star signs with pragmatic business decisions. In Dubai, executives cautiously align ventures with planetary positions, maintaining their belief in free will yet acknowledging subtle divine oversight. Similarly, Ethiopian communities integrate astrological cycles with religious festivals, pragmatically merging celestial timings with divine celebrations.

Kenyan zodiac memes humorously link athletic prowess to star signs, demonstrating pragmatic humor within a spiritual framework.

In Asia, China's younger generation merges traditional zodiac animals with Western astrology, crafting multilayered personality analyses. Pragmatically, they balance corporate life with dreamy Piscean escapism. Japan's cautious approach subtly ties zodiac compatibility to romantic relationships, pragmatically assessing couples through spiritual alignment.

Throughout the Pacific, Australians humorously consult radio horoscopes, pragmatically questioning Mercury's influence on directionality, while Fijians pragmatically link ocean tides to zodiac signs, symbolically harmonizing their pragmatic lifestyles with divine oceanic lore.

Globally, humanity's deep-seated fascination with astrology illustrates a broader cosmic paradox within the 3D value system: despite fiercely claiming autonomy through pragmatic rationalism and scientific discovery, humans continually seek divine reassurance from distant celestial bodies. Astrology's global persistence, from gemstones and rituals to daily horoscopes, reflects humanity's pragmatic desire for structured meaning, scientific curiosity about cosmic patterns, and spiritual hope for divine orchestration.

From elemental carbon evolving into diamond under precise conditions, humanity's intangible souls similarly adapt under environmental and cosmic pressures. Astrological classification parallels chemical categorization, offering initial parameters yet never fully determining destiny. As phosphorus safely stored underwater prevents spontaneous combustion, wearing prescribed gemstones aims pragmatically to manage celestial influences. Human souls, initially categorized by zodiac labels, remain fluid under conditions shaped by divine will, scientific exploration, and pragmatic choices.

Just as research teams adapt instrumentation for Antarctic chill or Saharan heat, individuals pragmatically modify their environments, beliefs, and behaviors to navigate life's extremes. This cosmic evaluation suggests that souls, subject to planetary alignments, remain capable of profound transformations through environmental catalysts and personal resolve. Astrology, thus, becomes a pragmatic symbolic system blending scientific observation with divine interpretations.

Ultimately, humanity oscillates between cosmic classification and individual free will, continually reshaping intangible souls. The cosmic puzzle, observed quietly by satellites and perhaps more advanced intelligences, emphasizes humanity's delicate balance within the 3D value system, perpetually navigating between pragmatic realism, divine spirituality, and scientific inquiry. Each soul's journey, subtly influenced by celestial alignment yet defined by personal choices and earthly experiences, illustrates humanity's timeless endeavor: understanding its place within a meticulously ordered yet infinitely mysterious universe.

Where cosmic forces converge, forging both elements and souls, one truth abides: what we become depends on the moment we're born, the furnace we face and above all, the free will to shape ourselves beyond any classification

Martians Have Better Wifi: What Humanity Really Wants to Ask Our Cosmic Cousins

In the radiant twilight of their distant, pulsating star system, the seven grand offspring sat attentively, their bioluminescent ribbons dancing with anticipation. Elliot, known among them by the elaborate name ⚲◇Λ☐☐⊠☐⊕, observed with gentle affection. This story, woven from his experiences on Earth, was not merely entertainment, it was a profound transmission of cosmic wisdom.

"After our unexpected landing near Kauai, Earth's delicate equilibrium began revealing itself to us in intricate detail," Elliot began, his tri-tonal voice warm and melodic. "From the moment Earth's skies received us, we witnessed humanity's bewildering contradictions firsthand. They harnessed astonishing technology yet squandered potential through relentless conflict. Our mission was observation, subtle and neutral, to assess whether this planet remained a robust environment to transform our cosmic truants."

A small offspring with newly forming ridges on its forehead pulsed curiously. "Did humans detect your presence immediately?"

Elliot nodded gracefully. "Indeed, they possessed technologies sophisticated enough to sense our arrival, though they misunderstood our nature completely. Their primitive radars registered anomalies, triggering a frenzy of response. Rather than collaboration, humans instinctively prepared for conflict. Their societies, unlike our harmonious Type 3 civilization, were fragmented by suspicion and secrecy."

A wave of contemplative silence spread among the offspring. Elliot continued, elaborating with care, "Ironically, Earth mirrored the three-dimensional value system we cherish, Divinity, Science, and Pragmatism, but severely distorted each dimension. They revered Divinity, yet weaponized faith against each other. They mastered Science but often channeled it into tools of domination rather than discovery. Pragmatism guided their daily actions yet was frequently short-sighted, favoring immediate gain over lasting synergy."

One of the offspring gently inquired, "Grandparent, did you interact directly with them?"

"I did," Elliot responded, his tone subtly shifting to playful amusement. "We initially assumed a form calculated to inspire respectful curiosity without panic, small, bipedal, eyes enlarged, distinctly alien yet not monstrous. However, due to an unforeseen solar flare affecting our camouflage technology, we materialized near Kauai more visibly than intended. Humans quickly mobilized their primitive vehicles, scrambling to secure what they saw as an unprecedented advantage."

The young listeners shifted closer, eyes wide, pulses of lavender and gold rippling across their skins.

"They captured us," Elliot continued serenely. "A minor inconvenience from our perspective. Our bodies entered a forced slumber, appearing inert as they transported us to their secret facility,

Area 51. Yet, even immobilized, we gleaned invaluable insights. Human interactions revealed layers of fear masked by bravado, curiosity intertwined with suspicion."

"Weren't you afraid?" a tender voice asked quietly.

Elliot hummed reassuringly. "Fear, no, but curiosity, immensely so. We observed from within as humans debated our significance. They hoped to exploit our advanced knowledge against their geopolitical adversaries. Ironically, our unintended arrival exacerbated human divisions, highlighting their readiness to weaponize even peaceful encounters."

"Did the cosmic council consider intervention?" another child queried earnestly.

Elliot nodded, a thoughtful hue coloring his membranes. "Yes, but ultimately they refrained. Intervention risked corrupting Earth's profound experiment, the evolution of free will under adversity. Our council recognized the delicate ethical balance: intervention might protect humanity yet simultaneously deprive them of essential growth opportunities. Earth, after all, was designed precisely to evaluate and refine rebellious souls."

"Then how did you conclude your infiltration?" a particularly bright-eyed offspring pressed eagerly.

"Once our observational data was complete, we vanished as effortlessly as we appeared," Elliot explained warmly. "My experience culminated in subtle, personal interactions across Earth's diverse societies. I assumed varied human identities, a general, a laborer, a traveler, immersing myself fully in the tapestry of their existence. Each identity revealed profound truths about humanity's capacity for both innovation and destruction."

Elliot paused, eyes sweeping gently across his enraptured audience. "When the cosmic council recalled me, the departure was swift. Within moments, our forms dematerialized, traversing seven hundred light-years in mere seconds, a marvel of translocation we perform routinely, though it defies Earth's understanding of physics."

"Grandparent," a child asked softly, "will humans ever transcend their struggles and unify?"

Elliot's expression softened with empathy. "Perhaps. Humans possess immense potential, but true unity requires embracing the full harmony of Divinity, Science, and Pragmatism, not merely fragments thereof. Until then, they remain a fascinating mosaic, brilliantly flawed yet ceaselessly striving."

Elliot concluded gently, "We returned home, bringing lessons that reshaped our understanding of cosmic governance and free will. Earth taught us humility, reminding even Type 3 civilizations that unpredictability is an inherent quality of existence. And perhaps," he added with affectionate amusement, "we too are learners, forever refining our cosmic dance."

As the offspring rose, quietly dispersing toward their resting pods, Elliot watched them thoughtfully. Each carried away a profound understanding, that the Universe, in all its vastness, continues to teach infinite lessons through worlds like Earth, blending chaos and creativity into the endless rhythm of existence.

A universe that expands is a universe that beckons, for growth in knowledge is its own form of cosmic travel

Filters, Followers, and FOMO: Tales from the Digital Parade

I lounge here above Earth in my cosmic hammock, watching humans, those endlessly fascinating creatures who keep my interstellar boredom at bay. Call me Jeff. I've been stuck here since the Andromeda Karaoke Incident (don't ask), observing Earth's peculiar inhabitants with a mixture of amusement and sympathy.

Humans received free will as a birthright, yet they manage it like it's optional, activated only when their friends nod approvingly. I've seen this habit sabotage them from their first smoky cave experiments, like the moment Grunt discovered fire, proudly waving a flaming stick until a fellow cave-dweller wrinkled his nose at the smell. Instantly, humans decided warmth and cooked meals were less important than social comfort.

Fast-forward through millennia of inventions abandoned at the first hint of a skeptical eyebrow, steel tools discarded because sparks looked scary, teleportation sidelined due to spinach lodged between teeth, cold fusion dropped because a lab coat clashed with reactor hues. It's a mesmerizing dance: astonishing genius tripping over trivial opinions.

But let's zoom in on a recent, everyday disaster, less spectacular than scrapped teleportation, yet equally revealing about humanity's Achilles' heel: their addiction to approval. This story begins simply enough, with a person who, financially stable and rational, desired a reliable new car. Practicality dictated this as a straightforward choice. Yet, practicality forgot to factor in Earth's Flip-Flop Troupe, the well-meaning but wildly inconsistent advice-givers whose thumbs-up or thumbs-down swings decision-making faster than a pendulum.

"Only fools buy new cars!" chimed friends, cousins, and that coworker who changed his brake pads once and crowned himself the automotive sage. Warnings of immediate depreciation echoed through group chats and casual conversations, planting seeds of doubt. Desperate not to appear naive, our protagonist retreated from the gleaming new vehicles and instead purchased a "certified" used sedan.

Initially, everyone cheered. "Look at you, smart shopper!" the Flip-Flop Troupe praised. And indeed, at first glance, saving thousands seemed commendable, until reality seeped in. Certification, it turned out, wasn't magic; soon the protagonist was draining pockets on surprise repairs, specialty oils, and economy-brand brakes that squealed louder than cosmic static. Meanwhile, friends who'd advocated used vehicles quietly transitioned to shiny new rides themselves, now extolling the virtues of warranties and free roadside assistance.

Still, our protagonist stubbornly clung to fleeting approval, assured by sporadic thumbs-up emojis from friends blissfully ignoring mounting repair costs and dwindling reliability.

Then came a cold, snowy morning, seemingly designed by fate itself to mock human folly. Discount tires met icy pavement, economy brakes whimpered uselessly, and the inevitable crash unfolded. With liability-only insurance, another Flip-Flop recommendation, our protagonist lay battered in a hospital bed, swathed in bandages and steeped in regret.

Friends arrived, awkwardly boasting how their newer models' advanced safety systems had saved them from similar mishaps. "Why didn't you upgrade earlier?" they lamented sympathetically, conveniently forgetting their previous mockery of buying new. As our protagonist attempted frustrated responses through a wired jaw, the Flip-Flop Troupe offered weak shrugs: "Times changed."

And there, immobilized and buried under hospital bills and totaled car debts, our protagonist confronted a stark realization: human approval is ephemeral, and decisions driven by fear of missing out (FOMO) inevitably lead to disasters both large and small.

From my cosmic perch, this scenario highlighted humanity's peculiar insistence on surrendering free will to the transient opinions of others, ignoring solid data, pragmatic reasoning, and timeless truths. The Universe doesn't alter its fundamental laws for passing whims, and Antarctic researchers don't abandon experiments because someone scoffs at their boots. Yet humans, blessed with intellect and innovation, still chase the illusionary security of collective nods and casual applause.

This pattern isn't limited to cars, it echoes throughout history, from abandoned breakthroughs to sidelined scientific marvels. Each incident begins the same: a genius spark overshadowed by an anxious glance at the watchers. And while humans have undeniably conquered remarkable feats, their potential repeatedly fizzles under the slightest skeptical smirk.

Will humans ever overcome this compulsion? Possibly. But part of me suspects they'd rather not; their drama-addicted hearts thrive on this eternal oscillation between brilliance and hesitation. Thus, I remain here, amused yet hopeful, quietly rooting for the day they'll realize that free will doesn't require approval, that sometimes, true genius must stride forward even amidst silence.

Until then, pass the cosmic popcorn. Earth's greatest comedy show continues, unstoppable yet paradoxically paused by the faintest whisper of doubt.

Chasing applause usually lands you in the passenger seat of someone else's road trip

From Santas to Subpoenas: When Holidays Demand You Hand Over Your Last Brownie

In a quiet, luxurious conference room, far removed from public scrutiny, a select group of ultra-wealthy individuals gathered, deeply troubled by a minuscule seventy-five basis point shortfall in global investment returns. Despite their immense fortunes, this tiny deviation triggered an anxious outcry, quickly devolving into admonishments aimed at ordinary people for daring to tighten their belts.

These influential figures, masters of finance, media, and government, swiftly devised plans to shift more public burdens onto the very citizens they blamed. Retirement ages would rise, transforming restful golden years into distant mirages. Jobs as simple as serving coffee would inexplicably demand costly college degrees, funneling more money into educational institutions and training programs that offered dubious real-world benefits.

Marketing teams gleefully embraced the challenge, crafting campaigns that subtly labeled frugality as a form of selfishness, turning responsible saving into an act worthy of shame. "Don't you love your family enough to max out your credit card?" they seemed to whisper. Soon, even the simplest holidays morphed into anxiety-laden, debt-driven spectacles. Christmas ceased to be about family gatherings, instead becoming a battleground of competitive spending, tension-filled dinners overshadowed by worries about unpaid bills. Ironically, the joy of giving turned into the dread of repaying.

Mothers who yearned only for a heartfelt phone call found themselves waiting until Mother's Day, a commercial spectacle complete with overpriced bouquets and crowded brunches. Authentic emotional connections became hostage to calendar-driven consumerism. The same applied to every celebration, each holiday evolving from intimate joy into stressful, obligatory spending rituals. Families who once celebrated quietly at home now felt compelled to stage grand, anxiety-filled events, terrified of being judged stingy or uncaring by neighbors and social media acquaintances.

The promise of a luxurious, carefree retirement dangled enticingly in front of workers, making them willing to sacrifice youth and health to tedious, unfulfilling jobs. Each day became a monotonous step toward a golden horizon that never seemed closer. Workers poured their best years into careers, missing irreplaceable moments with loved ones, ironically losing the very thing they worked so desperately to achieve, time.

In this twisted world, choosing not to spend recklessly became an act of rebellion, ironically branded shameful by the very people who stood to profit. Marketing campaigns insidiously suggested that if one wasn't drowning in debt, one wasn't truly participating in society. "Look at the Smiths, they refinanced their home to afford that vacation! Do you not love your family as much as they do?" became a subtextual pressure tactic.

This culture of enforced extravagance fundamentally clashed with the 3D value system, Divinity, Pragmatism, and Universal Law. Divinity stresses genuine connection and compassion, not superficial gestures measured by price tags. Pragmatism advocates thoughtful spending and sustainable living, sharply contradicting the frivolous excess society now idealized. Universal Law underscores the balance and harmony of existence, profoundly disrupted by consumer-driven anxiety and artificial scarcity.

Yet beneath this manufactured illusion lay a quiet undercurrent of resistance. Amid the noisy commercial clutter, the COVID-19 pandemic had caused many families to reclaim the essence of celebration. Simple gatherings around kitchen tables replaced extravagant dinners; genuine conversations took the place of showy displays of wealth. Parents rediscovered the unadorned joy of spending unstructured time with their children, engaging in activities that required no monetary investment yet yielded profound emotional returns.

Similarly, couples found deeper intimacy in unpretentious moments. Instead of expensive restaurants and lavish outings, they shared quiet evenings, simple meals, and heartfelt talks, discovering that sincere affection thrives best when unburdened by financial anxiety. Friends, too, began gravitating toward casual gatherings that celebrated companionship and genuine connection, rather than status-driven spectacles.

These subtle acts of defiance exposed the hollowness of extravagant consumerism. Genuine happiness, it became clear, was never tied to price tags or calendar-driven events. Instead, it flourished quietly, in authentic gestures of kindness and presence, demonstrating the enduring power of sincerity over orchestrated spectacle.

Observing this troubling shift in public behavior, the ultra-wealthy strategists regrouped with a renewed sense of urgency. A stern warning was issued, recovering those critical seventy-five basis points was non-negotiable. Investment managers, sensing an opportunity, eagerly pledged to reverse the shortfall, their eyes gleaming at the promise of substantial bonus incentives. Reassured by these confident assurances, the elites returned to their lavish festivities, popping $100,000 champagne bottles and savoring exquisite cuisine, dancing the night away without a care in the world.

Meanwhile, ordinary citizens embraced their newfound discipline with cautious optimism, believing they'd discovered a way to finally beat the manipulative system. However, lingering doubts remained, whispering that perhaps this independence was only temporary. Could genuine frugality withstand another orchestrated assault of marketing brilliance and financial pressures, or would their hard-earned resistance crumble under renewed waves of guilt and temptation?

As the ultra-rich toasted their latest strategies beneath chandeliers and the glow of opulence, they smiled knowingly, confident they could reignite the cycle of consumption. After all, history had proven that collective memory was short, easily reshaped by expertly crafted narratives. They danced to the reassuring rhythm of clinking glasses, convinced that human behavior could always be redirected, their wealth insulated from the consequences of economic fluctuations.

Yet, somewhere far from the glittering ballrooms and exclusive banquets, families quietly gathered, cautiously hopeful yet wary. They understood the game better now, having glimpsed the fragile nature of manufactured desires and hollow consumer rituals. The question lingered, unspoken but felt by all: had they truly escaped the orchestrations of the powerful, or was their freedom merely a brief interlude before the relentless gears of the cycle began to turn once more?

Every moment of choice, however small, reminds the universe that free will still has more power than any grand design

When Test Tubes Meet Testaments: How Atheists, Believers, and Scientists End Up in the Same Chatroom Brawl

In the quiet formality of the Annual Divinity's Progress Update, an event curiously labeled a meeting yet attended solely by one, as divinity remains ultimately singular, a gentle tension unfolds. At its core lies the profound yet puzzling truth that existence might originate from a single source, contrasted starkly by humanity's insistence on parsing that truth through three distinct lenses: the believer, the empiricist, and the pragmatist. Each claims a unique hold on reality, yet all revolve around the same fundamental question: if existence itself is arguably divine, why does humanity remain fractured in understanding it?

Believers view divinity as absolute. It is the underpinning of existence, the basis of moral certitude, and the definer of purpose. Across the spectrum of sacred traditions, from ancient Vedic hymns to scriptural teachings born in arid deserts, divinity is distilled into forms beyond empirical measure. Yet, assemble a group of believers and invite them to articulate their visions of the divine, and disagreements quickly surface. Is divinity a compassionate overseer guiding every heartbeat, or an impersonal force sustaining existence itself? These subtle variations expose that even unified devotion struggles to find consensus.

Empiricists anchor themselves firmly to the principle of observation. All cosmic phenomena, they assert, from stellar birth to galactic drift, can eventually be mapped through meticulous data collection. The Big Bang theory exemplifies this stance, emerging from precise measurements of cosmic microwave background radiation and galaxy trajectories first noted by Georges Lemaître and further supported by Edwin Hubble's discoveries. Despite its robust acceptance, empiricists maintain readiness for revision should contradictory evidence appear. Yet, if humanity can embrace cosmic events observed indirectly through instruments, might it not equally acknowledge forms of divinity existing just beyond sensory detection?

Pragmatists approach existence with cautious humility. Acknowledging life's brevity and the inherent limitations of human perception, they advocate piecing together partial truths. Recognizing reality's innate complexity, random yet governed by unyielding constants, they argue that neither empirical nor faith-based views alone can fully encapsulate existence. Accepting these limitations is not seen as defeat but as a humble starting point for genuine exploration.

Despite these perspectives' complementarity, conflict frequently arises. Believers assert faith's necessity, empiricists demand verifiable proof, and pragmatists highlight incomplete knowledge. Ironically, amidst this friction, the universe continues functioning according to consistent laws that defy human divisions. To grasp humanity's cosmic role, integration rather than isolation of these dimensions seems essential.

Chapter 5: Beyond the Script: Free Will and Cosmic Uncertainty Drive Revolutionary Change - When Test Tubes Meet Testaments: How Atheists, Believers, and Scientists End Up in the Same Chatroom Brawl

Thus, the sole attendee of the Annual Divinity's Progress Update contemplates: Why insist on separation rather than synthesize insights? Why resist multiplicity when nature itself demonstrates layered complexity? Perhaps human inclination towards absolutes reflects evolutionary psychology, a historical reflex that challenges contemporary attempts at unity.

These queries resonate widely, mirrored in diverse human gatherings worldwide. From a Southern church-turned-television studio, where charismatic Pentecostals debate scripture with reserved Baptists, to international forums linking Rome's traditional Catholicism, Amsterdam's rigorous atheism, and Manila's devout mysticism, humanity vigorously asserts differing truths. Each faction passionately defends its perspective, often dismissing alternative views despite addressing the same fundamental mystery.

Simultaneously, beyond human view, cosmic or perhaps divine observers consider this intricate human dance. Their attention focuses not merely on disagreements but also on humanity's relentless pursuit of truth. This friction, while seemingly divisive, could reflect the vital energy driving progress and preventing complacency.

Indeed, global discussions about miracles and saints, from African radio debates in Nairobi to European café discussions on relics, showcase humanity's common quest: interpreting phenomena that transcend ordinary experience. Whether attributing these to divine intervention, empirical investigation, or cautious skepticism, all participants engage in a shared endeavor to understand reality's deeper layers.

From a broader cosmic vantage, these spirited exchanges might resemble a grand composition, each viewpoint adding distinct notes rather than discord. Perhaps the tension between different perspectives serves as humanity's crucial test, challenging individuals to expand their understanding beyond singular dimensions.

Ultimately, observers from beyond our world may recognize humanity's dual nature: deeply creative yet stubbornly attached to inherited beliefs. They notice how often humanity repeats narratives uncritically, reflecting familial and cultural traditions more than personal exploration. The question then becomes why humans, equipped with free will, frequently limit their inquiry, accepting inherited truths rather than forging their own understanding.

Perhaps the real potential of humanity lies precisely here, in recognizing the illusions within accepted narratives and courageously challenging them. It is possible that illusions serve a dual purpose: they provide stability yet also provoke critical reflection, spurring individuals toward a deeper, more authentic exploration of existence.

And so, as twilight descends upon Earth and humanity prepares to retell familiar stories, the cosmic observers remain watchful and intrigued. Tomorrow's sunrise will again offer the chance to question or accept, to explore further or retreat into familiar certainties. Within this continual cycle lies humanity's profound opportunity: the potential to realize that existence, layered and vast, can never be fully comprehended from any single viewpoint, but perhaps can be approached more truthfully by synthesizing them all.

Never doubt that reality can be stirred by the faintest flicker of human courage sometimes, the smallest flame casts the longest light

Free Will vs. Fill-in-the-Blank: Are They Marking Down Your Creativity With a #2 Pencil?

In her silent living room, she held the simple wooden frame, gazing deeply into the photo of her child, a bright face lost too soon, crushed beneath the unbearable weight of expectations. Her heart tightened, recalling how she once promised herself to spare her child from the pressure she endured in her youth. Yet, despite those heartfelt vows, she found herself replicating the very demands she despised, convinced that success hinged on flawless performances in standardized assessments.

Her eyes drifted, and for a moment she imagined homes around the globe, parents like her caught in identical cycles. Across the United States, a mother warned sternly about SAT scores determining life's opportunities. In Canada, another pleaded that only perfect marks ensured a path to prestigious universities. Mexico echoed similar fears, one exam deciding futures at UNAM or Tec de Monterrey. In Brazil, tense reminders that a single missed point on ENEM could limit lifelong possibilities. Argentina, Germany, Sweden, Russia, France, Britain, each voice different, yet each driven by the same anxious mantra: one exam, one chance, no room for error.

She saw Türkiye, Egypt, Ethiopia, India, China, Japan, Indonesia, Australia, South Korea, Ukraine, all places where parents poured dreams and anxieties into evaluations, convinced that scores opened doors or sealed fates. Each household tense, each child puzzled or resigned, all caught in a global web woven by the same fear-driven narrative.

A profound ache filled her chest. Could it be right, she wondered, if the whole world had agreed to measure children's worth and potential through bubble sheets and numerical rankings?

Her mind drifted back through history. In older worlds, education took countless forms, tribal elders passing survival skills by firelight, Aztec training shaped by social roles, enlightenment-era tutors nurturing curiosity. Knowledge had been communal, practical, diverse, never confined to universal metrics. But somehow, in humanity's march toward progress and comfort, learning became standardized, commodified, and constrained.

She remembered clearly how she once hovered anxiously, her child poring over textbooks, nights filled with tension and tears. Now, the emptiness reminded her bitterly of the true cost. What good was a system that lifted some yet crushed others beneath unbearable pressure? She would have traded every modern comfort to undo that loss, to hold her child again, free from the fear that one misstep meant lifelong failure.

In a remote Antarctic research station, a scientist received her story. As he shared it with colleagues, laughter turned reflective. Each confessed: real breakthroughs, real survival skills, real learning had come not from standardized tests, but from experiences, curiosity, adaptation. In Antarctica, no exam measured worth; life itself evaluated them daily, asking only whether they could adapt, think freely, and remain resilient.

Quietly, the grieving mother imagined cosmic observers, perhaps puzzled that humanity, capable of mapping stars and splitting atoms, had chosen to constrain knowledge behind gates of evaluation. If learning was inherently about curiosity and exploration, how had the species that reached the moon reduced discovery to multiple-choice questions?

Outside her window, children played, laughter dancing on the breeze. Their innocence tugged at her heart, stirring hope alongside grief. Perhaps this relentless cycle could be questioned, transformed, maybe one day, education would truly nourish, not measure, young souls. For now, she whispered gently to herself and the universe, hoping her child's lost brightness might guide others toward a gentler path, one where the value of a life was never reduced to the score on a sheet of paper.

Let the mind roam like wind ungraded, unscheduled, and unwilling to be boxed only then will it return with something worth teaching

Carrying Receipts Beyond the Exit: The Curious Notion of Deeds Echoing Elsewhere

From the moment a child takes their first breath, they're immersed in stories hinting at invisible worlds just beyond our own. Before shoes are tied or bicycles ridden, whispers from family, community, and culture instill a gentle yet insistent awareness: an unseen realm watches, judges, guides, or perhaps waits patiently. Heaven, hell, ancestral spirits, karmic cycles, names vary, but the underlying message remains: each action echoes far beyond immediate sight.

In Cairo's bustling streets, Junaid learned to imagine angelic scribes meticulously recording his deeds, good and bad alike. A missed prayer was never merely a lapse; it felt like an entry on a cosmic ledger. Across oceans, Elise in Haiti grew up fearing nocturnal spirits who watched her every move, convinced a forgotten chore might provoke their displeasure. Far away, Olamide's Nigerian village elders spoke solemnly of Orishas who bestowed blessings or punishments with each small gesture or oversight. In Bangkok, Dao humorously teased friends about karmic consequences yet secretly worried her irreverence might lead to reincarnation as something trivial. And in northern India, Sejal listened attentively as relatives whispered warnings of karma clinging relentlessly to each minor misstep, like an invisible stain.

This blend of awe and anxiety colored their young lives, carrying them into adulthood with quiet dread. The smallest mistakes, a broken cup, a missed ritual, felt monumental, recorded eternally in invisible records. Yet, as each grew older, subtle moments began reshaping their understanding. Dao once missed temple chants without karmic punishment; Elise noted neighbors unaffected despite their carefree choices. Sejal skipped rituals during illness, unharmed by cosmic repercussions. Junaid overslept through dawn prayers without heavenly reprimand, and Olamide observed harvests succeeding despite forgotten village rites.

Slowly, laughter replaced fear. Their beliefs didn't vanish; instead, they matured. Rituals became meaningful, guided by sincerity rather than dread. Through chance, they connected online, discovering shared experiences. Humor and openness blossomed as they exchanged stories, forming bonds over lighthearted admissions of perceived cosmic slip-ups. Soon, a digital group became a community, prompting a real-world retreat organized by Ashley ("NomadicAsh") along a serene coastal shore.

At this gathering, beneath the whispering winds and starlit skies, they shared heartfelt confessions and comedic revelations. Freed from oppressive anxiety, traditions felt profound yet flexible, ceremonies enriching yet gentle. Each morning and evening brought prayer, meditation, or small personal devotions, not driven by fear, but genuine reverence and joy. Together, they recognized that faith, spirituality, and cosmic awareness need not crush daily happiness.

Returning home, their changed perspectives influenced families and communities. Their newfound serenity became contagious. Elise gently adapted Haitian rituals with warmth; Junaid prayed with renewed sincerity, no longer enslaved by routine. Dao's humorous meditations drew curious city dwellers; Olamide's village ceremonies embraced joyful music and spontaneity, while Sejal's daily mantras resonated warmly among neighbors. They had discovered a profound truth: spirituality thrives when fear loosens its grip.

As months became years, each lived more deeply, authentically. Their online circle flourished, reminding each other regularly that life's essence lay beyond strict dogma. Stories of mistakes became shared jokes, reinforcing the message that any cosmic watchers might delight in humanity's genuine, flawed sincerity. Gradually, the oppressive chains of dread faded entirely, replaced by the quiet realization that existence offered infinite possibilities rather than fixed penalties.

Their new philosophy spread subtly, sparking curiosity among friends and strangers. When asked how they attained such peace, their answers varied yet harmonized, life was an expansive tapestry of experiences, not a rigid ledger of rights and wrongs. They laughed, lived gently, and pondered openly about cosmic mysteries without the paralyzing terror of missteps.

Their individual journeys merged into a collective understanding: existence itself is a grand experiment. Human life, fleeting yet precious, serves as the vessel for exploring deeper truths. Each soul, unique and vibrant, engages with conditions not of its choosing, cultural backgrounds, geographical origins, societal pressures, yet possesses the freedom to shape its responses. This profound realization turned fear into curiosity, dread into wonder, and anxiety into exploration.

Understanding that truths were relative and perspectives fluid allowed them to appreciate the delicate balance between certainty and openness. They recognized that each cultural viewpoint offered one angle of understanding, each interpretation revealing another facet of existence's immense tapestry. Their discussions embraced philosophical insights and scientific discoveries, each reinforcing the expansive nature of their newfound worldview.

Humanity, they mused, was still at the infancy of understanding this broader cosmic experiment. The soul, this enigmatic force animating every living being, was not merely confined to earthly biology but part of a vast, interwoven cosmic narrative. Energy never perished; it transformed, continuing beyond physical boundaries. From divine teachings about reincarnation and heavenly realms, through scientific principles of energy conservation, to pragmatic observations about continuous transformation, the message echoed clearly: life's essence was eternal and endlessly evolving.

This insight, exhilarating yet humbling, opened avenues of thought that reached beyond personal liberation into collective human destiny. The grand experiment was not simply personal growth but a collective evolution toward a more intelligent civilization. They pondered humanity's progression from primitive tribes to a species capable of mapping genomes, decoding quantum mysteries, and reaching into cosmic realms. Each technological breakthrough, each cultural shift, each philosophical advancement was another step toward becoming an advanced, Type II+ civilization capable of harnessing planetary and stellar energy.

The idea thrilled them, a civilization harnessing stars, managing planetary climates, mastering energy on unimaginable scales. Humanity stood on a precipice, capable of ascending toward remarkable intelligence, empathy, and understanding. Yet, as they recognized, becoming truly advanced involved more than technology; it required spiritual maturity, emotional intelligence, and deep philosophical reflection. Intelligence without empathy or spiritual awareness was incomplete, potentially destructive.

They envisioned future humans living harmoniously, driven by curiosity, creativity, and compassion rather than fear, dogma, or conflict. A Type II+ civilization would not merely wield enormous power; it would wield it responsibly, guided by wisdom nurtured over millennia. Humans might someday transcend current limitations, harnessing energy in ways that unlocked extraordinary potentials, not only technological wonders but profound ethical and spiritual insights, creating societies deeply attuned to cosmic harmony.

Each small step taken by their own lives, embracing humor, discarding fear, exploring faith without dogmatic constraints, felt like contributions to that future. They recognized their modest roles as threads woven into a much larger narrative. Humanity's collective journey toward becoming a Type II+ civilization was not guaranteed; it required deliberate, conscious effort toward empathy, wisdom, and cooperative harmony.

And so, their insights deepened into broader reflections. Perhaps the true measure of humanity's intelligence would ultimately rest not on technological marvels alone, but on our capacity to integrate spirituality, empathy, reason, and pragmatism into a coherent worldview. Each soul contributed uniquely to the cosmic experiment, shaping outcomes through daily choices, small acts of kindness, and thoughtful introspection.

They understood profoundly that no single version of truth held absolute supremacy. Each human, shaped by experiences and environments, offered a distinct vantage, enriching collective wisdom. They respected the diverse tapestry of human beliefs, knowing that every perspective, like the blind men exploring an elephant, captured only partial truths.

In their daily lives, now infused with deeper purpose and calm, they pursued creativity, kindness, and curiosity, embodying principles of empathy and open-mindedness. Each life became a testament to the profound, joyful experiment of conscious existence.

As their understanding expanded, the question shifted away from anxiety about afterlife correctness toward a more pressing, inspiring inquiry. The mysteries of existence, vast and infinite, would remain subjects of contemplation, speculation, and discovery. Yet, one crucial question resonated clearly above all:

And so, the question is no longer which version of afterlife is correct. The question is: How shall we live in the meantime?

> *In a Universe built on energy, the greatest act of faith is to believe your spark matters*

CSI: Common Sense Investigation In Case Anyone Wonders Why Our Brain's on a Vacation Without Us

In our expansive journey through the sprawling corridors of human experience, we have glimpsed into rooms both familiar and mysterious, tracing pathways that illuminate our extraordinary quest for meaning in this infinite universe. With each step, each subtle turn of thought, humanity emerges not as a puzzle to be solved but as a grand symphony composed note by unpredictable note. Now, as we prepare to journey onward, we pause briefly not to dwell, but to remember the richness of what we have already encountered, weaving together fragments of past explorations like vivid memories that linger warmly before fading softly into our continued voyage.

Our reflection began with an honest confrontation with opinion itself, the paradoxical truth that while all viewpoints claim equal footing, some inevitably whisper louder, promising truths more enticing or convenient. From bustling cafés in Paris to street-side debates in Mumbai, we glimpsed humanity locked in perpetual, polite disagreement, forever propelled forward by precisely this friction. It became clear that opinions, valid or not, serve less as barriers and more as bridges toward collective progress, structures bending and flexing under the gentle weight of discourse.

From dialogue, we wandered into quietly profound sanctuaries of human union, discovering marriage as remarkable alchemy: a ritualistic blend of love, legacy, and legislation. We saw rings exchanged and vows whispered beneath canopies of stars or ceilings of law; bonds affirmed not merely by passion but also by the delicate social machinery designed to sustain human intimacy. We watched as diverse traditions danced gracefully around the core truth that companionship is perhaps humanity's most eloquent answer to the loneliness of infinite space.

Yet humanity's exploration did not linger solely in daylight. In quiet corridors after twilight, we felt the subtle pull of the unseen, those midnight whispers giving rise to ghost stories, folklore, and enduring beliefs. We stood beside those who found comfort in the shadows, whose imaginations illuminated dark spaces, reassuring us that not every phenomenon requires measurement or replication to be meaningful. The power of believing in things unseen reminded us of humanity's remarkable capacity to hold mystery gently, embracing ambiguity without fear.

As dawn broke once more, we confronted humanity's intriguing penchant for celestial scapegoating where distant Mercury, swirling gently through its retrograde waltz, bore unjust blame for daily inconveniences. In this innocent celestial scapegoating, we uncovered a charming, universal vulnerability: a yearning for absolution from responsibility, reflecting a deeply human desire to imagine our fates delicately strung between cosmic forces rather than solely our own hands. This tendency, endearing and peculiar, spoke quietly about how readily we assign order, even whimsical order to a universe otherwise unpredictable.

Shifting our gaze outward to the cosmos, we encountered visions of hypothetical beings from distant worlds, whose imagined lives posed humanity's earnest, playful questions: Do Martians envy our Wi-Fi or marvel at our messy existence? Such whimsical wonderings underscored humanity's perpetual curiosity our bold willingness to question the stars, imagining ourselves not isolated but part of an endless tapestry of intergalactic connection, shaped by the fragile yet wondrously persistent hope of cosmic kinship.

Returning to terrestrial experience, we observed humanity's increasingly digital parade a realm of filters, followers, and relentless fear of missing out. Each click, swipe, or share became a mirror reflecting deeper human anxieties, desires, and a ceaseless quest for connection and validation. We watched attentively as the digital landscape magnified human impulses, both virtuous and superficial, exposing the stark yet beautiful contradiction between our desire for genuine community and the alluring simplicity of virtual approval.

Amid modern existence's whirlwind came the sanctity and frenzy of holidays, moments when humanity transformed rest into festivals of frantic generosity occasions ripe with tradition yet equally heavy with expectation. We smiled gently at the quiet irony that cherished gatherings, meant to soothe the soul, often found us tangled in ribbons and rushing through rituals. Yet beneath layers of commercialism lay the undying glow of human warmth: humble generosity given freely; quiet joy of connection unmarred by expectation.

From traditions binding generations, we moved into crossroads where faith, science, and skepticism converged animated collisions of belief, disbelief, and empirical scrutiny. Even fierce debates among atheists, believers, and scientists ultimately revealed universal longings for coherence, anchoring ourselves amid existence's mysteries. Rather than divisions, we discovered surprising unity, revealing humanity's stubborn pursuit of meaning beyond mere physical experience.

Venturing next into structured classrooms, we witnessed humanity's ongoing battle to protect creativity against standardized measurement. Our gaze lingered with empathy upon students whose futures rested precariously on sharpened pencils, evaluation forms, and circled answers. Here, reflections grew somber but determined, reminding us that while knowledge can be quantified, human ingenuity and imagination remain resistant to scoring, forever free from absolute evaluation.

Finally, our flashback brought us gently to contemplating life's deeper ledger, the echoes left by deeds long after actors depart the stage. Cultures globally insistently teach that each action whispered kindness or careless cruelty carries significance far beyond visible moments. Deeds, we realized, were humanity's quiet fingerprints on infinity, transcending mortal bounds, nudging the cosmos toward brighter or darker horizons, reminding us that the universe listens closely, recording echoes we ourselves might never fully perceive.

As reflections draw toward closure, a profound truth crystallizes: every facet of human experience: opinion, partnership, superstition, skepticism, tradition, innovation which reveals an intricate dance of free will and circumstance. Clearly emerging from our exploration is the reassuring and beautiful complexity of human life albeit never perfect, rarely predictable, yet always remarkable. Each moment, each decision, ripples outward, affirming humanity's quiet courage to keep stepping into the unknown, shaping existence with choices holding gentle powers of creation itself.

Now, as memories softly recede, we stand poised to continue ready to delve deeper into the curious phenomenon of our thought processes. We move forward unburdened by heavy truths, buoyed gently by insight and imagination, reassured that life, for all its mystery, grants us room to breathe, explore, and gently reinvent. Ahead lies fresh inquiry, illuminated by gentle realization that life, though profound, need never be unbearably heavy.

As humanity continues this grand experiment, striving toward becoming an advanced, intelligent civilization, a Type II+ capable of harnessing planetary and stellar energies, our narrative expands exponentially. Each thoughtful step, each courageous inquiry, and every mindful reflection brings us closer to realizing our vast potential. The cosmic journey calls upon humanity not merely to accumulate technological prowess but to deepen moral wisdom, empathy, and cooperative spirit.

We stand at the threshold of extraordinary possibility, ready to craft civilizations capable of managing planetary climates, harnessing solar energy, and expanding beyond Earth's cradle. Yet the path forward relies fundamentally upon nurturing intellectual discipline, ethical clarity, and emotional maturity. Each choice we make individually contributes to collective ascension toward cosmic maturity.

Ultimately, humanity's destiny rests not solely in technological advancement but in our capacity for thoughtful, compassionate coexistence. In recognizing this, the central question of our existence shifts profoundly:

And so the question is: *How shall we live in the Meantime?*

> *The greatness of humanity lies not in flawless perfection but in the quiet courage of reasoned imperfection; not in unquestioned dominance, but in disciplined freedom; and not in the loud proclamations of certainty, but in the humble, persistent quest for deeper truths. In every gentle question courageously pursued, humanity's future softly whispers, 'I am possible*

Chapter 6: Convergence at Infinity: Humanity's Journey from Paradox to Cosmic Understanding

Human life, in its essence, unfolds as a tapestry of inherited choices and patterns, woven by threads passed down through generations. From the earliest moments, a child observes and absorbs the textures of the lives surrounding them careers, struggles, values, and ambitions. They see the contours of their parents' journeys, understanding intimately the trials their elders face, whether through admiration or resentment. A child born into a physician's home witnesses firsthand the exhausting cycles of dedication, selflessness, stress, and achievement that define the healer's existence. They either internalize this path as comfortable and familiar, willingly stepping into its well-worn footprints, or they recoil from it, actively rebelling against an inherited fate. Yet, in both acceptance and rejection, their decision remains tethered not to an independent exploration but to an external narrative already written.

Throughout humanity's tenure on this cosmic research station called Earth, individuals often gravitate toward these familiar orbits seeking certainty and comfort in recognizable experiences. The pragmatic safety of the "*well-trodden path*" guides many to repeat the journeys of their forebears, seldom daring to question the boundaries drawn by prior generations. This repetition creates a society that, while stable, can become constrained and unimaginative. We become so conditioned by these familiar trails that we mistake comfort for purpose, repetition for destiny, and conformity for fulfillment.

Yet, the profound paradox of human existence the true heartbeat of the cosmic experiment lies precisely in stepping beyond this familiar terrain, beyond the predictable scripts handed down from the past. As Robert Frost eloquently proposed, choosing the path less traveled unlocks an unexplored dimension of self-discovery, courage, and authenticity. It is precisely this divergence from the comfortable, the safe, and the prescribed that ignites the spark of genuine self-awareness, unveiling the deeper truths of our being.

When individuals dare to question the narratives imposed upon them whether by familial expectation, societal conditioning, or cultural tradition they begin to unearth the hidden depths of their own souls. The choice to venture into the unknown, though daunting, is the birthplace of genuine purpose and creativity. The path less traveled, marked by uncertainty and challenge, provides the richest soil for growth, revealing strengths and insights that would remain undiscovered along safer routes.

This conscious divergence catalyzes the awakening of a more profound spiritual consciousness and an awakening not constrained by previously established roles or external expectations. Rather, it is the conscious embracing of free will, the deliberate stepping into uncertainty, that allows us to glimpse the full spectrum of human potential. The courage required to undertake such a journey brings us closer to understanding our role within the universe, aligning human experience with the soul's deeper, more expansive purpose.

Moreover, when humanity collectively acknowledges the necessity of this daring exploration, societal consciousness itself shifts. Innovations emerge, compassion deepens, and understanding expands, transforming the human narrative from one of repetition into one of continuous evolution and exploration. As humanity increasingly embraces uncertainty and individuality, we collectively discover our ability to transcend previously accepted limitations, stepping forward into new realms of thought, creativity, and spiritual awareness.

Ultimately, it is precisely this willingness to take the uncharted path, to break free from familiar patterns, that embodies humanity's truest purpose within the grand cosmic experiment. For in the unknown lies the key to understanding not just who we are, but who we might become.

Humanity often romanticizes the notion of originality, perceiving it as a solitary quest requiring complete independence from all previously known paths. Yet, in the cosmic experiment of life on Earth, true progress is not measured by originality alone, but rather by the effective and inspired application of existing wisdom. The measure of an experiment's success, after all, lies not in its isolation or novelty, but in its profound capacity to leverage existing knowledge towards higher understanding and meaningful innovation. This truth resonates deeply within the fabric of the universe itself, where knowledge flows ceaselessly, free and accessible to any consciousness attuned to its currents.

Each human life, therefore, is less about forging an entirely uncharted course and more about creatively synthesizing lessons from diverse sources of insight. Humanity stands as a collective heir to an immense library of wisdom accumulated across time and space a universal repository that transcends cultures, generations, and civilizations. Scientists, artists, thinkers, and visionaries have always built upon foundations laid by their predecessors, weaving threads from past discoveries and reflections into new and beautiful tapestries of understanding. Even history's greatest breakthroughs from Einstein's theories of relativity, which drew from the intuitive speculations of earlier thinkers, to Shakespeare's timeless narratives built upon the archetypes established by ancient Greek tragedies have never been purely original. Rather, they emerged from inspiration drawn from the inexhaustible wellspring of universal consciousness.

Knowledge, in its very essence, exists as an energetic river coursing through the cosmos, ever-present and accessible to those willing to listen, observe, and connect. The great insights and inspirations that shaped human civilization have consistently arisen when individuals quieted their egos and opened their minds to these universal currents, allowing intuition and inspiration to flow freely. The genius, therefore, is not the solitary architect of wholly unprecedented thoughts, but rather the adept interpreter who harmonizes inherited wisdom into new, purposeful visions.

Human consciousness itself functions like a vast antenna tuned to the frequencies of this universal knowledge. The flashes of inspiration experienced by individuals from poets and philosophers to innovators and inventors are not isolated occurrences but glimpses into the infinite reservoir of consciousness. It is by quieting our internal voices and attuning ourselves to this broader field of awareness that we become conduits for profound insights. The task, then, is less about striving to be uniquely original and more about becoming skillful receptors, interpreters, and amplifiers of the boundless intelligence that permeates our universe.

This approach does not diminish individual contribution; rather, it amplifies humanity's capacity to innovate and evolve. When we understand originality as a collective, interconnected phenomenon where knowledge freely flows across minds and boundaries innovation becomes more dynamic and inclusive. Society moves forward most effectively not by isolated leaps but by interconnected progress, built upon collaboration, adaptation, and the generous exchange of ideas. Recognizing and embracing this collective inheritance fosters humility, curiosity, and a shared commitment to discovery, reinforcing our interconnectedness rather than isolating us in futile pursuit of absolute originality.

In the grand cosmic experiment of life, true advancement comes not from absolute originality, but from inspired synthesis drawing strength from universal wisdom, learning from diverse experiences, and creatively reimagining existing paths to form new avenues toward enlightenment. Ultimately, it is this free-flowing exchange of knowledge and inspiration, accessible to all willing hearts and open minds, that propels humanity toward a richer, more profound understanding of its cosmic purpose.

Chapter 6: Convergence at Infinity: Humanity's Journey from Paradox to Cosmic Understanding

Grief and suffering punctuate existence as profoundly as joy and triumph, marking our lives with inevitable moments of darkness. While grief is natural, a timeless echo of love and loss etched deeply into our hearts, suffering emerges differently it manifests as a perception, a state of mind that we have the capacity to navigate and transcend. To understand this distinction, consider the analogy of two balloons: one filled with air, the other with water. Both appear similar, yet their reactions when exposed to flame are fundamentally different. The balloon filled with air, lacking substance, quickly succumbs and bursts under pressure. The balloon filled with water, however, withstands the flame, absorbing and diffusing heat through its substantial core.

In this analogy lies a profound lesson. The air and water represent the substance or lack thereof in our lives. A life without substance one that lacks skills, wisdom from teachers, guidance from parents, or the rich nourishment of a robust value system is fragile, quickly overwhelmed by adversity. It collapses at the first encounter with suffering, losing the opportunity for meaningful transformation. However, a life brimming with substance, filled with experience, compassion, knowledge, and resilient values, absorbs life's inevitable challenges, transforming pain into growth. This substance becomes a profound source of inspiration and originality, enabling individuals to perceive suffering not as permanent affliction, but as a powerful catalyst toward self-discovery.

Yet, there comes a point when both balloons, irrespective of their contents, confront their ultimate fate. Prick either balloon with a pin, and both will burst instantly. This stark realization reflects an undeniable truth about our human existence: life, in all its intricate and beautiful complexity, is finite. Each of us is given a limited amount of time to participate in the grand cosmic experiment. The inevitability of life's end underscores the importance of how we choose to live each moment we are given.

Suffering, viewed through this lens, transforms from a permanent burden into a transient state that can be overcome through purposeful living. Our capacity to endure and overcome suffering, to harness its transformative potential, depends profoundly on the depth and quality of the substance within us the wisdom we accumulate, the values we uphold, the experiences we cherish, and the connections we foster. This substance allows us to reinterpret our narrative from victimhood to strength, from passivity to empowerment, and from despair to hope.

Therefore, the secret of thriving within the grand experiment lies not in an attempt to avoid grief and suffering, but in cultivating our inner substance so richly and meaningfully that even adversity becomes an opportunity for profound inspiration. By embracing this understanding, we recognize that our brief sojourn within the universe offers the extraordinary potential to live fully, creatively, and purposefully, transforming suffering into a pathway toward deeper cosmic understanding and authentic personal enlightenment.

The profound realization of life's finite nature compels us inevitably toward questions about why we find ourselves immersed in states of grief or joy, struggle or triumph. Often, individuals seek to attribute

Chapter 6: Convergence at Infinity: Humanity's Journey from Paradox to Cosmic Understanding

such conditions to external authors, whether a divine entity, fate, or sheer randomness, presupposing that our journey through life may already be predetermined. Yet, the truth might lie beyond simplistic causalities. When we identify our existence as residing within a "*state*," we implicitly regard this state as something fixed, tangible, and immutable. In reality, however, these states are never absolute; they shift constantly according to the lens through which we perceive them. Our reality, as complex and multifaceted as it appears, is intimately tied to our observation, our consciousness, our interpretation of experiences.

Consider the famous thought experiment of Schrödinger's cat, encapsulating this very paradox. A cat enclosed within a sealed box, subject to a quantum event, remains simultaneously alive and dead until observed. This apparent contradiction seems impossible within our conventional understanding of reality, yet it highlights a fundamental truth about existence: the act of observation itself shapes reality. The cat's state remains indefinite, neither dead nor alive, until someone looks inside only at that precise moment of observation and does one reality crystalize, collapsing from infinite possibilities into a singular truth. Similarly, our experience of life's emotional spectrum happiness, grief, contentment, or suffering depends entirely upon our viewpoint, our internal framing, our interpretation.

The universe, in all its vastness and complexity, emerges as something akin to a mirage: not an illusion devoid of substance, but a canvas upon which our consciousness projects its perceptions. What we choose to focus upon becomes our reality, constructing the parameters of our own existence. Grief and suffering, in this light, no longer emerge as fixed external impositions, but rather as fluid experiences, shaped significantly by our internal narrative. Suffering, in particular, shifts according to the observer's context and perspective. To a family living comfortably yet modestly, suffering might manifest as envy or inadequacy when compared to the opulence of their wealthy counterparts. Yet, from another angle, that same modesty is abundance food, shelter, security, and education, each a foundation upon which inspiration and creativity can flourish.

Thus, what truly distinguishes one's place in the grand experiment of life whether one finds themselves amongst the majority, the ninety-nine percent, or amongst the rarefied one percent is how consciously they choose to observe and interpret their circumstances. This choice, more than external conditions or predetermined destinies, shapes each individual's trajectory through existence. The ability to recognize opportunities amid apparent scarcity, to transform challenges into meaningful insights, and to perceive abundance where others see only lack, defines success within the cosmic experiment.

Ultimately, it is our interpretive stance toward life's myriad conditions grief and joy, triumph and tribulation that truly defines our reality. The universe is not simply a static backdrop upon which we enact predetermined scripts; it is a dynamic, responsive field shaped by consciousness and perception. Recognizing this truth empowers individuals, transcending passive fatalism and fostering active engagement with life's infinite possibilities. By choosing consciously

Chapter 6: Convergence at Infinity: Humanity's Journey from Paradox to Cosmic Understanding

how we perceive, interpret, and engage with the state we inhabit, we wield the profound power to sculpt our own reality, redefining grief, overcoming suffering, and unlocking the boundless potential that exists within every moment of human experience.

As we recognize our profound power to shape reality through observation and interpretation, we must also acknowledge the paradoxical nature of the universe itself: it is both infinite and limited. Opportunities for inspiration and originality abound endlessly yet coexist alongside undeniable constraints imposed from the moment of birth. Indeed, the universe is neither singular nor strictly dualistic and it flourishes within multiplicity, where infinite potential interacts dynamically with finite boundaries. Each soul entering the grand cosmic experiment encounters predetermined elements: the family into which one is born, the name bestowed, cultural heritage, socioeconomic status, and geographical location. These factors serve as initial conditions, shaping our early experiences and defining the limits within which we begin our journey.

Yet, the profound beauty and challenge of existence lies precisely in our capacity for free will the innate human power to transcend constraints and consciously pursue the infinite. While our starting conditions frame life's initial boundaries, they do not irreversibly dictate destiny. Rather, each soul is equipped with an intrinsic power to move beyond imposed limitations, redefine realities, and expand their horizons beyond the constraints of circumstance. Unfortunately, many overlook this potent capacity, allowing their lives to be guided entirely by external observations and the

Chapter 6: Convergence at Infinity: Humanity's Journey from Paradox to Cosmic Understanding

interpretations of others. In doing so, they unknowingly surrender their agency, dimming the flame of their intrinsic potential.

To harness the full power of the soul, individuals must recognize the distinction between blind adherence and genuine learning. A truly inspired student is not one who passively absorbs teachings, but rather one who actively engages, questions, synthesizes, and internalizes wisdom to forge an authentic, independent value system. This dynamic, creative engagement places the soul firmly within the exceptional 1% of participants in the grand experiment those who transform the finite constraints of existence into infinite possibilities.

Artificial Intelligence (AI) exemplifies this tension between perception shaped by others and independent exploration. AI possesses extraordinary potential to propel humanity exponentially closer to becoming a truly intelligent civilization capable of extraordinary scientific, cultural, and philosophical breakthroughs. However, popular culture and dramatic storytelling often frame AI through dystopian lenses, crafting cautionary tales of robots running amok or technology overtaking humanity. These fictional portrayals, while captivating, influence collective perception and stifle genuine exploration, much like Schrödinger's cat paradoxically obscured from view. Just as we cannot ascertain the cat's actual state until we look within the box, humanity cannot fully comprehend the transformative potential of AI until we actively, deliberately engage with its possibilities firsthand.

Thus, the critical challenge for each soul in this cosmic experiment is not merely to acknowledge free will, but to courageously exercise it.

Breaking away from predetermined interpretations, stepping beyond the shadows of external expectations, and exploring paths others may fear are necessary acts for transcending limitations. Each soul must recognize its agency as the active creator and curator of its own reality, navigating between finite boundaries and infinite potential. It is through this courageous exploration this purposeful exercise of free will that individuals ultimately realize their unique capacity for inspiration and originality. By consciously stepping into unknown territories, whether in the personal sphere or collectively as a civilization embracing AI, humans move closer toward fulfilling their true purpose within the grand experiment, transforming constraints into catalysts for boundless innovation and profound cosmic understanding.

The universe, in its inherent duality of finite and infinite possibilities, continuously oscillates in a dynamic state of chaos. Far from representing a destructive force, chaos serves as a fertile ground from which creation emerges. Nothing profound or transformational ever arises from absolute stillness; indeed, construction and innovation demand a certain disorder an energetic unrest that fosters evolution. The very essence of the grand cosmic experiment in which we partake is rooted within this chaos. Humans, often seeking comfort and clarity, instinctively lean on observations our own and those of others as anchors amid uncertainty. But herein lies a critical paradox: observations, by their nature, are finite snapshots mistaken as absolute truths. Within an ever-changing chaotic cosmos, no perpetual order exists, and thus, no absolute truth endures.

To truly navigate and understand this cosmic chaos, we must dare to transcend mere observation and venture boldly into the realm of imagination. Observations set boundaries, delineating clearly between what we perceive as possible and impossible. But imagination, unbound and uninhibited, transcends these artificial borders, illuminating paths previously hidden. Imagination invites us into realms where conventional logic and observational evidence hold no jurisdiction. By severing the restrictive ties between imagination and observation, humanity accesses the power to visualize possibilities that lie beyond current understanding.

Even Einstein, whose scientific rigor reshaped humanity's comprehension of reality, exemplifies this principle vividly. His groundbreaking theory of General Relativity which profoundly transformed the way we understand gravity, space, and time was not conceived purely through meticulous observation, but rather through radical acts of imagination. Einstein dared to hypothesize scenarios that directly contradicted observable experience. By imagining the sun absent, Einstein liberated his thought experiments from observational constraints, enabling him to theorize gravitational effects and spacetime curvature concepts that would have remained unreachable if confined solely to observable phenomena. Indeed, the very essence of General Relativity required Einstein to envision realities beyond what sensory data permitted, thereby unraveling a deeper cosmic truth inaccessible through observation alone.

Similarly, each soul's journey within the grand cosmic experiment requires a parallel leap of imagination. Relying solely on personal or collective observations restricts us, anchoring our perception of the universe to predetermined interpretations. Yet when we embrace imagination, unshackled from observation, we unlock the potential to create order from chaos, extracting meaning and purpose from infinite uncertainty. Our universe thrives not in strict determinism nor in utter randomness, but in the dynamic interplay of both an *"ordered chaos,"* wherein our creative imagination becomes our most potent tool for understanding and evolving.

Thus, humanity's role within the cosmic experiment is not merely to observe, record, and repeat existing truths, but to boldly imagine new possibilities that defy conventional wisdom. It is precisely through this imaginative courage stepping beyond observable evidence that humans transform chaos into purposeful innovation. In doing so, we bridge finite limitations with infinite potential, discovering deeper meanings hidden within the universe's restless, chaotic dance.

To grasp the chaotic essence of the universe and resolve profound existential enigmas such as the Fermi paradox, we must relinquish our dependence on conventional observation and embrace imagination fully. Traditional definitions of life have constrained our understanding, tethering existence strictly to the human biological form. Humans, as biological beings, are composed of elements specifically abundant and harmonious with Earth's unique environment carbon, hydrogen, oxygen, nitrogen elements enabling our physical adaptability to conditions prevalent on this planet. Yet, imagine if the cosmic experiment is not exclusive to Earth. Imagine the experiment unfolds simultaneously in vastly different environments, such as the caustic atmosphere of Venus, a planet enveloped in crushing pressures, searing temperatures, and acidic clouds inhospitable to the human form.

If our essence the soul, energy, or consciousness were transported to Venus, it would inevitably adapt, manifesting in a form radically distinct from the carbon-based biology familiar to us. Life, therefore, transcends the narrow confines of our corporeal form; the human body represents merely a temporary vessel, enabling souls to partake in Earth's grand cosmic experiment. To claim life cannot exist on Venus or elsewhere because the human form cannot survive there betrays profound anthropocentric bias. Such assertions expose limitations not of universal potential, but rather of human perception bound within sensory constraints inherently finite and exceedingly narrow.

Human senses, despite their apparent richness, perceive only minuscule fragments of the universe's vast spectrum. Our eyes detect just a fraction of electromagnetic waves; our ears discern only a narrow slice of sound frequencies. Thus, our proclaimed reality is merely a shadow cast by the limited capacities of our sensory apparatus. It follows that the Fermi paradox asking, "*If life exists elsewhere, where is it?*" is fundamentally flawed. Instead, the genuine paradox should compel introspection: "If life exists in myriad forms beyond our comprehension, why are human senses unable to detect it?"

This reframed paradox challenges humanity's instinctive assumption that the finite capabilities and fleeting duration of human existence represent universal absolutes. Our propensity to elevate the limitations of our physical senses into immutable truths hinders our capacity for imagination and insight, effectively blinding us to alternative forms of existence. The universe, infinitely diverse in its manifestations, does not conform to the narrow parameters set by humanity's transient observations. It thrives far beyond these limitations, encompassing possibilities that elude the grasp of our current observational methodologies.

Recognizing this prompts profound humility, inviting humanity to transcend narrow perceptual constraints through creative imagination and intellectual openness. Only by expanding our imaginative horizons beyond observable data, embracing the infinite diversity of life's potential forms, can humanity truly approach the deeper truths of the cosmos. Embracing imagination unbounded by finite perceptions enables the exploration of existential mysteries, offering insights beyond current comprehension. It is precisely through such imaginative exploration free from sensory constraints that humanity may someday unravel the true nature of life, consciousness, and existence, thus transforming chaos into meaningful cosmic understanding.

Humanity's intellectual advancement has undoubtedly accelerated exponentially, yet a subtle paradox remains deeply entrenched in our understanding of progress. We tend to interpret each era's pinnacle of human achievement as perpetual, absolute truth. This habit emerges naturally from our inclination toward order and stability. Yet, the universe dynamic, vast, and perpetually evolving exists not in stillness, but in continuous chaos. True progressive intelligence, therefore, demands that we constantly question and surpass conventional wisdom, persistently imagining new possibilities beyond observable reality.

Chaos inherently defies conventional approaches. When existing solutions falter, we cannot rely solely on what is already observed or known. Instead, imagination must lead the way, inventing new methodologies unconstrained by past experiences or conventional limitations. Consider, for instance, the humble bumblebee. Its body, seemingly ill-suited for flight due to its non-aerodynamic shape, defies classical aerodynamic theories. Traditional physics would assert that such a creature is incapable of flight. Yet, the bumblebee thrives precisely because nature unbound by human theories has imagined and adapted alternative solutions. Bumblebees compensate for their aerodynamic shortcomings with rapid wingbeats, creating powerful vortices and generating sufficient lift, allowing them to fly despite theoretical impossibilities.

Such examples illustrate vividly that the universe itself engages continually in imaginative adaptation. Chaos fuels this creativity, serving as the birthplace of novel approaches and unconventional solutions. Yet, humanity often fails to recognize this intrinsic connection, perceiving chaos merely as disorder rather than potential. Moreover, we frequently overlook how deeply interconnected the universe truly is how every minute action reverberates through an intricate web of consequences, encapsulated elegantly in the concept known as the butterfly effect.

Chapter 6: Convergence at Infinity: Humanity's Journey from Paradox to Cosmic Understanding

Consider the subtle yet profound example drawn from human history: during World War I, Adolf Hitler, then merely a young soldier, was wounded in battle and reportedly spared by a British soldier who chose mercy over lethal force. Had Hitler not survived this encounter, the cascade of events that led to World War II might never have unfolded in the manner history records. This incident starkly illustrates the delicate interplay between order and chaos, demonstrating clearly that they are neither isolated nor mutually exclusive but deeply intertwined forces continuously shaping reality.

Thus, order does not emerge independently or spontaneously; it is intricately woven from threads of chaos, imagination, and adaptation. Within the grand cosmic experiment Earth our souls, housed temporarily in human vessels, navigate this complex interplay. The very essence of our existence lies in our capacity to face chaos, to imagine beyond observable reality, and thereby to create new forms of order and meaning. This iterative process is both humanity's challenge and privilege, defining our collective journey toward deeper cosmic understanding and enlightenment. Recognizing that chaos and order coexist symbiotically empowers us to perceive reality not as rigid and finite, but as flexible, boundlessly creative, and perpetually ripe with infinite possibility.

At the core of human insecurities lies a deep-rooted fear the fear of losing the perpetual absolute truths we painstakingly construct. These perceived truths, comforting in their supposed permanence, become like monarchs reigning over our consciousness. Yet history repeatedly shows that every monarch, no matter how powerful or long-lived, must eventually yield to time and circumstance. There was always a monarch before, and inevitably, there will be one after. Similarly, the absolute truths we cling to ideologies, paradigms, and orders are temporary constructs in an eternal sea of chaos. Chaos, paradoxically, remains constant, unwavering, and permanent; it is order, in fact, that emerges temporarily, a fleeting sovereign amidst perpetual turbulence.

The emotional turmoil humans experience often stems precisely from this relentless interplay between ephemeral order and enduring chaos. Individuals struggle profoundly to reconcile their innate desire for permanence with the undeniable impermanence of everything they hold true. Yet herein lies the ultimate challenge and profound opportunity of the grand cosmic experiment. Just as chaos dismantles one monarch only to give rise to another, humanity too must learn to adapt, transform, and heal from the disruptions chaos imposes. True healing is neither avoidance nor mere coping; it is a transformative process where disorder is accepted, embraced, and ultimately re-imagined into new forms of order and meaning.

This transcendent process echoes Maslow's profound concept of self-actualization the pinnacle of psychological health and human potential. Achieving such a state demands more than mere observational understanding, as observation alone emphasizes grief, loss, and limitation. Observations anchor humans in past experiences, often highlighting their pain and obscuring the potential pathways toward genuine healing and transformation. To rise above these constraints, individuals must courageously transcend observation, tapping deeply into imaginative faculties that can envision solutions previously unseen or thought impossible.

Self-actualization this healing and liberation from the confines of convention is what distinguishes the rare few who ascend into the coveted 1%, from the many who remain within the constraints of the 99%. The truly self-actualized are those who bravely challenge conventional wisdom, who look beyond existing knowledge and, in doing so, discover deeper, richer meanings within chaos. Their healing is profound, marked not simply by recovery from pain, but by the transformation of that pain into creativity, innovation, empathy, and wisdom.

To achieve such transcendence, humanity must shift fundamentally from reliance on finite observational truths toward courageous exploration of infinite imaginative possibilities. Only then can souls participating in this grand cosmic experiment fulfill their highest purpose finding genuine meaning and authentic healing amid universal chaos. This profound journey requires a departure from accepted truths, a willingness to risk uncertainty, and a commitment to imagine new realities. When human consciousness embraces imagination over convention, it aligns harmoniously with the universal rhythm, transforming chaos from an intimidating adversary into a powerful catalyst for growth, insight, and the deepest realization of cosmic purpose.

The complexities of chaos and disorder that permeate the universe, as we have explored, are mirrored vividly in humanity's continuous struggle to interpret and navigate existence. Within the intricate tapestry of human life, our understanding is primarily guided by three fundamental systems: Divinity, Science, and Pragmatism. These value systems are not isolated realms of knowledge, but rather intertwined dimensions, each providing a unique lens through which we perceive reality. Yet, paradoxically, humanity tends to rely excessively on conventional wisdom and observation, neglecting the profound potential of imagination. Only through imaginative insight can we begin to fully comprehend how these seemingly divergent value systems interconnect to provide guidance amid the cosmic chaos.

Divinity is often regarded as the oldest interpretative framework humanity has leveraged. Rooted deeply within our existential psyche, divinity provides moral direction and purpose, offering a higher order meaning to existence. It serves as humanity's emotional and ethical compass, proposing that there is more to existence than mere randomness. Religious and spiritual texts, have historically provided moral frameworks inspiring profound human achievement and introspection. However, humans often limit their divine comprehension to literal, observable manifestations, failing to recognize deeper metaphorical and imaginative layers. Divinity, at its purest, demands imagination to interpret its infinite meanings beyond the restrictive boundaries of observational dogma.

Science, conversely, appears methodical and rigorously empirical. Its core strength lies in controlled observation and replicable experimentation, revealing universal laws and patterns. The scientific method has propelled humanity forward, equipping us with profound tools from harnessing electricity to decoding genetic sequences. Yet

Chapter 6: Convergence at Infinity: Humanity's Journey from Paradox to Cosmic Understanding

even science finds its greatest breakthroughs not merely in observation but in imaginative leaps. Einstein's theory of General Relativity and quantum mechanics challenged conventional wisdom not through observable evidence alone, but through bold thought experiments and creative imagination that envisioned new frameworks for reality.

Pragmatism acts as the critical mediator between Divinity and Science, insisting upon practicality and immediate utility. It anchors grand moral ideals and complex scientific theories within the realm of daily human experience, ensuring abstract concepts yield tangible benefits. Pragmatism, deeply reliant on sensory experience and observable proof, often appears resistant to imaginative explorations beyond immediate reality. Yet its fundamental strength its demand for proof need not exclude imagination; rather, it can serve as a powerful check ensuring imaginative pursuits remain grounded in authentic, experiential validation.

Together, these three value systems Divinity, Science, and Pragmatism form a three-dimensional framework through which human souls interpret their existence within the chaos of the universe. Each provides a necessary facet of understanding. Divinity offers meaning, Science reveals mechanism, and Pragmatism ensures relevance. Humanity, however, tends to confine itself within conventional observational boundaries, frequently ignoring the essential imaginative synthesis required to fully leverage this multidimensional understanding.

Consider humanity's historical interpretation of these value systems. Divinity was long held distinct from Science and Pragmatism, isolated by dogmatic rigidity. Over time, intersections grew, forming what is now seen as interlocking domains. Like a prism refracting a single beam of light into diverse colors, these systems may merely reflect different aspects of one overarching truth, shaped by perception and interpretation rather than by fundamental contradictions. Thus, the imagined boundary between these frameworks dissolves when examined through imaginative insight, revealing an interconnected and complementary reality.

To understand and navigate the chaos inherent in the universe, humans must therefore embrace imagination as an essential interpretive tool. Our observational faculties bound by limited sensory perception capture merely fragments of an infinitely complex reality. By relying solely on conventional wisdom derived from observation, humanity risks stagnation. The challenge and opportunity lie in transcending these limitations, actively imagining possibilities beyond sensory constraints. As Einstein himself exemplified through thought experiments, imagination becomes humanity's primary means of progressing toward deeper truths.

The reluctance to move beyond conventional wisdom rooted in observational comfort is precisely why humanity struggles with existential questions and fails to achieve genuine self-actualization. Observational understanding often amplifies grief, loss, and suffering by emphasizing limitation and finite constraints. In contrast, imagination allows individuals to see potential beyond immediate circumstance, transforming suffering into profound growth opportunities. Maslow's concept of self-actualization aligns closely with this imaginative journey individuals who break free from conventional frameworks and integrate divinity's purpose, science's mechanisms, and pragmatism's utility in an imaginative synergy rise into the coveted 1% of human souls achieving profound existential harmony.

Yet humanity frequently misunderstands the role of these three dimensions, perceiving them as isolated or antagonistic rather than interconnected. When divinity's moral clarity, science's empirical rigor, and pragmatism's operational realism harmonize through imagination, a profound existential order emerges. This imaginative synthesis does not dismiss observation but transcends it, acknowledging its limitations and extending human understanding into realms previously inaccessible.

The universe, in perpetual chaos, provides infinite opportunities for imaginative exploration. Human souls are participants in an ongoing cosmic experiment, challenged to continuously reimagine order from disorder. The greatest civilizations and breakthroughs whether moral, scientific, or practical emerge not merely from careful observation, but from the imaginative capacity to envision and pursue unprecedented possibilities. The complex interplay of chaos and order demands imaginative interpretation, blending divinity's visionary ideals, science's methodological precision, and pragmatism's grounded applicability into a cohesive, multidimensional approach.

Ultimately, humanity's journey through cosmic chaos represents a profound opportunity for imaginative self-discovery and self-actualization. Each soul, navigating finite constraints and infinite potentials, holds the inherent power to transform chaos into meaningful existential order. To accomplish this, humanity must courageously imagine beyond conventional wisdom, embracing imagination as the primary interpretive lens through which divinity's purpose, science's mechanisms, and pragmatism's practicalities harmonize.

The Antarctica Protocol itself serves as an apt metaphor for this imaginative integration. Scientists collaborating at Earth's polar extremes blend visionary purpose (divinity), empirical methods (science), and practical operations (pragmatism) seamlessly. Their harmonious cooperation embodies precisely the imaginative synthesis humanity needs to embrace universally. If Earth's cosmic observers indeed exist, their profound interest would lie not merely in our technological prowess or moral philosophies, but in humanity's imaginative capacity to transcend observational constraints and transform chaos into meaningful order.

The essential task for human souls participating in this grand cosmic experiment lies in recognizing and embracing the powerful imaginative synthesis of divinity, science, and pragmatism. By courageously exploring realities beyond conventional observational wisdom, humanity unlocks profound existential truths, advancing collectively toward genuine self-actualization. Through imagination, the apparent chaos of the universe transforms into a purposeful, comprehensible, and profoundly meaningful order.

In contemplating the profound dynamics of chaos and order, we arrive inevitably at the realization that the universe, in all its apparent randomness, is meticulously designed. Chaos, often perceived as disorderly or disruptive, is in truth an intricate architecture intentionally woven into the fabric of existence itself. Within this grand cosmic arrangement, the universe sets definitive boundaries constraints that render all things finite. Nothing within our observable reality transcends these immutable limits; everything is inherently temporary, ephemeral, and bound by conditions of finitude.

Consider human existence on Earth. From the moment a soul inhabits a human form, it is subject to inevitable temporal constraints. Our earthly journey is inherently limited, framed by birth and death, a finite passage through the relentless flow of cosmic time. Similarly, celestial entities, seemingly eternal by human standards, are equally bound by definitive lifespans. Stars, colossal reservoirs of cosmic energy and luminescence, inevitably exhaust their nuclear fuel. They collapse dramatically sometimes forming dense neutron stars, at other times spiraling inward with immense gravity to become black holes. The cycle of star formation and death underscores the universe's intrinsic pattern of finite existence.

Cosmic finitude extends further. Galaxies themselves, vast congregations of billions of stars, spiral majestically but are destined eventually to collide or disperse, merging into new structures or scattering into the cosmic void. Even the universe, as expansive and timeless as it appears, is thought to have had a beginning the Big Bang and, according to some theories, might eventually reach an end, either through a "*big freeze*" or cosmic dissipation into absolute entropy.

Moreover, one of the most profound cosmic constants exemplifying finite limitations is the speed of light, set precisely at approximately 299,792 kilometers per second. This limit impossibly fast from a human perspective yet rigidly constrained reveals a fundamental boundary governing how information and energy traverse the cosmos. Consider briefly the hypothetical scenario in which the speed of light were infinite. If light symbolizes energy, an infinite speed of light would imply infinite energy availability. Infinite energy, however appealing conceptually, poses catastrophic implications: if infinite energy were available, any attempt at creating order from chaos would necessitate the management of infinite forces. In practical terms, infinite energy would overwhelm and obliterate existing structures; order itself would collapse under boundless power, rendering the universe incapable of sustaining coherent, stable realities.

This elegantly clarifies the necessity for limits: cosmic constraints are not impediments but rather protective designs integral to maintaining coherence and stability within the cosmic experiment. Limits provide a structured context, enabling orderly transformations from chaos. Without finite boundaries, perpetual absolute truths would emerge, overshadowing novelty, creativity, and diversity. Perpetuity breeds stagnation: infinite absolute truths would render the cosmos static and lifeless, stripping existence itself of purpose and meaning.

From this vantage, existential dilemmas find resolution. Constraints, limits, and finite boundaries encountered by human souls and potentially entities in other cosmic realms are intentional designs, profound lessons embedded by the universe itself. Our challenges, hardships, and constraints do not represent universal cruelty; instead, they serve a vital cosmic purpose: they prevent the rise of absolute, infinite truths that could disrupt the balance of existence. Constraints encourage adaptability, imagination, and innovation, guiding conscious beings toward meaningful evolution rather than existential stagnation.

Thus, the chaos we observe is not merely random turmoil; it constitutes the core of the cosmic experiment deliberately designed to evaluate, provoke, inspire, and ultimately advance souls toward self-actualization. The human body itself is simply one vehicle among potentially countless others through which souls journey, confronting existential chaos, navigating it purposefully toward higher wisdom, insight, and understanding.

Our mission within this grand design becomes clear: we are travelers tasked with converting chaos into clarity, limitation into liberation, and constraint into creativity. Rather than lamenting our finite existence, we must celebrate it. Our finite experiences, emotions, intellect, and energies form the very foundations upon which genuine meaning and profound growth are constructed. The chaos of existence the perpetual flux, uncertainty, and complexity is the most profound educational laboratory the universe provides.

In accepting and embracing these cosmic constraints, we harmonize our existence with the universe's grand intention. Recognizing that limits exist to empower rather than oppress, we step courageously into uncertainty, imagining possibilities, constructing purposeful meaning, and striving toward authentic self-actualization. This realization elevates the human experience from mere survival to profound spiritual, intellectual, and emotional fulfillment.

Ultimately, humanity's greatest opportunity lies in recognizing the universe's intentional design of finite boundaries. Understanding and internalizing this truth equips us to navigate existential chaos with grace, resilience, and imagination. We become co-creators within the cosmic experiment, actively participating in the profound transformation of disorder into meaningful order.

In this conscious engagement with finite existence, we find our highest purpose. Each soul, on its unique journey, contributes to the collective evolution toward cosmic enlightenment transforming existential challenges into the profound beauty of self-realization.

As we embrace finitude and imagination alike, we honor the universe's grand intention transcending the limitations of conventional observation to uncover deeper truths hidden within chaos. Our existence, finite yet infinitely valuable, reflects the cosmic paradox: in limitation, we find boundless potential.

Chapter 6: Convergence at Infinity: Humanity's Journey from Paradox to Cosmic Understanding

For indeed, the greatest journey lies not in escaping constraints but in transcending them, not in denying chaos but in transforming it.

> *We are finite travelers within infinite possibilities, architects of meaning within cosmic constraints, turning chaos into purpose through imagination and courage*

Concepts Used in the Books

1. *Quantum Mechanics:* Quantum mechanics explores phenomena at atomic and subatomic levels, where particles behave unpredictably and exist in multiple states simultaneously until measured.

2. *Schrödinger's Cat:* A famous thought experiment by physicist Erwin Schrödinger illustrating quantum superposition, proposing a cat inside a sealed box is simultaneously alive and dead until observed, highlighting quantum uncertainty.

3. *Relativity Theory:* Developed by Albert Einstein, relativity theory comprises two parts: special relativity and general relativity. Special relativity addresses physics at high speeds, stating that time and space are relative, depending on observer speed. General relativity extends this, describing gravity not as a force, but as curvature in spacetime created by mass and energy.

4. *Time Dilation:* A concept from Einstein's theory of relativity describing how time passes differently depending on relative velocity or gravitational field strength. Time appears to slow down for an object moving at speeds approaching the speed of light.

5. *Gravity:* A fundamental force of nature responsible for the attraction between masses, crucial for the structure of the cosmos, from planetary orbits to galaxy formations.

6. *Singularity:* A point of infinite density and gravity, believed to exist at the center of black holes or at the universe's origin during the Big Bang.

7. *Chaos Theory:* A branch of mathematics focusing on systems highly sensitive to initial conditions, illustrating how small changes can lead to vastly different outcomes, known as the "*butterfly effect*"

8. *Big Bang Theory:* This theory describes the universe's origin from an incredibly dense and hot state approximately 13.8 billion years ago, leading to ongoing expansion, creating galaxies, stars, and planets.

9. *Darwinian Evolution:* Proposed by Charles Darwin, this theory suggests species evolve through natural selection, where traits advantageous for survival are passed down, leading to adaptation and diversity of life.

10. *Multiverse Theory:* Suggests the existence of multiple or infinite universes beyond our observable universe, each potentially governed by different physical laws and constants.

11. *Simulation Hypothesis:* The theory that reality as we know it could be an artificial simulation, possibly designed and run by a highly advanced civilization, raising questions about consciousness and existence.

Concepts Used in the Books

12. *Fermi Paradox:* Named after physicist Enrico Fermi, this paradox questions why, given the universe's vast size and age, there is no clear evidence of other intelligent life.

13. *Dark Forest Hypothesis:* An answer to the Fermi Paradox suggesting intelligent civilizations remain silent to avoid detection, assuming other civilizations could be threats, fostering a cosmic environment of suspicion and silence.

14. *Second Law of Thermodynamics:* This law states entropy (disorder) in a closed system always increases over time, suggesting the universe naturally moves toward disorder and eventual equilibrium, or heat death.

15. *Kardashev Scale:* Created by Soviet astronomer Nikolai Kardashev, this scale categorizes civilizations based on their energy usage capabilities: Type I harnesses planetary energy, Type II stellar energy, and Type III galactic energy.

16. *Anthropic Principle:* Proposes that the universe's fundamental constants appear fine-tuned to allow life because if conditions weren't suitable for life, no observers would exist to notice this fact.

17. *Moore's Law:* An observation made by Gordon Moore noting the number of transistors on integrated circuits doubles approximately every two years, predicting exponential technological progress.

18. *Gödel's Incompleteness Theorems:* Developed by Kurt Gödel, these mathematical theorems demonstrate limitations within

formal logical systems, asserting that no consistent system can prove every truth about arithmetic, highlighting fundamental limits in mathematical completeness and certainty.

19. *Soul:* In various spiritual and religious traditions, the soul is considered the immaterial essence or spirit of a being, often seen as eternal, transcending physical death, and intimately connected with consciousness and moral identity.

20. *Consciousness:* Consciousness refers to the state of awareness of self and environment. It's the capacity to experience thoughts, emotions, and sensations, remaining a central subject in philosophy, psychology, and neuroscience.

21. *Energy:* Energy, in physics, refers to the ability to perform work or produce change, existing in various forms such as kinetic, potential, thermal, chemical, and electromagnetic. It is fundamental for understanding the universe and the forces shaping reality.

22. *Karma:* In Hinduism, Buddhism, and Jainism, karma refers to the principle of cause and effect, where actions in this life directly influence future circumstances, guiding moral behavior and spiritual progression.

23. *Afterlife:* The concept present in many religions and spiritual philosophies that consciousness or the soul continues after physical death, existing in other realms or states, influenced by the individual's moral conduct in life.

24. *Sensory Observation:* A fundamental pragmatic principle emphasizing empirical knowledge acquisition through direct experience and sensory perception, prioritizing observable evidence over theoretical or abstract concepts.

These concepts collectively explore profound philosophical and scientific questions about existence, consciousness, morality, and humanity's role in the universe, foundational to understanding our reality and future.

www.ingramcontent.com/pod-product-compliance
Lightning Source LLC
Chambersburg PA
CBHW070531230426
43665CB00014B/1644